Street Protests and Fantasy Parks

Edited by David R. Cameron and Janice Gross Stein

Street Protests and Fantasy Parks: Globalization, Culture, and the State

UBC Press · Vancouver · Toronto

09 08 07 06 05 04 03 02 5 4 3 2 1

Printed in Canada on acid-free paper ∞

National Library of Canada Cataloguing in Publication Data

Main entry under title:

Street protests and fantasy parks

Includes bibliographic references and index.
ISBN 0-7748-0880-2 (bound); ISBN 0-7748-0881-0 (pbk)

1. Globalization – Social aspects. 2. Culture – Social aspects. 3. State, The. I. Cameron, David, 1941- II. Stein, Janice
JZ1318.S77 2002 303.48′2 C2001-911554-7

Canada

UBC Press gratefully acknowledges the financial support for our publishing program of the Government of Canada through the Book Publishing Industry Development Program (BPIDP), and of the Canada Council for the Arts, and the British Columbia Arts Council.

UBC Press gratefully acknowledges the Policy Research Initiative of the Government of Canada for its generous support of this publication.

Printed and bound in Canada by Friesens
Set in Stone by Neil and Brenda West, BN Typographics West
Copy editor: Tara Tovell
Proofreader: Judy Phillips
Indexer: Annette Lorek

UBC Press
The University of British Columbia
2029 West Mall
Vancouver, BC V6T 1Z2
604-822-5959 / Fax: 604-822-6083
www.ubcpress.ca

Contents

Preface

This volume arises out of a large research endeavour, known as the Trends Project, organized and financed by the Government of Canada's Policy Research Secretariat and the Social Sciences and Humanities Research Council of Canada (SSHRCC), in Ottawa. After extensive consultation, these two agencies identified eight different "trends" for sustained research and analysis by multidisciplinary teams of social scientists. Team leaders were named for each of the trends – in the case of globalization, Janice Gross Stein and David R. Cameron – and were asked to join a committee to choose the members of the various teams by means of a competitive process. Requests for proposals were posted on the Social Sciences and Humanities Research Council Web site, and the team members were selected from the pool of applicants who responded.

From the start, the team leaders responsible for the globalization trend intended to approach this complex phenomenon as a social and cultural process. A great deal has been said and written about the economics of globalization, but less about its social and cultural dimensions. The request for proposals placed a premium on imaginative ideas, and we were delighted by the variety and creativity of the projects we were able to select. We understood from the outset that a systematic and comprehensive examination of the social and cultural dimensions of globalization would be beyond the reach of this enterprise. However, we believe that the essays in this volume address some of the most important but less studied dimensions of globalization as a social and cultural process, as well as its consequences for Canada. The essays should be regarded as explorations of a highly complex phenomenon central to modern human existence and to Canada's fate in the coming decades.

We would like to take this opportunity to thank the people who made this project possible. Laura Chapman, the head of the Policy Research Secretariat in Ottawa, offered her strong support to the Trends Project in general and to our globalization project in particular. We are grateful to her for her unremitting encouragement. Our colleagues at the University of Toronto, Joy Fitzgibbon and Joshua Goldstein, were indispensable participants as well; their energy, organizational skills, and unfailing courtesy made doing yet more work and meeting yet more deadlines something close to a pleasure. Ann Medina, Melissa Williams, and Franklyn Griffiths offered all of the authors creative commentary and advice at a critical stage in the development of the project; their insights have improved the book in many ways. The two anonymous reviewers of the manuscript contributed criticism and suggestions that have been of great assistance in putting the collection into final form. We also extend a big thank you to Emily Andrew, our editor par excellence at UBC Press; Emily did a marvellous job of shepherding this enterprise to a successful conclusion. Finally, as co-managers of this project on globalization, we would like to express our appreciation to our colleagues and fellow authors. Multi-authored books can be a nightmare to execute. This one wasn't, largely because of the people with whom we have had the good fortune to work. Our thanks to you all.

1
Street Protests and Fantasy Parks

David R. Cameron and Janice Gross Stein

Globalization: "Real Time" and "Virtual Space"

Globalization shrinks distances through networks of connections. It is the set of economic, environmental, technological, political, cultural, and social processes that first connect and then integrate societies, fragmenting and transcending the traditional social structures they confront. Globalization is centuries old and has proceeded throughout history at an irregular pace and with uneven intensity. Although globalization is not new at all – the Roman Empire connected and integrated societies from Edinburgh to Jerusalem – economic and cultural globalization accelerated again late in the twentieth century, after almost fifty years of regression. The reduction of trade barriers in the 1950s was followed by liberation of capital flows and the deregulation of financial markets in the 1970s and 1980s. In the last two decades, integration deepened as foreign direct investment increased and multinational enterprises spread their chains of production worldwide. More and more, national economies are now integrated into a single global marketplace through trade, finance, production, and a dense web of international treaties and institutions.[1] Increasingly, cultural products with widely recognized icons are shared globally.

The speed and intensity of global connection and integration in the last twenty years have provoked serious debate about the cultural and social consequences of these processes, and, in this context, deep concern about the continuing capacity of the state to provide social justice. In this volume, we focus on two dimensions of globalization: the cultural and social dimensions of global connection and integration, and the uneasily shifting role of the state in a globalizing world. We argue that global processes are integrating societies and economies more deeply, but that obituaries for the state are premature, if not wholly inappropriate. The constraints imposed by globalization on the postindustrial state are looser than stylized portraits suggest. Furthermore, not only are the constraints less restrictive but the state has significant degrees of freedom in the way it reconfigures itself in postindustrial society.[2] In this volume, we examine the options that states have and the consequences, for culture and society, of the choices they make. We find that, in reconfiguring themselves – whether by embracing or resisting globalization – postindustrial society and the state are becoming increasingly globalized as the institutional and cultural ground shifts beneath them. Change and choice are the twin threads of the narrative of state and society in their contact with global processes.

Globalization has been a long historical process, bumpy and uneven in its pace, at times reversing itself and at other times moving forward aggressively. Economic globalization – the connection of national economies through trade, finance, and production – is indeed not new at all. Transportation, communication, and exchange among widely separated societies have intensified in fits and starts over time.

Economic globalization peaked in the first decade of the twentieth century and then reversed itself dramatically in the context of world war and depression. Throughout most of that century, nations exhibited a marked retreat from economic globalization; only in the last twenty-five years has there been a return to the levels reached more than a hundred years ago. Labour is still less mobile than it was in the nineteenth century, when passports were unnecessary and people moved freely across national borders in search of work. In the nineteenth century, immigrating – especially to North America – was generally easier than it is today.[3] Trade is only now becoming as free as it was in the 1860s. Even after the recession of 1875 began in Europe, 95 percent of Germany's imports were free of duty. Trade was then almost as significant a component of the domestic economy as it is today. In the United States, for example, exports were 7 percent of GNP in 1899; in 1999, they were 8 percent. Capital movements as a proportion of economic output are only now reaching the levels of the 1880s.[4] In the nineteenth century, the dominant currency was not state controlled – it was credit created by private commercial banks. At that time, the gold standard severely restricted national fiscal and monetary policy. In the twentieth century, states captured control through the creation of central banks and, after 1973, via floating national currencies that enhanced state control over monetary and fiscal policies.[5] Only in the last three decades have levels of economic globalization begun to approximate those reached during the nineteenth century. Some of what seems historically inevitable at the beginning of the twenty-first century is indeed contingent and reversible, as evidence from the first half of the twentieth century demonstrates.[6]

Contemporary processes of globalization include far more than the connection of national economies to a global marketplace. The globalization of production, largely through intrafirm trade, is more widespread and deeply rooted.[7] In their current stage, moreover, processes of globalization are cultural as well as economic, and carry deep social and political consequences. The revolution in information technologies now permits active communication in "real time" and the creation of virtual space, with shared icons and common discourses, across cultures and societies. Contemporary information technologies, developed in part by "outsiders" who rejected authoritative structures, create both significant new social and cultural opportunities and formidable new constraints. Values, tastes, norms, and cultural products are diffusing worldwide and changing the context and meaning of local cultural expression.[8] The "globalization of the mind" – the ideological processes that have displaced traditional embedded liberalism and that enshrine efficiency through markets – is well advanced among Western intellectual, cultural, scientific, and technological elites. It sets the context for the cultural and social consequences of globalization that are the subject of this volume.[9] We begin with a brief look at economic globalization – usually the principal focus of attention – not to establish it as the focal point of our analysis, but rather to set the context for our subsequent examination of culture, society, and the state.

The Global Economy

The current global economy, made possible in part by information technologies that enable information to reach markets at the speed of light, has exponentially expanded capital markets, trade, the mobility of factors of production, and investment opportunities. In the last three decades, international trade and foreign direct investment have been expanding proportionally far more quickly than domestic trade and investment.

Knowledge and a deepening specialization of expertise are the signatures of this phase of the global economy. Knowledge has replaced other factors of production as the most important commodity. Unlike commodities that were important at earlier phases in the history of the international economy, knowledge is an infinitely renewable resource, only loosely related to geographic space. For the first time in history, we do not deplete our most important resource when we use it. Waste and conservation of this resource are not issues, as they were for other commodities in earlier periods of economic history.

In the global knowledge-based economy, knowledge products and services are becoming "customized." The standard model, in which products were made for mass consumption through mass production in command-and-control organizations, is less and less the norm. Knowledge products and services are targeted to niche markets, designed to meet specialized needs. The global knowledge-based economy promotes diversity, customization, and choice in the private marketplace.

These customized goods and services move increasingly through networks and other horizontal forms of organization. The importance of lateral organizations is growing in comparison to that of hierarchical, command-and-control structures.[10] These lateral organizations make monopoly and hierarchy more difficult, as information at times approaches the status of a public good. At its deepest level, the emergent knowledge-based global economy is non-territorial and less and less tied to political boundaries.[11]

The global knowledge-based economy has created significant wealth for those who are able to participate, directly and indirectly, in its processes. At the same time as the scope and pace of globalization have increased, however, income inequalities have grown, with serious consequences for the configuration of societies.[12] But the causal links between globalization and patterns of income distribution are deeply contested. Is it globalization that is intensifying inequalities? If so, which dimensions of globalization? And which kinds of inequalities is it intensifying – those between countries or those within countries? If those within countries, in what kinds of countries? How do globalization and growing inequality connect? Who is marginalized by current processes of globalization? All the critical terms, as well as the arguments, are the subjects of intense debate.

Some analysts argue that economic globalization has marginalized those who are geographically remote and cannot participate fully in international trade. Studies of interindustry trade have suggested that globalization marginalizes that part of the labour force in the developed world that does not have the literacy and the skills to participate, and disadvantages many of the highly skilled who remain in southern economies.[13] The United Nations Development Program makes the even stronger claim that global economic processes are widening the gap between rich and poor nations.[14] This is the argument that was made and heard on the streets of Seattle, Quebec City, Prague, and Genoa, where those constructing the new economic world order were confronted by wide-ranging, militant protest.

Others contest the important causal role of global trade and instead trace growing inequalities to the revolution in information technology and the differential lack of universal access to the skills needed to develop and use new technologies. Access to computer technology is highly skewed within and across societies: 26 percent of Americans use the World Wide Web, whereas only 3 percent of Russians, 0.2 percent of the population of Arab states, and 0.04 percent of South Asians do so. The United States has more computers than the rest of the world combined. A knowledge-based economy, critics argue, marginalizes those who are not skilled enough to access, understand, and convert information into knowledge, just as earlier globalizing processes marginalized segments of society that could not innovate and exploit the new technologies of the day.

The evidence, however, suggests a more complex story than either an incapacity to participate in trade or a lack of access to technology. Inequalities between nations were already pronounced in the nineteenth century, in the early stages of industrialization. At the end of that century and until the Depression, income inequality between countries declined while inequality within countries rose. For the next forty years, the pattern was reversed: within-country inequalities declined, but between-country inequalities increased. Now, at the beginning of the twenty-first century, between-country inequalities have increased and are greater than they have been for two centuries. Two different patterns of within-country inequalities have developed. Within the core group of technologically advanced countries, inequalities among households have declined: most countries, including Canada, have had relatively stable levels of inequality, while others – Britain, the United States, Australia, and New Zealand – have experienced a sharp rise in inequality in the last two decades. In the semi-periphery and periphery, inequalities have declined within many countries in Asia, but have increased dramatically in China and in Africa. Clearly, we need a more differentiated argument about the impact of globalization to account for these significant differences in changes in inequality over the last two decades.[15]

What explains these uneven patterns of changes in inequality? One intriguing analysis gives us a stylized yet textured portrait. It looks to mass migration as the driver in the first period; to the uneven development of states in the second period, *before* the current wave of globalization accelerated; and to the expansion of markets and supranational organizations in the contemporary period.[16] Around the turn of the twentieth century, global migration exploded – barriers to entry were limited, passports were rarely required – and reached levels that have not since been equalled. Mass migration had contradictory consequences for inequality. It was associated with a decline in between-country inequalities, as it generally increased the relative size of the population of the rapidly growing countries and decreased the relative size of the population of the lower income and slower growth countries. Since average income per capita is generally used to measure the differences among nations, these differences decreased as the proportion of unskilled labour grew in receiving countries. At the same time, mass migration increased within-country inequalities as it swelled the supply of unskilled labour in receiving countries, and decreased inequality within sending countries as the supply of labour was reduced.

In the second period, from the 1930s to the 1970s, the state assumed a much more active role in regulating domestic markets to promote industrialization and, in the context of broadening processes of democratization and a deepening concept of citizenship, intervened actively to limit migration and promote the welfare of its population. Although models of state intervention varied widely, states were far more active than they had been fifty years earlier, and state activism generally led to a decline in within-country inequality. However, the relative capacities and effectiveness of states varied widely among countries in the core, the semi-periphery, and the periphery, and the gap grew as the twentieth century progressed. Particularly in the periphery, states were unable to promote innovation and development effectively, and, concomitantly, were unable to provide the supports for the welfare of their populations. This difference in state capacity provides a rough explanation of the growing inequalities between states during this period. Here we have the early threads of the story that will twist and turn throughout this volume – the differing capacities of states to mediate global processes.

The latest phase of globalization joins two quite different stories about the state. New leadership in Britain and the United States in the 1980s led a challenge to the "social welfare" state and to a reliance on market mechanisms of allocation. In the semi-periphery, particularly in Latin America and Eastern Europe, the failures of state-led strategies of development also encouraged a turn to market-centred strategies of growth. Leaders of the dense network of international institutions that are charged with the management of the global economy enshrined market liberalism as the governing orthodoxy. The state, as the engine of growth and as the guarantor of welfare, directly through the services it provided and indirectly through redistribution, came under attack from within and from without. This phase of globalization through markets, unlike the period a hundred years ago, excludes mass migration as a leveller of the inequalities between nations; the construction of citizenship has deepened, but has also narrowed. Given the uneven development of states throughout the last century, it is not surprising that inequalities between states have sharpened, as have inequalities within the least effective states. Market-led growth has gone in diverse directions in different countries, and a critical difference has been the mediating impact of the state.

Globalization and the State

The impact of the global economy on the national economy and on the state is similarly controversial. It is no surprise that ideological debate rages about the scope and consequences of contemporary globalization. Critics of globalization have conceptualized strong and weak versions of the constrained state in a globalizing economy. The strong version suggests that globalization narrows the scope and autonomy of the state; that it constrains what states can do; and that it limits the capacity of governments to address inequalities, to promote and protect cultural identity, and to construct a national narrative in a globalizing society. The weaker version suggests that the dominant orthodoxy of market liberalism creates ideological pressure to be competitive, and that this pressure leads to a smaller public sector and to convergence of policy across societies. In both the strong and the weak versions, the continuing economic and political pre-eminence of the state is no longer accepted conventional wisdom.

There is, Thomas Courchene argues in the strong version, a growing mismatch between an increasingly globalized private sector and a public sector that continues to operate largely at the national level. The argument goes wider, and deeper. As globalization has deepened, control – although not authority – has moved up and out from the state. It has migrated up to a thickening network of international and transnational institutions and laws, some newly created and others newly strengthened.[18] There has been an explosion of international agreements, treaties, and tribunals, yet most remain heavily bureaucratic – thickly insulated from popular pressures, although not from protest.[19] In response to the broadening writ and unprecedented reach of international institutions, groups of citizens are using the Internet to mobilize in fragile global civil society networks to try to hold these institutions accountable. Thousands came to Seattle, to Prague, to Quebec City, and to Genoa to demand greater transparency from international institutions that make decisions behind closed doors, decisions that have important consequences for far-flung local societies.

Power has also leaked out to non-governmental organizations (NGOs) and transnational associations that work across state borders. In Africa, it was not governments but *Médecins sans Frontières* (Doctors without Borders), a transnational non-governmental organization, that led the global campaign to reduce the price of drugs for AIDS in poor societies. In South Africa, where the epidemic of AIDS rages most fiercely, solutions to local health problems can no longer be national. Multinational pharmaceutical companies, international institutions, and non-governmental organizations have joined with national governments in an attempt to seek collaborative solutions. South Africans, like many others, live today in overlapping communities of fate, and cannot look only to their government to provide the most fundamental public good – treatment for an otherwise deadly disease – at a price they can afford. The strongest critics of globalization argue that, as the state's capacity diminishes, its ability to fulfil the most basic elements of the social contract with its citizens is eviscerated.

That postindustrial states are tied more deeply to global markets and institutions is largely correct. But what are the consequences? Here, the controversies begin. The most forceful critics of globalization argue that there is a growing mismatch between an increasingly globalized private sector, a transnational voluntary sector, and a public sector that continues to operate largely at the national level. It is the public sector that has been traditionally responsible for social entitlements and for the reduction of inequality within nation-states. The Keynesian welfare state, constructed originally to manage the risks of private domestic markets, now faces a much more formidable challenge from global markets and global institutions.

As economic decision making migrates to global markets and institutions, it becomes more difficult for national governments to fulfil their traditional responsibilities to provide a social safety net and basic public goods.[20] The state, the argument goes, is becoming increasingly "hollow," precisely because its borders no longer correspond broadly to "national" economic, cultural, and social spaces.[21] Not only goods and services, but ideas, culture, and new kinds of organizations travel easily across state borders that have become more porous and fluid.

The disconnect is clear. Political boundaries continue to remain largely fixed, while cultural and economic spaces are changing, expanding, and reshaping.[22] In this shifting landscape, a continuing retreat of the state, critics conclude, is both inevitable and irreversible. The state may become one among many institutions bidding for the loyalty of citizens in a competitive marketplace of public and private spaces.[23] A retreat by the state will have disturbing consequences for its capacity to provide public goods, and for legitimate and accountable governance. Some even predict an end to the era of the modern state as we have known it for the past 300 years.

This kind of argument – one that is widespread – does not stand up to the evidence. It is far too pessimistic a view. Processes of globalization do pose formidable challenges to the state – and to the citizen. The story is, however, more complicated than the critics suggest. Global markets and global politics are certainly expanding, but they do not constrain the state from fulfilling its social contract with its citizens. States still have real and significant capacity, both to provide public goods to their citizens and to mediate the impact of global economic, social, and cultural forces. While it is true that some postindustrial states have shed some responsibilities, they have also assumed new ones: helping their citizens to acquire the skills and knowledge to become competitive; and innovating in the way in which they organize and regulate the delivery of public goods. What states do is largely a function of institutional tradition, ideological bent, political culture, and policy choice. The story of globalization that we tell matters.[24]

Those who argue that globalization weakens the state and limits its capacity to provide public goods point to some convincing evidence. Global capital and firms have an unparalleled opportunity to move, to "exit" to more attractive environments, while the nation-state is fixed and immobile. That national financial markets are weaker relative to global financial markets is also now widely accepted. Globalization has also weakened national production as a natural economic space and, indirectly, leached control from the state.[25] State capacity to wield monetary and fiscal policy to lever growth and control cyclical economic downturns has consequently diminished. That state autonomy to manage monetary and fiscal policy has diminished is not in dispute, but the consequences of this diminution of state capacity are. If it were correct that a reduction in the capacity of the postindustrial state to run deficits seriously constrains its capacity to finance its social obligations to its citizenry, this would be a significant fault line in the future trajectory of the state and its capacity to meet the expectations of its citizens for social justice. Existing constructions of the social contract would weaken badly and within-nation inequality would logically increase.

Geoffrey Garrett acknowledges the impact of globalization in limiting the capacity of governments to run deficits, but finds that the increased financial discipline imposed by globalization has not had the expected effect of reducing the size of government in member countries of the Organisation for Economic Co-operation and Development (OECD). Nor has it resulted in the convergence of fiscal policies, much less the feared race to the bottom.[26] Surprisingly, postindustrial states are not reducing the proportion of the gross domestic budget they spend. Indeed, the post-industrial states that trade the most have the largest budgets as a proportion of their gross national product.[27] The most open economies – those most heavily engaged in the global economy – have the largest capacity to provide public goods to their citizens. Contrary to conventional wisdom, globalization has not reduced the capacity of the state to invest in public goods.

States are also less porous than critics of globalization suggest. Borders still matter. In 1996, the typical Canadian province traded twelve times as much with another Canadian province as with a state in the United States of similar size and distance. Within the European Union, the most densely integrated economy, significant border effects are still in place for goods, services, and capital. The markets for domestic goods are still much tighter than international markets. Although national border effects are weaker than they were thirty years ago, they are still significantly stronger, John Helliwell concludes, than those that cross borders. "Despite many increases in the strength and depth of international linkages over the past 40 years," Helliwell argues, "countries' internal economic and social structures remain much tighter than is commonly believed ... Small countries remain as viable and vibrant as they were decades ago ... The smaller countries seem to do particularly well on broader measures of welfare."[28] Globalization does not severely constrain the viability of even the smaller postindustrial countries, much less the choices their leaders can make. Indeed, some analysts argue that globalization can be understood as the product and consequence of the political choices of governments.[29]

The state is changing its shape in postindustrial societies, but not in the way critics of globalization expect. The postindustrial state has not reduced its investment in public goods, but it has changed, in fundamental ways, the way it provides public goods to its citizens. Some suggest that the emerging role for the state is that of financier of public goods rather than direct provider – increasingly a regulator and referee, rule-maker and rule-monitor, a guarantor of quality, and the locus of heightened transparency and accountability.[30] The state is not absent, or hollow, or shrunken, or even residual. It is changing, not simply in response to pressures from global forces, but also in response to changing expectations from citizens who increasingly live in multiple worlds and bring a global sensibility with them. The state sets the rules of the game, and then allows an ever-increasing number of social actors to join together to reframe the social contract constructed in the twentieth century. Relevant here is the radically different capacity of the various social sectors to speak and act within the newly emerging sociopolitical order. The face that the postindustrial state is showing to its citizens is changing, but this change in the face of the state cannot be explained only, or even largely, by the growth of global markets and global institutions.

The Global Citizen in a Global Culture

Processes of globalization have been fuelled by faster and cheaper technologies of transportation, information, and communication. These technologies have direct consequences for the construction of social and cultural spaces, a process that is at times unmediated by the state. Here, too, these changes raise important – indeed fundamental – political questions for the state.

In Chapter 3, Lloyd L. Wong examines evolving notions of citizenship in an era of globalization. He focuses on the emergence of transnational identities and diasporic communities, now understood as communities in which a continuing balance of membership and identity is maintained between home and host societies. Throughout the twentieth century, as we have seen, the concept of citizenship in industrial societies simultaneously deepened and narrowed. After a hiatus of fifty years, immigration and emigration are growing again worldwide as people's horizons of opportunity are broadened, partly as a result of contemporary communication technologies. As Wong points out, with contemporary forms of migration and population movement, new forms of identity align badly with the territorial notions of citizenship associated with the traditional nation-state. Diasporic public spheres are growing across borders as a new arena of political action.[31] This increased movement of people will likely have significant consequences for inequality between nations and within nations.

In a global society, as Wong demonstrates, "transilient" citizens – people who do not settle permanently in one locale – become crucial nodes in a thickening network of interconnections. They are also important resources as they move in and out of Canada, taking the Canadian "brand" with them back and forth, to and from their original homes. The current tightening of citizenship policy seeks to strengthen national narratives in the face of multiple cultural stories but, as Wong concludes, it works directly against the transnationalization of identities and the transilience of citizens in a global society.

The information revolution and the thickening global economy are also making possible a nascent global culture. We understand culture as the pattern of shared values that give meaning to individual and collective action in a community.[32] Culture is the repository of a community's shared understandings that facilitate collective action. These shared understandings are intimately linked to identity: they reciprocally reinforce one another. In the last several hundred years, it has been commonly assumed that culture has helped to define the nation and that the state gives formal expression to culture as collectively defined and experienced. Through this came the shorthand concepts of "nation-state" and "national culture."

Globalization works to transcend and even, at times, to supersede national cultures. Its processes create a common cultural environment where everyone who is "connected" has access to the same messages, the same icons, and the same calligraphy, produced and disseminated through the tightly controlled transnational corporate media networks of television and film. Many of these networks are currently headquartered in the United States and their products increasingly dominate global cultural markets.[33] These products no more reflect the diversity of American culture than they do the diversity of other cultures. For the first time, global cultural product is mass rather than elite based.[34]

In Chapter 2, John Hannigan examines the "global entertainment economy," and the branded cultural products and images that are being transmitted along these ever-wider and more rapidly moving corporate conveyor belts. Important as economic product, these "brands" are even more important as shared cultural icons. Themed fantasy parks are dominating the cultural discourse of urban centres around the globe, as brand recognition pulls consumers in and away. Culture is becoming deterritorialized, detached from the community, and commodified in the global marketplace. Local forms of culture, in this environment, are under assault. These local cultures are becoming more important as people activate differentiated identities in response to increasingly homogenized global cultural space. However, they are becoming more difficult to produce and reproduce, not only as cultural product grows in economic importance, but also as new global regulatory frameworks constrain what governments can do to sustain local cultures.

The Internet works in the opposite direction, by encouraging direct, unhindered individual participation, free of supervision and largely beyond the reach of authority. Nevertheless, like other global media, it too promotes cultural and social integration, the development of a common language – cyberspeak melded with English – and the creation of virtual communities.[35] On the World Wide Web, the least structured contemporary cultural environment, English is the language of choice for 80 percent of the sites.

The increasingly accessible technologies of information and communication not only erode difference and foster homogenization, but simultaneously promote particularization and differentiation as communities appropriate, use, and transform global cultural product even as they rediscover the individuality of local culture. The multichannel universe and magazines and music tailored to niche markets accentuate particular differences and local specializations. The "customization of cultural product," so characteristic of global economic product, allows individuals and communities to meet their specific needs in ways that would have been impossible even two decades ago. In this fashion, new technologies have enabled actual and virtual groups to define and empower themselves in opposition to, or even without reference to, dominant cultures. In doing so, these same processes contribute to social fragmentation and to the proliferation of specialized subcultures that have little in common.

As global processes simultaneously promote cultural homogenization and fragmentation, cultural boundaries – historically an essential component of national identity – are beginning to diverge from national political spaces even more than economic boundaries are.[36] As Marc Raboy argues in Chapter 5, the "national," is weakened as the primary reference category for identity. The choices states make in the face of new global regulation, global cultural product, and locally active and differentiated cultures will be crucial to the retelling of national narratives. In Canada, this is not a new challenge, but one that is taking on a radically different complexion. Canada has traditionally adopted a mixed approach to cultural policy, somewhere between the market-driven US system and the more nationally driven European approach; this sometimes ambivalent policy posture is often expressed in contemporary international negotiations, with the economic ministries inclining in one direction and the cultural ministries inclining in the other. Raboy argues that, given the powerful internationalizing forces shaping modern culture and communication, there is an acute need to develop the capacity to articulate a global public interest in the field that is more than the sum of transnational corporate interests. As he points out, "the sites of policy making have shifted, vertically, from the national to the transnational, and horizontally, from the state to the boardroom" (p. 133).

Historically, culture has been fundamental in constituting a shared terrain for all kinds of action. We have a particular interest in political culture, that dimension of culture that constitutes the ground for political action.[37] Political culture, conceived as shared political meanings, values, and practices, can be understood much more broadly than much of the contemporary analysis of the displacement of national culture would suggest. There may be a nascent global political culture, empowered by new technologies and constituting a new terrain for global political action.

Ronald J. Deibert's analysis, in Chapter 4, of the international opposition to the Multilateral Agreement on Investment (MAI) demonstrates the capacity of private actors, using new technologies, to connect across borders and engage effectively on a public global issue. He concludes that the Internet played a key role in the resistance movement in three ways: by permitting swift communication of information among members of the anti-MAI lobby; by publicizing information about the MAI – and the activists' interpretation of the MAI – to a broader community of Internet users and beyond; and by offering opponents a tool to put direct pressure on politicians and policy makers in member states. Interestingly, his work reveals a fairly robust continuing network of activists that has sustained itself after the issue that gave birth to it was halted. While the anti-MAI groups cannot be regarded as a community, they are more than a coincidental coordination of isolated groups. The Internet, Deibert says, "has become the sinew of power for the coalescing nebulae of global civil society" (p. 90). In this case, and in others like it, the state has ceased to be the primary arena of political contestation or action, although its role as a political actor in the international policy-making environment remains central. Individuals and groups living in Canada reach out across borders to connect with like-minded others.[38]

The narratives of opposition to the MAI and of protest against the WTO in Seattle in 1999, and against the Summit of the Americas in Quebec City and the G8 Summit in Genoa, both in 2001, are evidence of the capacity created by the new technologies for concerted political action in the global arena. These are, however, narrative threads in a far more complex tale. Private groups have worked not only in opposition to states, but also with states as lead partners: they did so recently, for example, to create a treaty to ban anti-personnel land mines and to create a new global institution, the International Criminal Court. It is apparent that globalization is opening up new terrain for political action and that cross-border political cultures are beginning to emerge. How accountable these communities are, how representative they are, and how they are empowered to act is far less clear. Nor is it obvious how these global political cultures will intersect with and relate to national political spaces and action.

Our review of globalization as a set of embedded historical processes suggests that the connection and integration of societies have proceeded over time in uneven fits and starts. In their current phase, processes of globalization are enabling the emergence of nascent cultures and opening up new terrain for political action, both above and below the state. Culture and identity, two of the important bulwarks of the modern state, are becoming deterritorialized. Globalization is giving voice to communities that have often found it difficult to be heard within national structures, but it is also muffling the voices of others. The processes of globalization pose new challenges to the state – and to the citizen – given their capacity to flow around, over, and under existing national political communities, and to shift economic, cultural, and social spaces in lumpy aggregations away from territorial borders. Nevertheless, as we will argue in the final chapter, the state remains the critical mediating force among the global, the local, and the national. The choices political leaders make will prove critical to the telling and retelling of national narratives. They will also shape who is listening and who hears.

Globalization, Identities, and the Politics of Inclusion

The narrow construction of the state as authoritative referee and regulator is problematic, we have argued, for the legitimization of the capacity of the state to provide social justice. It is also troubling with respect to the sustainability of national identities over time. Citizens rarely cheer for umpires; they tend to give their loyalty to teams. The erosion of boundaries, the opening of new terrain for global political action, and the diminishing overlap of state borders with cultural spaces also make the sustainability of national identities over time more difficult.

Central to any concept of identity is differentiation: a distinction between "you and me," between "them and us." Research in social psychology confirms that categorization and boundaries play a defining role in establishing differentiation; indeed, identity would be impossible to create were all borders eradicated. Globalization works, however, to eradicate borders and connect across divides. Information and communication technologies facilitate the breakdown of time and space barriers; they encourage connection and integration, and the creation of a common cultural vocabulary. When barriers erode and a global culture creates shared and easily recognizable icons, a "national identity," tied to political borders that no longer coincide with economic, cultural, political, or even social boundaries, is increasingly problematic.

The problem may prove to be more apparent than real. Social psychology speaks precisely to the prevalence of multiple identities and the importance of situational triggers. We are partners at home and professionals at work, and see no conflict between these identities; each is triggered by different situations. Similarly, we may be members of our local communities when we join together to support a school, citizens of our country when we vote in a federal election, and citizens of the world when we contribute to a non-governmental organization that works to alleviate the suffering of refugees around the globe. In each case, different triggers activate identities appropriate to the situation. This sequencing of identities is sustainable, and even mutually reinforcing, as long as the identities are compatible with one another.

Our analysis suggests, however, that the triggers of national identity will decline as globalization intensifies. If "national" borders coincide largely with political boundaries – and less and less with the economic and the cultural, and only partly with the social – then the triggers to national identity cannot help but diminish over time. What is activated less and less over time cannot help but become less important. If our argument is correct, national identities will become less and less salient among the multiple political identities people tend to hold.

History teaches us that collective concepts evolve over time, in response to a changing constellation of social, economic, and political forces. This capacity to adapt suggests the more optimistic hypothesis that "national identity" will be reconfigured as a focal point of identity in response to globalizing processes. It may well become a "niche" or "customized" identity, a place of loyalty within shifting spaces.

The weakening of national identities, moreover, is not an entirely negative development. It is easy to imagine, for example, that a strengthened global identity, drawing on shared cultures and values and more vibrant local political identities, could provide valuable focal points for political action and institution building. Indeed, we have begun to see fairly significant institutional creativity and political activity at the global level in recent years. Marc Raboy, in Chapter 5, examines the nascent global communications regime and the challenges it creates for state and private stakeholders who seek to influence its development in a new arena of political action. And Ronald Deibert, in Chapter 4, explores the capacity of widely separated groups from different societies to use the new information technologies to engage politically on a global issue. Lloyd Wong's depiction, in Chapter 3, of "transilient citizens" of no fixed address raises interesting questions in this context; from a national perspective, their instrumental loyalty can be cause for concern to the states with which they are associated, but perhaps they are global citizens-in-waiting, prefiguring emerging forms of global citizenship and identity.

The opening up of new arenas for political action at the global and local levels will benefit citizens only if the new structures are representative and accountable. Many at the local level are, but most at the global level are not. As long as they are not, they cannot substitute effectively for authoritative states embedded in constitutional legal systems. Without strong national identities as supports, however, state structures of authorization, representation, and accountability may weaken more quickly than alternative global structures of accountability can be constructed.[39]

It is possible that, within a broader field of salient identities, national identities may become largely instrumental rather than constitutive. Loyalty to a state for what it can do rather than for what and whom it represents is, however, a significantly weaker basis for political authority. Here, the politics of inclusion become central. Social psychology tells us that identity is created in part through processes of identification. Whether people identify with a particular group is a matter of choice and, in choosing an identity, people struggle between the contradictory imperatives of inclusion and differentiation. People choose to sustain an identity or to assimilate to it when they regard it as favourable and strong and when the barriers to entry are not high; identification becomes a strategy of entry and opportunity. We only choose to differentiate ourselves when core identities are incompatible and we think that an identity that is important to us is threatened or that the barriers to inclusion are strong.[40]

The construction and maintenance of a national narrative in the global surround can succeed if citizens hear the national narrative as positive, compatible with other important identities, and open to inclusion. Here, the threads of the cultural and the social stories join. If social inequalities grow, and the state chooses to retreat, to become residual, citizens are unlikely to sustain a strong version of the national narrative. As processes of globalization continue to thicken, political leaders and citizens must examine and reconfigure the ground on which the legitimacy of the state stands. They must also redefine the national project if states are to continue to be a vibrant focal point of identity in a global field.

As we will argue in the closing chapter, the state remains the guardian and authoritative interpreter of place in a landscape of shifting tectonic plates. The state faces the formidable challenge of redefining itself in space so that it retains political loyalty as an authoritative, legitimate, representative, and accountable arena of political action. We are just beginning a new dialogue of place amid newly opened and shifting spaces.

Notes

1 Jeffrey Sachs, "International Economics: Unlocking the Mysteries of Globalization," *Foreign Policy* 110 (Spring 1998): 97-111; and Manuel Castells, *The Rise of the Network Society* (Cambridge, MA: Blackwell, 1996); and *End of Millennium* (Cambridge, MA: Blackwell, 1998).

2 Keith Banting, George Hoberg, and Richard Simeon, eds., *Degrees of Freedom: Canada and the United States in a Changing World* (Montreal: McGill-Queen's University Press, 1997).

3 Jeffrey Williamson, *Globalization and the Labor Market: Using History to Inform Policy* (Milan: Lezioni Raffaele Mattioli, Banca Commerciale Italiana, Universita' Commerciale Luigi Bocconi, 1996), 16, 18, Table 2:1. See also Stephen Krasner, *Sovereignty: Organized Hypocrisy* (Princeton, NJ: Princeton University Press, 1999).

4 M. Obstfield and A.M. Taylor, *The Great Depression As a Watershed: International Capital Mobility over the Long Run* (Cambridge, MA: National Bureau of Economic Research, Working Paper no. 5960, 1997); Krasner, *Sovereignty: Organized Hypocrisy,* 13; and Linda Weiss, *The Myth of the Powerless State: Governing the Economy in a Global Era* (Cambridge: Polity Press, 1998), 172-6.

5 Peter F. Drucker, "The Global Economy and the Nation-State," *Foreign Affairs* 76, 5 (1997): 159-71. See also Paul Doremus, William Keller, Louis Pauly, and Simon Reich, *The Myth of the Global Corporation* (Princeton, NJ: Princeton University Press, 1998); and W. Ruigrok and R. van Tulder, *The Logic of International Restructuring* (London: Routledge, 1995).

6 Paul Hirst and Grahame Thompson, *Globalization in Question: The International Economy and the Possibilities of Governance* (Cambridge: Polity Press, 1996); and Robert Wade, "Globalization and Its Limits: Reports of the Death of the National Economy are Greatly Exaggerated," in *National Diversity and Global Capitalism,* ed. S. Berger and R. Dore (Ithaca, NY: Cornell University Press, 1996), 60-88.

7 Wolfgang H. Reinicke, *Global Public Policy: Governing without Government* (Washington, DC: Brookings Institution Press, 1998), 11-51, especially 19.

8 William Watson, *Globalization and the Meaning of Canadian Life* (Toronto: University of Toronto Press, 1998).

9 Globalization is considered as a "hegemonic discourse" that alters ideas and expectations about the role of the state in society. Philip Cerny, "Globalization and Other Stories: The Search for a New Paradigm in International Relations," *International Journal* 51 (1966): 617-37; and Harry W. Arthurs, "Globalization of the Mind: Canadian Elites and the Restructuring of Legal Fields," *Canadian Journal of Law and Society* 12 (1997): 219-46.

10 For an analysis of knowledge networks, see Janice Gross Stein, Richard Stren, Joy Fitzgibbon, and Melissa MacLean, *Networks of Knowledge: Collaborative Innovations in International Learning* (Toronto: University of Toronto Press, 2001).

11 Countervailing tendencies also exist: knowledge can also be a source of competitive advantage, and the current state-led attempt to strengthen the international regime protecting intellectual property rights seeks to reterritorialize knowledge and convert it into a private good. We are grateful to our anonymous reviewer for this interesting point about the privatization of knowledge.

12 Sachs, "International Economics."

13 Paul Krugman, *Development, Geography, and Economic Theory* (Cambridge, MA: MIT Press, 1995); and Paul Krugman and Robert Lawrence, "Trade, Jobs, and Wages," *Scientific American* (April 1994): 44-9 argue that the direct effects on US income distribution of global trade have been small. They attribute the rising income inequality within the United States not to global trade and investment but to the impact of technology. They argue that the proportion of the labour force in developed economies in direct competition with low-skilled workers in the south is far too small – about 5 percent in the US labour market – to explain the dramatic increase in income inequalities of the last two decades. For a contrary perspective, see Robert Frank and Philip Cook, *The Winner-Take-All Society* (New York: Simon and Schuster, 1995).

14 United Nations Development Program, *Tenth Annual Report* (New York: United Nations, 1999).

15 Glen Firebaugh, "Empirics of World Income Inequality," *American Journal of Sociology* 104 (May 1999): 1597-631.

16 Roberto Patricio Korzeniewicz, Timothy P. Moran, and Angela Stach, "Trends in Inequality: Towards a World-System Analysis" (paper presented at the "Conference on Re-Inventing Society in a Changing Global Economy," University of Toronto, 8-10 March 2001).

17 Thomas J. Courchene, ed., *The Nation State in a Global Information Order: Policy Challenges,* proceedings of a conference held at Queen's University, 14-15 November 1996 (Kingston, ON: John Deutsch Institute for Economic Research, 1997).

18 David Held, Anthony McGrew, David Goldblatt, and Jonathan Perraton develop the concept of "thick" and "thin" globalization in *Global Transformations: Politics, Economics, and Culture* (Stanford, CA: Stanford University Press, 1999).

19 Mark Zacher, "The Global Economy and the International Political Order," in *The Nation*

State in a Global Information Order, ed. T. Courchene, 67-95. See also Michael Th. Greven and Louis W. Pauly, eds., *Democracy beyond the State? The European Dilemma and the Emerging Global Order* (Lanham, MD: Rowman and Littlefield, 2000); and David Held, *Democracy and the Global Order: From the Modern State to Cosmopolitan Governance* (Stanford, CA: Stanford University Press, 1995).

20 For a sceptical view, see Louis Pauly, *Who Elected the Bankers? Surveillance and Control in the World Economy* (Ithaca, NY: Cornell University Press, 1997).

21 Kenichi Ohmae, *The End of the Nation State* (New York: Free Press, 1995), 5. Ohmae argues that "traditional nation-states have become unnatural, even impossible business units in a global economy." Susan Strange makes a similar argument: "The impersonal forces of world markets ... are now more powerful than the states to whom ultimate political authority over society and economy is supposed to belong ... The declining authority of states is reflected in a growing diffusion of authority to other institutions and associations, and to local and regional bodies." Susan Strange, *The Retreat of the State: The Diffusion of Power in the World Economy* (Cambridge: Cambridge University Press, 1996): 4.

22 Castells, *Rise of the Network Society;* and John Ruggie, *Winning the Peace: America and World Order in the New Era* (New York: Columbia University Press, 1996).

23 Yale Ferguson and Richard Mansbach, *Polities: Authority, Identities, and Change* (Columbia, SC: University of South Carolina Press, 1996).

24 Bob Rae, *The Three Questions: Prosperity and the Public Good* (Toronto: Viking, 1998); and Thomas Courchene, ed., *Room to Manoeuvre? Globalization and Policy Convergence* (Kingston, ON: John Deutsch Institute for Economic Research, 1999).

25 Sachs, "International Economics."

26 Geoffrey Garrett, "Global Markets and National Politics: Collision Course or Virtuous Circle?" *International Organization* 52 (1998): 787-824. See also Geoffrey Garrett and Peter Lange, "Internationalization, Institutions, and Political Change," in *Internationalization and Domestic Politics,* ed. H. Milner and R. Keohane (Cambridge: Cambridge University Press, 1996), 48-75; and A. Hurrell and N. Woods, "Globalization and Inequality," *Millennium: Journal of International Studies* 24, 3 (1995): 447-70.

27 Dani Rodrik, "Why Do More Open Economies Have Bigger Governments?" *Journal of Political Economy* 106, 5 (1998): 997-1032.

28 John F. Helliwell, *Globalization: Myths, Facts, and Consequences,* C.D. Howe Institute Benefactors Lecture 2000 (Toronto: C.D. Howe, 2000), 3ff, 41, 46.

29 Philip G. Cerny, "Globalization and the Changing Logic of Collective Action," *International Organization* 49 (1995): 595-625.

30 Janice Gross Stein, *The Cult of Efficiency* (Toronto: Anansi, 2001).

31 Arjun Appadurai, *Modernity at Large* (Minneapolis: University of Minnesota Press, 1996).

32 For a similar definition of culture, see Franklyn Griffiths, "The Culture of Change" (paper presented at "Analysing the Trends: National Policy Research" conference, Ottawa, 25-6 November 1999).

33 Raboy points out (in Chapter 5 of this volume) that, in 1998, contrary to popular myth, only three of the seven leading global cultural industry corporations were actually owned by Americans, although all of them had their main operational headquarters within a twenty-block area of central Manhattan.

34 Held et al., *Global Transformations,* 427.

35 Barry Wellman, *Networks in the Global Village: Life in Contemporary Communities* (Boulder, CO: Westview Press, 1999).

36 It is striking that even within the United States, the dominant producer of global cultural product, concern about the viability of culture is growing. Culture and the arts are the second largest American export, after technology. The Pew Charitable Trusts, the foundation that funded the pioneering work on global warming, civic journalism, and campaign finance reform, has committed itself to shaping a "national" cultural policy. Over the next five years, the Pew plans to encourage policy makers to focus on the financing of the arts, intellectual property rights, zoning in historic areas, and an arts curriculum for public schools. Animating the project is the view that culture is a national responsibility,

essential to "preserving and enabling American creativity." Judith H. Dobrzynski, "Heavyweight Foundation Throws Itself behind Idea of a Cultural Policy," *New York Times,* 2 August 1999, B1.

37 See Griffiths, "The Culture of Change," for a discussion of political culture.

38 See also Sylvia Ostry, "Dissent.Com: How NGOs Are Re-Making the WTO," *Policy Options* (June 2001): 6-15.

39 We are grateful to Ann Medina and Melissa Williams for these helpful points.

40 D. Abrams and M.A. Hogg, eds., *Social Identity Theory: Constructive and Critical Advances* (New York: Harvester Wheatsheaf, 1990); and M.B. Brewer, "The Role of Distinctiveness in Social Identity and Group Behavior," in *Group Motivation: Social Psychological Perspectives,* ed. M. Hogg and D. Abrams (New York: Harvester Wheatsheaf, 1993), 1-16.

2
The Global Entertainment Economy

John Hannigan

Sometime soon, downtown Toronto will reinvent itself as midtown Manhattan. Across from a reconfigured Eaton Centre, "Metropolis," five levels of retail anchored by a thirty-screen cinema and a Virgin megastore, will sprout up in a block now occupied by dollar and discount stores and street-level amusement arcades. Billed as a "Times Square concept," the $90 million redevelopment project will also include a public square and, to give it an extra dash of pizzazz, New York-style neon signage. Just around the corner, the International Olympic Committee plans to erect an entertainment centre of its own, with an Olympic sports theme. With an estimated cost of $32 million, "Olympic Spirit" will take the form of a fifty-metre-high media tower in the shape of the Olympic torch. Five hours down Highway 401, a similar development plan has already transformed the Montreal Forum, formerly the temple of hockey for generations of Quebeckers. Promoted as a "Times Square-style" entertainment complex, the redeveloped Forum, now called the Pepsi Forum Entertainment Centre, features a twenty-two-screen megaplex and "Jillian's," a restaurant complex that includes such entertainment facilities as virtual and real bowling alleys, a blues stage, and a disco.

The "Manhattanization" of downtown locations in Canada's two largest cities is the leading edge of a "global entertainment economy" organized around the merchandising of American popular culture brands and celebrities. In the United States, which has the most developed entertainment and media industry, as a percentage of household spending entertainment (5.4 percent) currently ranks ahead of clothing (5.2 percent) and health care (5.2 percent), generating US$480 billion in business each year in a US$8 trillion economy. Expected to double in a handful of years, entertainment is, according to American media consultant Michael Wolf, "fast becoming the driving wheel of the new world economy."[1] In the United Kingdom, annual expenditure on leisure activities rose by 50 percent between 1992 and 1997. By the end of the 1990s, British consumers spent more on leisure and tourism than on food, rent, and local taxes put together.[2] In Canada, the consumer market for entertainment services grew by almost 50 percent in real terms in the decade between 1986 and 1996, to reach $5.8 billion.[3] Since Statistics Canada's figures do not include such activities as dining at a themed restaurant or patronizing a casino, this figure can be seen as being substantially higher in the developing fantasy cities of the future. European cities, long resistant to American-type commercial developments, are on the verge of undergoing a major transformation. Major urban entertainment projects are already under way in Brussels and Barcelona. Symbolizing Berlin's economic renaissance, the new Potsdamer Platz, along the former East-West boundary, is crowned by the Sony Centre, Europe's largest private sector development. Under a soaring V-shaped canopy composed of sail-like fabric and glass panels, an oval-shaped Forum, an IMAX theatre, the German Film Institute, several themed cafés, and a Sony store can be found. Across the road is a private neighbourhood that contains a casino, an Imax/Discovery Channel theatre, a three-storey retail mall, and numerous themed eateries. Despite the "Asian flu" that has battered most economies in the Pacific Rim, countries in the region are poised to welcome some major entertainment developments. New urban theme parks are being built by both Disney and Universal in Japan, and the former has announced plans to open an international entertainment facility in 2006 on Lantau Island, Hong Kong, the site of the former colony's new airport.

While rooted in the "global communications environment," the impact of the entertainment economy is profoundly felt at the level of the local urban community. Speaking at a 1998 real estate development conference in Toronto, Vancouver architect Clive Grout predicted that "entertainment and experience will begin even more strongly to shape the ways that architecture, design, merchandising, shopping, travel and leisure define themselves in our cities."[4] Elsewhere, I have described how a new form of urban development has emerged in which cities have come to represent themed fantasy experiences.[5] These "fantasy cities," as I have termed them, are often promoted as antidotes to the decades-long decline of those inner cities that have suffered from the steady exodus of manufacturing jobs and middle-class residents. However, there are indications that rather than reawakening downtown vitality and urban sociability, these new themed developments may well impose an iron cage of uniformity in which local initiative and identity are stifled and private space replaces public space. In the ageographic city of the future, with its "generic urbanism inflected only by appliqué," ties to any specific space could be replaced by a universal particular that is favoured by globalized capital, electronic means of production, and uniform mass culture.[6]

Of course, the cultural invasion of American mass culture and the resulting "globalization and homogenization of values, culture and consciousness"[7] is by no means of recent vintage. Over a quarter of a century ago, in his book *Mass Communication and American Empire,* the media theorist Herbert Schiller denounced the juggernaut that flattens local identities and cultures while substituting a uniform and predominantly American character.[8] Today, even as America's hegemony in other industries ranging from automobiles to consumer electronics has been shattered irrevocably, global consumer culture has remained almost an American monopoly and is said by some scholars to have effectively eclipsed both high culture and the culture of traditional societies worldwide.[9] With the fall of the Soviet bloc, "literally the entire planet is being wired into music, movies, news, television programs and other cultural products that originate primarily in the film and recording studios of the United States."[10]

Nevertheless, the global entertainment economy in the early twenty-first century has some distinctive features as compared to its earlier forms. Of particular importance has been the merging of corporate globalization strategies with those that emphasize creating and building brand-driven synergies. To describe this process, political scientist Benjamin Barber has coined the term "McWorld": "McWorld is an entertainment shopping experience that brings together malls, multiplex movie theaters, theme parks, spectator sports arenas, fast-food chains (with their endless movie tie-ins), and television (with its burgeoning shopping networks) into a single vast enterprise that, on the way to maximizing its profits, transforms human beings."[11]

The expanding universe of entertainment described by "McWorld" pivots around the convergence of three types of consumer purchases: screened products (movies, television, computer games); packaged products (home videos, toys); and leisure activities (amusement parks, casinos, cruise ships).[12] These are brought together under the umbrella of "brand empires," colonies of products and services that draw their sustenance from a single strong and readily recognizable corporate brand. Wolf observes that brands do more than just carry a product's attributes; they convey a simple, powerful idea: family, taste, money, or fun: "Disney doesn't simply mean animated features or theme parks anymore: it means family. Martha Stewart doesn't mean a magazine or a TV show; Martha equals glamorous good taste. Bloomberg is not just a terminal on a trader's desk; it is instantaneous financial news and analysis. The NBA isn't about watching tall men put the ball in the hoop with a high degree of accuracy; it's about a fast, urban, street lifestyle, with all the glitz and glamour of showbiz."[13]

Factors Promoting the Growth of the Global Entertainment Economy

Demographic and Lifestyle Factors

To understand why the global market for entertainment has become so large, it is first necessary to recognize some of the key demographic features and lifestyle choices of contemporary consumers.

About a third of the Canadian population, the largest single cohort, constitute the so-called "boomer" generation, born between 1947 and 1966. Of these, the majority are "front-end" boomers – that is, those entering or about to enter their fifties. During the decade of the 1980s, many of the older boomers spent considerable time at home rather than going out. Pop marketing guru Faith Popcorn labelled this stay-at-home behaviour "cocooning" and claimed that it was the future trend in cities, which were increasingly overwhelmed by crime and other urban problems. However, University of Toronto economist and demographer David Foot rejects this forecast, arguing that once the boomer generation's children became old enough not to require constant supervision, their parents once again began to go out in search of fun. Solidly established in their careers, entering their peak earning years, and having already made most of the major consumer purchases – most notably a house – the front-end boomers are now primed to shift to a leisure-spending mode.[14] Some have emulated the "forty-something" Vancouver trial lawyer, cited in a *Globe & Mail* article from the late 1990s, who opted for a high performance sport coupe "before I get too old to enjoy it."[15] But others have rejected new luxury consumer durables in favour of shopping and entertainment "experiences." Comparing figures from 1969 and 1996, Statistics Canada reports that spending on recreation services was especially increased for the highest income households, a category that encompasses many of the more affluent front-end boomers. Of this group, 60 percent reported attending "live staged performances," 40 percent said they had paid admission to museums, exhibitions, and the like, and 36 percent went to "live sports spectacles."[16]

Smaller in number than the front-end boomers, "Generation X," those now in their thirties, have also been important in spurring the growth of the new entertainment economy. Weaned on MTV and MuchMusic, high tech video games and computers, the Generation Xers are said to be media savvy, both multitaskers and multimedia users.[17] Furthermore, they display an entirely new outlook toward television, eschewing loyalty toward a particular channel or network in favour of the program itself. One of the consequences of this "postmodern" orientation has been to break up the long-standing domination of the airwaves by the major television networks, thus opening up access to a new flock of competitors, including

MTV, Fox, Nickelodeon, and CNN. Turow calls these channels "lifestyle parades" that invite their audiences to belong to an "ad-sponsored community" that resonates with their personal beliefs and helps them chart their position in the larger world.[18]

These qualities are even more pronounced in "Generation Y" (or the "Echo" generation, as Foot labels them), the children of the front-end boomers who are just beginning to enter the working world. According to figures cited by Michael Wolf, these "children of the multimedia" spend US$130 billion annually and are estimated to influence the spending of an additional US$250 billion.[19] Members of Generation Y are particularly avid moviegoers. Accustomed from childhood to watching videotaped movies at home, they are also more likely than older generations "to go to the cinema," and they therefore "form an important component of movie audiences."[20]

New Leisure Patterns

Contemporary leisure analysts are split on the issue of whether our leisure time is shrinking or expanding. One prominent researcher, John Robinson of Pennsylvania State University, has presented data for the period 1965-1995 that demonstrates a steady rise in the leisure time of Americans in the 18 to 64 age range.[21] Other social scientists have argued that people today are "overworked"[22] and are experiencing a "time bind"[23]; they are spending more time at paid jobs and less time in pursuit of leisure. What does seem to be clear is that the pace of both work and pleasure has increased significantly, leading to a perception that our free time has shrunk and has become a valuable commodity that must be rationed and be spent more carefully.[24] Drawing on data from three Canadian time-use surveys conducted between 1981 and 1992, Zuzanek and Smale detect a perception of significant time-related pressures in our lives – pressures that increased considerably in the 1990s. While they identify some gender and lifestyle differences, Zuzanek and Smale conclude that the mounting sense of time pressure "should be, at least in part, attributed to the harried lifestyles typical of modern industrial societies."[25]

Wolf contends that people today have begun to conceptualize time in a radically different way, treating it as a highly segmented grid – a series of small parcels or boxes that need to be filled. Leisure is no exception, requiring that free time be scheduled into manageable blocks distributed over the course of the week. This has led to a kind of "time surfer" mentality in which we choose recreational activities that can be consumed in bite-sized chunks, ranging from ten minutes to several hours. Wolf goes on to argue that not only has leisure time become segmented and broken into variable-length blocks, but it is something that can be most efficiently utilized by spending money. Time-pressed business executives, for example, hire "personal trainers" to put them through physical fitness routines either at the gym or at the office. The reorientation of leisure toward this type of commoditized time surfing has stimulated the growth of an entertainment marketplace in which audio books, video games, Internet "zines" (i.e., virtual magazines), and urban theme parks all figure prominently.[26]

An associated trend is what has been termed the "localization of leisure."[27] Rather than the traditional three-week summer vacation, middle-class consumers today prefer more frequent but shorter getaways scattered throughout the year. These take the form of long-weekend retreats to urban centres within several hours of a person or family's home, by air. According to a 1991 "Futures Project" survey conducted by the Hyatt Hotel chain, frequent short vacations were preferred by executives, on the grounds that they helped to alleviate work-related stress and could more easily be programmed into work schedules. While warm weather locales in Florida and the Caribbean are still popular, vacationers are increasingly flocking to regional destinations that are perceived as offering several days worth of entertainment value. The growth of tourism in second tier cities such as Cleveland, Pittsburgh, and San Diego is moving the urban entertainment economy beyond established fantasy cities such as Orlando and Las Vegas, into the heartland of the United States and Canada.

Economic Factors

Until the early 1990s, entertainment conglomerates relied on the first-run theatrical exhibition of motion pictures as their chief money-spinning operation. These were buttressed by "ancillary" markets (network television, pay TV, home video, syndication, foreign distribution) and "complementary" markets (theme parks, toys, video games, licensed merchandise, retail chains). Over the last decade, however, the role of ancillary and complementary markets has grown significantly, triggering a major expansion and restructuring of the global entertainment industry. This is reflected in the increasing emphasis on multiple revenue streams, the growth of synergies and brand empires (see above), and the accelerating pace of mergers and acquisitions resulting in "megamedia" formation.

The growth of ancillary markets has significantly altered the calculus of media economics. It is not unusual now to hear of Hollywood films that only break even or even lose money domestically, but which are very profitable because of strong sales abroad or on video. In some cases, a movie may go directly to video without first being exhibited in theatres. In the past, television networks in the United States were legally prohibited from holding syndication rights, by the so-called "Fin-Syn" rules enforced by the Federal Communications Commission (FCC).[28] The FCC's lifting of this prohibition in 1993 has encouraged the production of new programming and has made the networks more attractive prospects for takeovers by entertainment giants such as Disney.

Until relatively recently, the major player in complementary markets was the Disney Company. When he first opened Disneyland in Anaheim, California, in 1955, Walt Disney recognized that the venture's success depended upon the creation of synergistic linkages among the concept's television shows, motion pictures, theme park, and consumer products. The after-school *Mickey Mouse Club* TV show was a showcase for Disneyland as well as for related merchandise ranging from lunch pails to caps with mouse ears. Even more profitable was the *Davy Crockett* series, which was first shown on the Sunday night Disney prime-time television series on the ABC network (ABC held a one-third interest in Disneyland for the first decade, as well as receiving all profits from food concessions). The series about the Kentucky-bred frontiersman was enormously popular and was successfully spun off into theme park attractions (in the "Adventureland" area of Disneyland), merchandise (the coonskin cap worn by Crockett on the series became one of the biggest product fads of the era), theatrical releases, and even a chart-topping song, "The Ballad of Davy Crockett." As film scholar Douglas Gomery has noted, the "long-run Disney magic on TV consisted of fashioning a popular series that symbiotically promoted its core theme parks into world-class attractions."[29]

Despite Disney's success, other media conglomerates embraced complementary markets somewhat gingerly. A few other motion picture studios (Paramount, Universal Studios, and Warner Bros.) did enter the theme park market, as did Taft Broadcasting, a regional radio and television chain. In the late 1970s and early 1980s, several large entertainment companies invested directly in the toy and video game industries. After Disney had passed on the opportunity to buy in, Warner invested in the Atari home video game system while Universal/MCA flirted with toys and video games through its now long-defunct LJN Toys.

By most accounts, it was the enormous merchandising success of George Lucas's *Star Wars* that convinced entertainment companies that commercial licenses should be a "marketing goal" rather than a "marketing tool." The *Star Wars* trilogy generated US$2.6 billion worth of merchandise sales by the end of the 1980s and transformed the toy industry into a platform for branded products based on Hollywood characters. The huge sales of *Batman* merchandise in the early 1990s further reinforced this trend. With the stakes suddenly much higher, media conglomerates began actively to pursue expansion strategies designed to enhance complementary markets.[30] In one extreme case, *Space Jam,* a feature film with a mix of animated characters and human actors was produced primarily as a vehicle to promote sports merchandise associated with the movie's star, basketball player Michael Jordan.

The Changing Nature of Retail

The expansion of the global entertainment economy is also a reflection of the changing nature of retailing at the cusp of the millennium. This "entertainmentization" of retailing is in no small measure a strategic response to the decline of suburban shopping malls and the twin challenge from off-price retailers and online shopping.

In response to the corporate downsizing of the early 1990s, an increasing number of consumers embraced the concept of "value retail" – brand-name goods at prices below those offered by department and specialty stores. The threat posed by value retailers to suburban and regional shopping centres was exacerbated by the fact that value retailers succeeded in capturing higher-income shoppers as well as the expected lower-income ones.[31] The Factory Outlet Mall, just across the American border in Niagara Falls, New York, has taken this concept to a new level by transforming into a discount outlet for high fashion brands such as Polo/Ralph Lauren, Saks Fifth Avenue, and Jones New York. The 1990s witnessed the entry into Canada of the American "big box" stores – Costco, Staples, Home Depot – housed in stand-alone, warehouse-like structures, as well as the discount department store giant Wal-Mart. By 1997, retail analysts estimated that Wal-Mart was taking slightly more than one out of every four dollars spent at Canadian department stores, after only three years in this country.[32] Finally, there is the growing lure of online retailing. The full impact of Internet retailing has yet to be felt, but in some product areas, notably books and records, travel, and computer software, it has already challenged in-person shopping. With these alternatives newly available in the 1990s, shoppers began to desert existing shopping centres in droves. From 1994 to 1997, more than forty anchor stores left Canadian malls, either declaring bankruptcy or relocating in more profitable retail environments outside the malls.[33]

One major way in which retailers in Canada and the United States have responded to this decline of the shopping mall is to embrace entertainment as a way of bringing back the crowds. Some have retrofitted and expanded, adding megaplex cinemas, themed restaurants, high technology amusement arcades, and other leisure retailers. The more ambitious option has been to build completely new "super-regional" shopping centres that combine value retailing with entertainment components. The leader in taking this approach has been The Mills Corporation, of Arlington, Virginia, which builds facilities of 450,000 to 600,000 square metres (it is rare in Canada to find an enclosed shopping centre over 300,000 square metres). Grapevine Mills, two miles north of Dallas/Fort Worth International Airport, contains an AMC thirty-screen cinema, Imax Theatre, Virgin Megastore, Rainforest Café, Sega Gameworks virtual reality arcade, and, among its 150 retail tenants, Saks Fifth Avenue and Rodeo Drive (Beverly Hills) stores. Arizona Mills, in a suburb of Phoenix, has a megaplex, a Rainforest Café, and an American Wilderness Experience store among its attractions. The first Mills supermall is planned for a Toronto area location on Highway 400 near the Canada's Wonderland theme park, while a slightly smaller Mills mall in Vancouver is also on the drawing board. Both will be built as joint ventures with veteran Canadian developer Cambridge Shopping Centres.

More generally, retailers have reacted by attempting to make the activity of shopping itself more entertaining. This convergence of shopping, fantasy, and fun is known as "shoppertainment." Fashion floors in department stores frequently feature television monitors on which rock videos continuously play. Some leading-edge retailers are embracing the concept of "experiential retailing," which means that shopping is transformed into a themed retail experience complete with interactive exhibits (at the Nike store on Toronto's Bloor Street, patrons are invited to spin a basketball to call up milestone moments in the history of that sport). The new generation of bookstores comes complete with comfortable couches, in-store cafés, and celebrity authors (I once got to meet musician, songwriter, and television star Steve Allen at a local Chapters store). In a recent, much publicized dip into the world of the Internet, the Victoria's Secret lingerie chain broadcast a fashion show on its computer. Web site entertainment, then, has diffused out into the retail environment on a major, unprecedented scale.

Technological Factors

Most contemporary accounts of globalization accord a central role to communications technology. Tony Spybey, for example, stresses the convergence of various aspects of electronic technology in the "information super-highway" that runs between North America, Europe, and East Asia and that embraces telecommunications and computer networks with the aid of high-capacity satellites and fibre-optic cabling. Such technological advances in communications, Spybey observes, have contributed to potentiating and accelerating such major events of social change as the collapse of the Soviet Union and the resurgence of Islam, and have facilitated the contemporary development of global social movements in peace, feminism, and environmentalism.[34] Richard Barnet and John Cavanagh write that satellites, cables, Walkmans, videocassette recorders, CDs, and other marvels of entertainment technology have "created the arteries through which modern entertainment conglomerates are homogenizing global culture." In particular, they cite the daily beaming of MTV programming to 210 million households in seventy-one countries as "the most spectacular technological development of the 1980s."[35]

What is noticed less often, however, is the extent to which technologies developed for the defence and motion picture industries have been downsized and rolled out across a wide array of urban entertainment destinations. Motion simulators, for example, were derived from military and pilot training technologies of the 1970s. Their compact size and portability make them highly adaptable to use in theme parks, museums, festivals, shopping centres, and urban entertainment centres. One of the first examples of this miniaturization was the "Tour of the Universe" ride, introduced at Toronto's CN Tower in 1985. Developed by Douglas Trumbull, designer of special effects for motion pictures such as *Blade Runner* and *2001: A Space Odyssey,* it evolved five years later into the acclaimed *Back to the Future* ride which debuted at the Universal Studios theme park in California. By 1993, Trumbull had developed a simulator theatre with fifteen seats, which could fit into an approximately nine-metre-square space less than five metres high. In similar fashion, IMAX Corporation, the pioneer of large-format movie technology, has introduced the new SR projection system, which is small enough to fit into multiplex cinemas and yet costs two-thirds less to build than a conventional venue. The SR projection system is designed to bring this technology to urban markets with a population base as low as 500,000, unlike conventional IMAX theatres, which need a population of one million or more.[36] This type of technological downsizing is important because it facilitates the growth of the type of regional entertainment destinations that are being developed in response to the "localization of leisure" trend. On the other hand, conventional movie theatre technology is moving in exactly the opposite direction: megaplexes such as The Coliseum and Silver City contain larger screens, stadium seating, and digital sound.

Main Players in the Global Entertainment Economy

Herman and McChesney have characterized the worldwide communications market today as a "global media oligopoly" consisting of two tiers. At the top of the primary tier are the six largest and most fully integrated global media giants – Time-Warner, Disney, Bertelsmann, Viacom, News Corporation, and TCI. Rounding out the top ten are four other firms: Polygram, Seagram, Sony, and General Electric.[37] In the two years since Herman and McChesney compiled their list, Time-Warner has grown even larger, merging with Turner Broadcasting, and, pending regulatory approval, with America Online (AOL). Seagram, through its Universal Studios subsidiary, purchased Polygram, only to be taken over itself by the French utilities and media conglomerate, Vivendi. Most of the thirty or forty firms in the second tier are built on newspaper empires, cable broadcasting systems, or broadcast chains that have evolved into national or regional conglomerates. Of these, three are Canadian: Thomson Corporation, the Hollinger newspaper group, and Rogers Communications.

Rapidly entering the global media market are a number of new players such as computer software giant Microsoft and the telecommunications companies Bell Atlantic-NYNEX and U.S. West. In April 2000, Bell Atlantic Corporation (which had earlier taken over NYNEX), U.S. West, Pactel, and GTE merged to become Verizon, the largest wireless communications company in the United States. Such companies have taken advantage of the convergence of the telecommunications, media, and computer industries, usually entering the traditional media in joint ventures with existing media giants.

Most of the first tier media moguls have been leaders in recognizing the brand synergies attached to complementary markets (see above). Disney is one of the lead architects of this new landscape of leisure. In 1995, the Walt Disney Co. established a division to develop a wide range of new businesses, from location-based entertainment centres to sports restaurants, while its "imagineers" (designers) focused on ways to downsize theme park experiences for use in city locations.[38] Since then, the DisneyQuest entertainment arcades have been introduced, and the Disney-owned "ESPN Zones" in New York and Baltimore offer video games, batting cages, race car simulators, and big screen TVs on which a sports event is always being shown. One distinct advantage that Disney possesses is that it is able to debut and fine-tune its new entertainment initiatives at its theme park complex in Orlando, where a critical mass of patrons is already primed for entertainment experiences. Universal Studios, now a subsidiary of Vivendi, has been a leader in the themed entertainment industry. Universal's "CityWalk," a 460-metre private street that connects the Universal Studios Hollywood theme park with its megaplex theatre and amphitheatre, has come to be regarded as a template for urban entertainment projects and is being cloned by the company itself in Florida and Japan. Sony has joined forces with IMAX Corporation, a Canadian company, to build a series of advanced technology 3-D theatres. In New York, the Sony-IMAX theatre is located in a megaplex complex at Lincoln Square and has become the single highest grossing motion picture screen in the United States, while the four-storey Metreon centre, in San Francisco, is expected to draw over two million patrons per year.

While this global media oligopoly is a major player in the new entertainment economy, the two are not synonymous. The major initiative behind many of the urban entertainment destinations now being built or on the drawing board in fact comes from a handful of long-established real estate developers that have branched out from erecting shopping centres and office buildings. In the United States, the leader has been Simon DeBartolo, of Indianapolis, the largest real estate investment trust in the country, with a market capitalization of US$7.5 billion. Under the direction of veteran developer Mel Simon, the company is involved in some landmark projects including the Forum Shops, an upscale themed mall attached to Caesars Palace casino in Las Vegas, which boasts its own hand-painted, computer-controlled sky. The major Canadian player is Peter Munk's TrizecHahn Corporation. TrizecHahn is constructing a shopping and entertainment complex at the foot of the CN Tower, in Toronto, and another at the totally rebuilt Aladdin casino-hotel in Las Vegas. Its highest profile project, however, is the "Hollywood and Highland" redevelopment along Hollywood Boulevard in Los Angeles. The brainchild of TrizecHahn executive David Malmuth, a former Disney developer, it will wrap a US$388 million urban-destination entertainment centre on Mann's Chinese Theatre and will include a new theatre that is to be the future home of the Academy Awards.

Since they lack experience in such key matters as determining the proper mix of retail tenants, global entertainment giants routinely join forces with experienced real estate developers. The latter usually welcome this collaboration because they need the branded concepts owned by the entertainment moguls.

Less visible than the big media companies or real estate developers, but worth watching, are a clutch of new competitors that are expanding rapidly in new and existing entertainment markets. One rapidly rising meteor in the entertainment industry is what was formerly called SFX Entertainment Inc. Now owned by Clear Channel Entertainment, a San Antonio, Texas, media company that controls 1,170 radio stations, eighteen television stations, and 700,000 outdoor advertising displays, it is aggressively expanding into the management and promotion of concert and theatrical productions. With exclusive booking arrangements in twenty-eight of the top fifty markets in the United States, Clear Channel's recent moves have raised some industry fears of an impending monopoly. In addition, Clear Channel recently acquired Integrated Sports Entertainment, a major sports entertainment company whose clients include National Basketball Association stars Hakeem Olajuwon, Jayson Williams, and John Starks; National Football League quarterbacks Steve Young and Vinny Testaverde; and corporate clients Burger King, Cadillac, Sports Illustrated for Kids, and General Mills-Wheaties. In another twenty-month spending spree in the 1990s, the company purchased four elite sports-agent firms, worth a total of about US$200 million, including super-agent David Falk's sports-management agency, FAME. What it is moving toward, suggests trade journalist Ray Waddell, is "hooking up" corporate America with live music tours that it both books and promotes, in the same way that the sporting industry now combines corporate sponsorships with live events.[39]

The Impact of the New Global Entertainment Economy

While economic development has long dominated the agendas and politics of urban governments, the new consumption-based versions associated with an international market culture appear to be particularly problematic. Reichl attributes this to the stultifying effect of Disneyesque places on social diversity and democratic social life. Assessing the recent redevelopment of Times Square in New York, he observes: "In an effort to create a place marketable to mainstream tourists and corporate tenants, a coalition of public and private elites imposed a Disney model of controlled, themed public space on an area of remarkable, if unsettling, diversity. In doing so, they sacrificed the provocative, raw energy produced by the friction of different social groups in close interaction for the stultifying hum of a smoothly functioning machine for commercial consumption."[40]

According to Andranovich, Burbank, and Heying, the well-crafted image of the city that we find in "tourist bubbles" such as Times Square contributes to the sense that downtowns are being reshaped for recreational users rather than for those who actually live in the city.[41] Julier notes that the conversion of focused pockets of the cityscape into outposts of the new cultural economy of postindustrial cities may be undertaken as "a local response to the globalization of capital and the demand to attract international investment," but it ends up as "a way of producing an illusion of the cultural capital of urban unity for the benefit and reward of upper- and middle-class commitment to urban living."[42] Each of these academic observers (Reichl, Andranovich, and Julier) similarly critiques the consumption-based development associated with the global entertainment economy on the grounds that it is undemocratic, socially exclusive, and rigidly predictable. The danger here is that the identities of our urban centres will be undermined even as global power relationships are being enforced.[43]

In further considering the implications of the trend toward theme-park-style urban development, three specific impact areas can be identified: urban governance, public space and community life, and Canadian cultural identity.

Urban Governance

In an article in a leading international urban studies journal, Australian social scientists Glen Searle and Michael Bounds describe some recent difficulties faced by the state government of New South Wales (NSW). With urban planning and development control constitutionally the responsibility of the states rather than the federal or local governments, New South Wales has found itself on the horns of a dilemma. On the one hand, changes in federal politics have favoured a shift to a market-driven economy in which government functions are downsized, privatized, and corporatized. At the same time, Australia has seen an escalating intercity competition to attract global capital, notably that attached to the entertainment industry. The NSW state government has reacted to this by implementing policies that favour the reduction of local impediments to development and the sale or lease of its own landholdings to entertainment entrepreneurs on favourable terms. Drawing on three case studies – the Eastern Creek Raceway, the Sydney Casino, and the Year 2000 Olympic Games, Searle and Bounds demonstrate how the pressure to bid for facilities and events associated with global entertainment and consumption led the NSW government to appropriate local planning powers in order to fast-track the projects and circumvent environmental challenges.[44]

As is the case in Australia, the increasing emphasis of urban governance in Canada and the United States has been on "public-private partnerships" oriented toward an explicit economic development agenda rather than the social, redistributional one that characterized the postwar period.[45] In this new policy environment, governments increasingly play the role of urban entrepreneurs, devising place-marketing strategies that they then direct toward the global "image bank" for consumption by media, sport, and leisure corporations.[46] But some major liabilities are attached to this form of cultural "smokestack chasing."

As Grant and Hutchison have discussed in the case of foreign manufacturing investment in American states, an incongruity is growing rapidly between the devolution of development functions to government units with smaller and fixed boundaries and the rising global economic reach of the corporations with whom they must deal. That is, state and provincial governments "are being inserted into a global economy and called upon to play a larger role in deciding their economic destinies, while the forces that shape those destinies are often too overwhelming or distant for them to manage."[47] Using time series data for the years 1978-85, Grant and Hutchison found that states that were drawn far beyond their borders into the game of "global smokestack chasing" soon floundered in deep water. Four supply-side "policy packages" are commonly used to lure foreign factories: debt financing programs that make or guarantee loans to business; geographically targeted policies meant to stimulate development in selected areas within states; labour market deregulation policies – such as abolishing the minimum wage – that lower labour costs for corporations; and regressive tax policies, such as corporate income tax exemptions, designed to reduce the tax burden imposed on corporations. Only the latter measure was found to have any significant effect or influence on corporate location decisions.

In their attempts to attract sports teams, casinos, entertainment malls, and hallmark events (e.g., Olympic Games), Canadian municipal and provincial governments are beginning to confront the same kind of pressures of a spatialized global economy that have dogged American smokestack chasers. Consider, for example, the case of the "Technodome," the most ambitious urban entertainment project heretofore proposed for a Canadian urban setting.

The "Technodome"

In 1995, the Urban Land Institute, a research and lobby group for the American real estate industry, began its sponsorship of an annual conference on urban entertainment development. Among those powerfully impressed by what they were hearing was Abraham Reichmann, president of Heathmount A.E. Corp., a private company that "exists to put Canada on the theme park map."[48] With his uncle Albert, former chairman of Olympia and York Developments, Ltd. (once the world's largest commercial real estate developer), on board as chairman and chief executive, Abraham set about making his mark. After unsuccessful efforts to put a movie studio attraction on the grounds of the Canadian National Exhibition (CNE), in Toronto, and build a $2 billion theme park near Niagara Falls, New York, Heathmount had its proposal accepted in principle for the $1 billion "Technodome."

Initially designed to be built on a corner of the 525-hectare former military base at Downsview in northwestern Toronto, the 600,000-square-metre Technodome was to include an indoor ski hill, a white-water kayaking facility, a beach, a rainforest, a thirty-screen multiplex cinema, a Hollywood-style movie studio and a re-creation of Bourbon Street in New Orleans. On hearing that the project had been given the green light, Mel Lastman, the mayor of North York (and subsequently the mayor of Toronto), proclaimed with characteristic hyperbole that the Technodome "will be the No. 1 jewel in all of the GTA [Greater Toronto Area]; there's nothing like it in the whole world."[49]

In March 1999, however, newspapers in Toronto and Montreal reported that the Reichmanns were considering moving the Technodome to Montreal, on the grounds that Canada Lands Company, the Crown agency in charge of the Downsview redevelopment, insisted on leasing the site rather than selling the land needed for the project. While Heathmount's first choice was said to be federal land in the westernmost part of the Port of Montreal, it was considering a site farther west at the "Technoparc," an underutilized, high technology industrial park next to the Bonaventure Expressway. This option was made even more attractive by the provincially run industrial development corporation Société générale de financement (SGF), which was reported to have offered to invest as much as 40 to 45 percent of the $135 million Technodome start-up costs. A month later, Heathmount made its decision public and official, announcing that the Technoparc locale had won out. Both the *Globe & Mail* and the *National Post* declared this to be a "development victory" for Montreal.

Some industry observers have suggested that the Technodome project is a white elephant that is too expensive ever to be built in either Toronto or Montreal; nevertheless, this episode has raised some pertinent questions about urban entertainment destinations and public policy. As financial journalist Eric Reguly noted in his *Globe & Mail* column, projects such as the Technodome are far too large to be guided by a small, virtually unknown Crown corporation whose specialties have been helping to dispose of surplus federal property and finding new uses for redundant military bases.[50] At the same time, local governments in both cities, caught up in a current of cultural smokestack chasing, do not seem to be capable of critically appraising whether the Technodome project is feasible, affordable, and environmentally compatible. They appear instead to see it simply as something that would give their city a competitive edge in the urban growth game. Thus the Montreal city councillor in charge of economic development was quoted as saying, "the price (of land) won't be an object, it won't be a major, determining consideration."[51]

More generally, the Technodome negotiations highlight what Leaf and Pamuk have identified as "the central dilemma of globalization." This is the tension between the conflicting roles of the state as a "facilitator" linking nations and communities with the global economy, and as a "guardian" seeking to protect its citizenry from the more negative impacts of global capitalism.[52] Reflecting on the rise and fall of property-led development in London and New York in the 1980s and 1990s, Rutgers University planning professor Susan Fainstein insists that economic restructuring and redevelopment, including the theme park development of the future, can be adequately directed only by understanding how the global and the local arenas interact. Furthermore, she recommends a new type of improved public-private partnership that would better balance the facilitator and guardian roles of the state. In Fainstein's view, it is inevitable that giant, multinational, service-producing corporations will come calling. Public policy makers therefore have to be prepared to "tap into their economic power" while making sure that urban populations do not "remain hostage to 'private' decisions shielded from democratic scrutiny despite their public significance."[53]

Public Space and Local Community Life

One of the chief attractions of the new entertainment economy has been its promise of reviving face-to-face interaction in urban settings. It is therefore treated by some observers as a much needed antidote to the disembodied form of communication found in Internet chat rooms and other such computer-mediated settings. Commenting on the recent boomlet in public lectures, *Globe & Mail* columnist Michael Valpy praised Toronto as a city of real, not virtual, meeting places: "If the cinema business knows what it is doing, cocooning is tottering. Huge multiscreen cineplexes are mushrooming through Toronto from the downtown to the suburbs. Ten thousand people throng the nightclub zone on a summer's weekend night. Lunchtime pulsates with neat little cafés. Telecommuting just hasn't happened."[54]

In Valpy's view, we are seeking out a more actively human experience than is possible by renting a video or surfing the Internet, although perhaps not as social as the bowling lionized by political scientist Robert Putnam as the key to civic economic success and democracy.[55]

Sociologist Craig Calhoun, in contrast, argues that new communications technologies such as the Internet have fostered the atomizing of the city into small-scale enclaves with weak local connections to each other. What he is thinking of in particular is the tremendous growth of gated communities in suburban and exurban areas. These gated enclaves are said to foster the compartmentalization of community life, something which is "antithetical to the social constitution of a vital public sphere."

Valpy and Calhoun share a conviction that urban public life based on propinquity is preferable to virtual communities, which rarely "pull beyond one's immediate personal choices of taste and culture." Calhoun's ideal seems to be the eighteenth-century European city, which was chock full of coffee houses, theatres, public festivals, and other "public spaces" in which people of different social identities were drawn into contact. By contrast, the industrial revolution, the rise of urban planning, and the new technologies of transportation and communication have collectively robbed cities of their public spaces and established an overwhelming plurality of what he terms "indirect social relations," those which involve no physical co-presence but instead exist only through the intermediation of information technology and/or bureaucratic organizations. Thus, sitting at the Lanterna, a café in Greenwich Village noted for its splendid apricot tarts, Calhoun concludes that electronically mediated groups and networks are limited in their capacity to enhance citizen power in democracies. Here he is reacting to a comment by William Mitchell in his book *City of Bits,* in which Mitchell refers to his computer keyboard as his "café." Calhoun counters that his café is in Greenwich Village, not the electronic village, contending that the Lanterna and the cybercafé down the street are both "sociable public space" where there are "dimensions of publicness and sociability [that are] reproduced poorly if at all in computer-mediated communication." Electronically mediated groups work best, he believes, as supplements to face-to-face encounters. With "cyberdemocracy" thus running far behind the "cybercapitalism" of globalized financial markets, local urban settings remain absolutely vital to preserving and enhancing public discourse.[56]

If Calhoun and Valpy are correct, then are the leisure-soaked, consumption-based cities that are created by the global entertainment economy hotbeds of civility and urbanity? Certainly, the promoters of fantasy cities like to think so. "Consumers crave the functionality of the city: dense, eclectic, spontaneous, pedestrian environments where entertainment, dining and retail options are in close proximity," suggest urban entertainment consultants Patrick Phillips and Jay Wheatley.[57] Reflecting on Berlin's future as a cultural capital, *New York Times* bureau chief Roger Cohen describes the Potsdamer Platz as a "sea of anonymous commercialism" but admits that "the development has proved hugely popular, one of the few places where 'Ossis' and 'Wessis' really mingle."[58] Other observers of the theme park city, however, detect a bleaker future. Paul Goldberger, the noted New York architectural critic, has identified the proliferation of "urbanoid environments," sealed-off private spaces which purport to be public places, but which lack all the energy, variety, visual stimulation, and cultural opportunities of the real thing. Intimately linked to the fusion of consumerism, entertainment, and popular culture, this counterfeit form of urban experience is measured, controlled, and tightly organized – cleaner and safer but also flatter and duller. Its shops and cafés are filled with consumers of culture, not with the makers and shapers of it.[59]

Another important aspect of this policy debate revolves around the influence of entertainment development on social equity and exclusion. According to Fainstein, this issue has two facets: the direct impacts of projects on different social groupings, and the extent to which the public receives the benefits of socially created gain in the value of property.[60]

Affordability constitutes one major barrier to accessibility. By and large, these new entertainment destinations are designed to attract out-of-town tourists and affluent suburban "day trippers" embarked on "leisure safaris into the depths of the postmodern metropolis."[61] As such, they remain beyond the financial reach of local residents. Referring to recent changes in contemporary Los Angeles, Mike Davis argues they mark the demise of what was once a genuine "democratic space" – free beaches, luxurious parks, and "cruising strips."[62] In some cases, these projects may also end up forcing the poor and disadvantaged out of urban spaces that they formerly occupied and utilized.

Furthermore, the economic "spillover" effects from leisure and entertainment development are not overwhelming. In one of the most comprehensive empirical analyses of its type, American economist Robert Baade charted the impact of new stadiums and professional sports teams on income levels for the eight major regions in the continental United States between 1959 and 1987. His results indicate that professional sports teams in fact have little impact on a city's economy.[63] In a similar fashion, Marc Levine failed to detect much economic spillover to local shops and businesses from the festival marketplace development around Baltimore's Inner Harbor in the 1970s.[64] It is still too early to know whether the urban entertainment destinations of today will create any economic ripples in surrounding neighbourhoods and communities, but this result can by no means be assumed.

Canadian Cultural Identity

In contrast to the topic of foreign media ownership and cultural protection policies, which has been extensively documented and analyzed, little is known about the effects of locality-based entertainment on Canadian culture and identity.

A little more than three decades ago, *Financial Post* journalist Robert Perry published a series of controversial *Post* articles in the form of a book entitled *Galt USA: the American Presence in a Canadian City* (1971). Near the beginning of the book, Perry profiled what he called "Popcult Galt," a New Jersey-style motel and fast-food strip along Hespeler Road, which ran between the city limits and the downtown. With its 7.5-metre-high rocket ship outside the Satellite Motel and a giant snowman guarding the entrance to the Thunderbird golf driving range, the Hespeler Road strip was perhaps an early harbinger of the coming of the theme park cities of the 1990s. Even the now long-defunct Red Barn hamburger drive-in, owned and operated by a Canadian, used American marketing techniques, standards, specifications, systems, and methods, giving its American franchisers, Perry observed, "the ultimate control."[65]

A decade later, Taft Broadcasting of Cincinnati, Ohio, added to their theme park chain by opening "Canada's Wonderland" near Maple, Ontario, just north of Toronto. In a remarkably blunt assessment recorded five years earlier, Provincial Treasurer Darcy McKeough had posed some potentially sticky questions to his cabinet colleagues:

1 Why can't a Canadian business take on this type of project? On the assumption that there may be room for only one such park in Southern Ontario, would we be shutting out the possibility of a future Canadian operation?
2 This thing could be seen as a Canadian "Disneyland" (or I guess it would be "Yogi Bear Land") and some people will argue about the cultural implications of putting it into the hands of an American operation.[66]

Despite McKeough's qualms, the provincial cabinet, under pressure from the Ministry of Industry and Tourism, readily blessed the proposed theme park, as did the federal Foreign Investment Review Agency. Yet aside from the name itself, very little in the park was in any way representative of Canadian life. Writing on the eve of its opening, York University geographers James Cameron and Ronald Bordessa issued this warning: "In spite of all its sophistication in marketing techniques, the Taft Broadcasting Company cannot altogether obliterate cultural differences though the sobering conclusion is that they almost certainly will become one of the agents promoting its steady erosion."[67]

Now, the next wave of foreign cultural content is about to descend upon Canadian cities. It is aggressively themed and is branded around American pop celebrities, sports stars, and cartoon characters. If there is a template for this, it could well be DisneyQuest, the entertainment giant's major new initiative into the urban entertainment market. A multistorey interactive indoor theme park that uses computer-based virtual reality technology, DisneyQuest can be described as a sort of "portable Disney World," designed to "deliver a piece of the Disney magic closer to people's houses."[68] From the swirling Hurricane Mickey logo on the exterior of the building to the video games and rides inside – Buzz Lightyear's Astro Blaster (based on a character from the Disney movie *Toy Story*), Aladdin's Magic Carpet Ride – DisneyQuest is meant to consciously exploit synergies with Disney's movie characters. With prototypes in Orlando and Chicago, Disney plans to franchise the project both domestically and internationally, including locations in Canadian cities.

Some scholars might respond to the planned rollout of the DisneyQuest model across the globe by citing the phenomenon of "glocalization," whereby the negative effects of a global consumer culture are progressively mitigated as they interact with local values and structures. For example, the contributors to editor James Watson's book *Golden Arches East: McDonald's in East Asia* (1997) demonstrate how East Asian consumers have eliminated the "fast" from fast food, transforming their McDonald's outlets into local institutions where the relations between staff and customers have become personalized (Beijing, Hong Kong) or politicized (Taipei). In many parts of the region, the Golden Arches have come to house leisure centres, after-school clubs, and meeting halls. One contributor to the book, David Wu, observes that in today's Taiwan two opposite forms of consumption, the "hyperlocal" (as symbolized by betelnut chewing) and the "transnational" (eating "Big Macs") coexist, and to a surprising extent reinforce one another as expressions of national identity.[69]

At first glance, it is difficult to envision how this glocalization process might operate in the Canadian context. While there are clear and documented differences in Canadian and American consumer tastes – we evidently prefer doughnuts, poutine, and Canadian Tire – our choices in music, clothing, and entertainment tend to be similar, suggesting that local values and structures are unlikely to mitigate the negative effects of global consumer culture. At the same time, some identifiable differences exist. Reporting on the most recent results of an annual poll that measures attitudes of Canadian versus American respondents on several social and cultural issues, Michael Adams of the Environics Research Group found that Canadians have fundamentally different views about dealing with conflict, about relating to their parents and children, and about relating to authority. For example, Canadians are more likely to favour accommodation rather than domination as a problem-solving strategy. "Globalization," Adams asserts, "may actually enhance the difference among cultures, rather than converge them."[70] While researchers have not provided comprehensive content analyses of the branded cultural products and images that are flowing into Canada as part of the expanding global entertainment economy, researchers have examined in great detail the ideological tropes contained in Disney movies and theme parks. These clearly emphasize such traditional American value themes as "America as the land of opportunity" and "the right to bear arms in defense of liberty"[71] When confronted with such lessons as part of the cultural discourse embedded in the current generation of high technology rides, games, and themed attractions, will Canadian teenagers be capable of maintaining a critical distance or will they accept these messages at face value?

Policy Implications and Options

In the past, cultural industries policy in Canada has been guided by two main arguments.[72] According to the *economic* (or industrial) argument, the federal government is compelled to intervene in the marketplace in order to nurture and protect Canadian-owned businesses that otherwise could not survive in the hurly-burly of intense international competition. In particular, Canadian companies are said to be potentially threatened by foreign-owned branch plants that supply imported content to the domestic market at a small fraction of the cost of generating comparable Canadian content.[73] The second, and perhaps more fundamental, argument used to establish cultural industries policy is a *cultural* one. This cultural argument maintains that telecommunications, broadcasting, film, publishing, and recordings are instruments for nation-building; they are the key to establishing and maintaining a distinct Canadian identity. Even in the midst of a continuous flood of American messages and images, Canadian personalities, viewpoints, and landscapes have continued to flourish, but only because they are shielded by a system of subsidies, tax breaks, and protective legislation.

In recent years, however, a crisis has been steadily looming. David Taras argues that the pace of envelopment by American popular culture has been accelerating as a consequence of structural changes in broadcasting, particularly television. He cites three changes that have been of special importance: new economies of scale enjoyed by the US television industry, which give it enormous advantages over its Canadian competitors;

the changing circumstances of the CBC, which has been reeling under fiscal strain and is unable to reconcile its obligations to serve a series of minority audiences with its financial need to capture a mass audience; and the advent of new technologies such as satellite, cable, and video, which have splintered audiences into narrow segments[74] and left Canadian television networks open to what Marc Raboy has called "the brutality of the gutted marketplace."[75]

What then of the rapidly diffusing global entertainment economy? Should the Canadian public policy response to this trend be neutral, supportive, or regulatory? If the latter, should it follow the dual direction that has been set by cultural policy in the past or carve out a new trail? To begin with, I detect two major difficulties.

As Magder has argued, the Canadian state is currently divided between agencies and departments that have business and economics as their focus and are committed to trade liberalization and neoliberal economics, and the cultural industries portfolio, which backstops a welter of protectionist policy measures "that muddy the marketplace transparency much in vogue."[76] As was noted earlier, this tension between the conflicting role of the state as "facilitator" and "guardian" constitutes one of the central dilemmas of globalization. The problem is even more acute when we turn to local politics and administration, where an "urban growth machine" promotes the development of tourism and entertainment destinations as one of its major objectives. As Rosentraub has noted with regard to the headlong rush to attract professional sports teams to North American cities, "the provision of subsidies to influence the location of capital has been a constant and frustrating component of local economic policy" and one which has been dictated in no small part by the "imperatives of global competition."[77] An outstanding example of this trend is the current scheme to massively redevelop the Toronto waterfront. Rather than being determined by an extensive and open public debate, the future of the Port Lands, the CNE grounds, and the Inner Harbour appears set to follow from the Fung Report (Toronto Waterfront Revitalization Task Force Report), which was written with one eye on Toronto's bid to "win" the right to stage the 2008 Summer Olympic Games. This area will therefore be developed into a sports, entertainment, and leisure corridor. Local space is thus (potentially) transformed into a globalized "hub" where flows of finance, information, people, goods, and services are temporarily targeted and assembled.[78]

Second, the global entertainment economy crosses so many jurisdictions and purviews that it cannot easily be fitted into a single policy area. Mostly, decisions about megamalls and megaplexes, sports stadiums and gambling casinos, end up being made narrowly on the basis of compliance to land use and zoning regulations, with no serious discussion of the social and cultural impacts. Too often, decisions are made about individual projects and proposals without situating them within a wider policy framework. What is sorely lacking in Canada is a national urban policy. Since the demise of Urban Affairs Canada in the 1970s, the responsibility for deciding on the future of cities has been downloaded onto the provinces and onto local municipalities that rarely take into account the larger picture. Those issues that do show up on the larger radar screen – the questionable effects of casino gambling, the advisability of tax subsidies to sports team owners – tend to be debated in relative isolation. At the same time, a nearly complete policy vacuum envelops other government programs and activities that fall outside the traditional watershed of cultural/communications policy; the disposal of surplus federal lands by Canada Lands Co. Ltd. (see the case study, above, on the Technodome controversy) is a good example of this.

Before concluding whether Canadian public policy should respond proactively to urban entertainment development with support, neutrality, or regulation, it is necessary to document the magnitude of this type of development in Canada, its organizational co-ordinates, and its effects on the local community. In a collection of articles on "Business Elites and Urban Development," published in 1988, editor Scott Cummings suggests four general themes related to the encounter between private enterprise and public policy in the urban context of the 1980s. First, it is necessary to identify: the preferred strategies for urban growth of urban business elites, who typically establish development coalitions and use public institutions to design and implement a growth agenda for their cities that is consistent with enhancing their own prosperity; and the conflicts that result between private benefits and the public good.[79] Second, we should consider the ability of real estate interests and others centrally implicated in the economic redevelopment of the city to mobilize resources from the local state and how this can be successfully countered by community and neighbourhood groups. Third, we need to look at how local development strategies are being influenced by extra-local events and investment trends, especially those that occur within an international economic context. Finally, it is important to document how changes in the organization of space, which are related to the changing economy, have produced a "dual city" marked by increasing class polarization.[80] Cummings's four themes can easily be applied to the case of the global entertainment economies and the city of the twenty-first century, and they provide a logical starting point for a systematic public policy analysis.

Conclusion

As the new millennium begins, corporate "brand empires" are rapidly hiving off from television, motion pictures, and professional sports, and "colonizing" urban downtowns and exurban malls, museums and schools, holidays and festivals. Much as fast-food giant McDonald's has already done, leisure developers such Nike, Disney, and Virgin "are trumpeting their brands by using comforting, familiar logos, thus attracting a large percentage of the population."[81] In doing so, they may well end up undermining communities of propinquity or place that for many Canadians remain a key source of identity and culture.

In its romanticized and overly simplified version of this process, Hollywood depicts a David and Goliath battle between the people-oriented "shop around the corner" and the profit driven megastore. In real communities, however, the tension between the global and the local is more subtle. Just before sitting down to write this, I went for a walk along Queen Street, the major shopping avenue in our east Toronto waterfront neighbourhood. Stopping for coffee at a Starbucks, I noted that the franchisee had mounted a new exhibition of paintings by local artists on the walls of the café and was advertising a series of poetry readings on Sunday afternoons. As I sipped my drink, I browsed through our community newspaper, noting a letter to the editor and a column by a local historian, both calling for a campaign to save a local boathouse, first built in the 1930s, which has fallen into a state of disrepair. On the way back, I saw a woman wearing a leather and suede jacket on which was prominently displayed the logo of "Silver City," a new megaplex cinema chain that has begun to ripple across the Canadian urban landscape. What these seemingly disparate events have in common is that each in some way indicates a differing brushstroke on the evolving canvas of the local/global community. Neighbourhoods like mine are fast becoming sites for contrasting "economies of signs and spaces."[82] Some, like the Silver Birch Boathouse, are viewed by long-time residents as pieces of area history that should be cherished and kept. Others, such as the Silver City jacket, are mobile advertisements for new entertainment brands. Starbucks is one of the hot global brands of the 1990s, but, here at least, it has made a token gesture toward supporting the local artistic and literary scene. Indeed, it is in the context of everyday community life that we can best find the nexus between traditional values and the new outlooks associated with globalization.

Attention must also be paid to the role of the state in responding to the emerging global entertainment economy. In his chapter in this volume, Marc Raboy observes that the pursuit of public policy objectives in culture and communication today requires a shift in focus from the national to the global policy arena and appropriate strategies for intervention through new global policy mechanisms. Yet are there any transnational fora that pertain to complementary markets and themed leisure retail experiences, as there are for telecommunications standards or intellectual property rights? Is there a disjunction between the spread of the global entertainment economy and the simultaneous movement of governance downward and outward to lower levels of the government, the market, and the community? How can we best rationalize the seemingly conflicting roles of the state as both cultural smokestack chaser and guardian of Canadian culture?

Muddying the waters somewhat is the recent surge of Canadian cultural exports, especially to the United States. According to a Statistics Canada report released in June 2001, exports of Canadian culture were worth $4.5 billion in the year 2000, up nearly 40 percent since 1996.[83] While this figure may be skewed by the massive sales of recorded music by a handful of Canadian-born performers – Shania Twain, Céline Dion, Alanis Morissette – it nevertheless also includes creative powerhouses such as Cirque du Soleil, which has become a fixture both in Las Vegas casinos and Disney theme parks. With culture becoming one of Canada's fastest-growing export sectors, governments need to become more pro-active in providing financial and marketing support to domestic producers and performers. One possible approach is to promote cultural exports more aggressively through the Export Development Corporation. Such a position would reinforce the situation that the editors of this collection have described as "the handmaiden state," in which public policy concentrates on facilitating entry into the global economy by producing a climate favourable to research and innovation and by providing higher levels of technical training. For example, the much heralded program in computer animation at Sheridan College, in Oakville, Ontario, can be seen as a template insofar as it provides Canadian-trained talent for Disney, DreamWorks, and other film studios that have re-embraced animated feature films. Despite such initiatives, however, the corporate conveyor belts from south of the border continue to bring in more cultural product than we export. Furthermore, Canadians must often necessarily work within the framework of American formulas for motion pictures, television shows, and themed attractions, which dictate a maximum branding potential and a minimum degree of moral complexity. As a result, national identities may erode over time, even as made-in-Canada cultural products achieve higher numbers. This is especially relevant at the level of local communities, which tend to become repositories of shared cultures and political loyalties in the face of the weakening of national identities.

Finally, as Cameron and Stein suggest in their conclusion to this volume, the process of globalization cannot be expected to "march in an uninterrupted, smooth, linear sequence" (p. 150). This statement is especially relevant with regard to urban entertainment development, which depends on ever-increasing flows of investment money, hot new global brands, and foreign tourists. Already, there are bumps in the road, with cinema chains facing bankruptcy because of the overcapacity created by an orgy of megaplex construction, and some of the better-known themed restaurant chains (Rainforest Café, Planet Hollywood) battling to stay alive. If city planners and politicians persist in investing significant sums of taxpayer dollars in infrastructure, subsidies, and promotions linked to the tourist economy while ignoring festering issues of poverty, homelessness, and widening social inequality, we most certainly risk ending up becoming, in Cameron and Stein's words, a "state of unrequited dreams" (p. 151). Governments, then, must find a better accommodation between their dual roles as "facilitators" and "guardians," both at the broad level of policy making and in the specific details that spell out the parameters of public-private partnerships.

Notes

1 Michael Wolf, *The Entertainment Economy: How Mega-Media Forces Are Transforming Our Lives* (New York: Times Books, 1999), 4.

2 Emma Rees, "Leisure Futures," *Design Week. The Big Picture: Leisure* (October 1998): 24-5. Cited in Guy Julier, *The Culture of Design* (London: Sage Publications, 2000), 146.

3 Louise Earl, "Entertainment Services: A Growing Consumer Market," *Service Indicators/ Indicateurs des Services – 3rd Quarter* (Statistics Canada) (1998): 17.

4 Albert Warson, "Entertaining Canada," *Building* 48, 3 (1998): 34.

5 See John Hannigan, *Fantasy City: Pleasure and Profit in the Postmodern Metropolis* (London and New York: Routledge, 1998).

6 Michael Sorkin, "Introduction: Variations on a Theme Park," in *Variations on a Theme Park: The New American City and the End of Public Space,* ed. Michael Sorkin (New York: The Noonday Press, 1992), xiii.

7 Jerry Mander, "Technologies of Globalization," in *The Case against the Global Economy: And for a Turn toward the Local,* ed. J.M. Mander and E. Goldsmith (San Francisco: Sierra Club Books, 1996), 350.

8 Herbert Schiller, *Mass Communication and American Empire* (Boston: Beacon Press, 1971).

9 Notably, David Rieff, "A Global Culture," *World Policy Journal* 10, 4 (1993-4): 73-81.

10 Richard Barnet and John Cavanagh, "Homogenization and Global Culture," in *The Case against the Global Economy,* ed. Mander and Goldsmith, 71-2.

11 Benjamin Barber, *Jihad vs. McWorld* (New York: Times Books, 1995), 97.

12 Jason Squire "What's Your Major? Entertainment Studies?" *The New York Times,* 19 April 1998, section 3, 13.

13 Wolf, *The Entertainment Economy,* 224-5.

14 David K. Foot and Daniel Stoffman, *Boom, Bust and Echo: How to Profit from the Coming Demographic Shift* (Toronto: Stoddart, 1997).

15 Jeremy Cato, "Muscle in on This Action," *Globe & Mail,* 15 March 1999, D12.

16 Louise Earl, "Spending on Selected Recreation Items in Canada," *Focus on Culture* (Statistics Canada) 10, 2 (1998): 3.

17 Bob Losyk, "Generation X: What They Think and What They Plan to Do," *The Futurist* 31, 2 (1997): 4.

18 Joseph Turow, *Breaking up America: Advertising and the New Media World* (Chicago: University of Chicago Press, 1997).

19 Wolf, *The Entertainment Economy,* 35.

20 Earl, "Entertainment Services," 27.

21 John P. Robinson and Geoffrey Godbey, *Time for Life: The Surprising Ways Americans Use Their Time* (University Park: Pennsylvania State University Press, 1997).

22 Juliet Schor, *The Overworked American: The Unexpected Decline of Leisure* (New York: Basic Books, 1991).

23 Arlie Hochschild, *The Time Bind: When Work Becomes Home and Home Becomes Work* (New York: Metropolitan Books, 1997).

24 See Elia Kacapyr, "Are We Having Fun Yet?" *American Demographics* 19, 10 (1997): 28-30.
25 Jiri Zuzanek and Bryan J.A. Smale, "More Work – Less Leisure? Changing Allocations of Time in Canada, 1981 to 1992," *Loisir et société/Society and Leisure* 20 (1997): 95.
26 Wolf, *The Entertainment Economy,* 38-40.
27 Michael S. Rubin and Robert Gorman, "Re-inventing Leisure," *Urban Land* 52, 2 (1993): 27.
28 The Financial Interest in Syndication (Fin-Syn) Rule(s) was adopted by the Federal Communications Commission (FCC) in the United States to prevent the three television networks (ABC, CBS, NBC) from restricting the market for television programming. The rule(s) prohibited the networks from owning re-runs; they were allowed only to lease them. In 1993, after a protracted and contentious set of hearings, the FCC finally opened the syndications business to the networks on the grounds that changes in broadcasting – the development of cable television networks – had undermined the theory that the three networks could control the market for video programming. See Robert Corn-Revere, "Economics and Media Regulation," in *Media Economics: Theory and Practice,* ed. Alison Alexander, James Owers, and Rod Carveth (Hillsdale, NJ: Laurence Erlbaum Associates, 1993), 71-90.
29 Douglas Gomery, "Disney's Business History: A Re-Interpretation," in *Disney Discourse: Producing the Magic Kingdom,* ed. E. Smoodin (New York and London: Routledge, 1994), 77.
30 See Dan Steinbock, *Triumph and Erosion in the American Media and Entertainment Industries* (Westport, CT: Quorum Books, 1995), 129.
31 Michael Beyard et al., *Developing Urban Entertainment Centers* (Washington, DC: Urban Land Institute, 1998), 11.
32 "Wal-Mart Romps ahead in Canada," *Building* 47, 5 (1997): 34
33 Albert Warson, "Born again Shopping Centres," *Building* 47, 5 (1997): 33.
34 Tony Spybey, *Globalization and World Society* (Cambridge: Polity Press, 1996), 111-12.
35 Barnet and Cavanagh, "Homogenization and Global Culture," 71-2.
36 H. Enchin, "IMAX Scores Its Biggest Deal in 10-Theatre Sale to Regal," *Globe & Mail,* 25 June 1997, B8.
37 Edward S. Herman and Robert W. McChesney, *Global Media: The New Missionaries of Global Capitalism* (London and Washington, DC: Cassell, 1997), 70.
38 Hannigan, *Fantasy City,* 111.
39 Ray Waddell, "SFX Pays $93.6 Mil. for Nederlander Interests," *Amusement Business,* 8 February 1999, 1, 6.
40 Alexander Reichl, *Reconstructing Times Square: Politics and Culture in Urban Development* (Lawrence, KA: University Press of Kansas, 1999), 179.
41 Greg Andranovich, Matthew J. Burbank, and Charles H. Heying, "Olympic Cities: Lessons Learned from Mega-event Politics," *Journal of Urban Affairs* 23 (2001), 115-16.
42 Julier, *The Culture of Design,* 28-30.
43 Steven Miles, "The Consuming Paradox: A New Research Agenda for Urban Consumption," *Urban Studies* 35 (1998): 1001-8.
44 Glen Searle and Michael Bounds, "State Powers, State Land and Competition for Global Entertainment: The Case of Sydney," *International Journal of Urban and Regional Research* 23 (1999): 165-72.
45 Stephen Graham and Simon Marvin, *Telecommunications and the City: Electronic Spaces, Urban Places* (London and New York: Routledge, 1996), 42.
46 See David Harvey, "Urban Places in the 'Global Village': Reflections on the Urban Condition in Late Twentieth Century Capitalism," in *World Cities and the Future of the Metropoles,* ed. Luigi Mazza (Milan: Electra, 1988), 23.
47 Don Sherman Grant III and Richard Hutchison, "Global Smokestack Chasing: A Comparison of the State-level Determinants of Foreign and Domestic Manufacturing Investment," *Social Problems* 43 (1996): 22-3.
48 Eric Reguly, "Reichmann: The Next Generation Takes a Shot," *Globe & Mail,* 6 April 1999, A10.
49 Alan Barnes, "Unveiled: A New Downsview," *Toronto Star,* 25 April 1997, A1.

50 Eric Reguly, "Downsview Debacle Needs Leadership," *Globe & Mail,* 25 March 1999, B2.
51 Estanislao Osiewicz and To Thanh Ha, "Montreal's $1 Billion Coup Infuriates Lastman," *Globe & Mail,* 26 March 1999, A1.
52 Michael Leaf and Ayse Pamuk, "Habitat II and the Globalization of Ideas," *Journal of Planning Education and Research* 17 (1997): 71-8.
53 Susan S. Fainstein, *The City Builders: Property, Politics, and Planning in London and New York* (Oxford, UK, and Cambridge, MA: Blackwell, 1994), 252-3.
54 Michael Valpy, "Flocking to Lectures: Live and in Person," *Globe & Mail,* 30 March 1999, A11.
55 Robert Putnam, *Bowling Alone: The Collapse and Revival of American Community* (New York: Simon and Schuster, 2000).
56 Craig Calhoun, "Community without Propinquity Revisited: Communications Technology and the Transformation of the Urban Public Sphere," *Sociological Inquiry* 68 (1998): 373-97.
57 Patrick Phillips and D. Wheatley, "Urban Chic," in *Developing Urban Entertainment Centers,* by M. Beyard et al., 19.
58 Roger Cohen, "Building a Capital Where Triumph Is Taboo." *The New York Times,* 11 April 1999, section 2, 33. This is especially true for the adjacent shopping mall where, during a recent visit, I observed local families sitting down for a traditional midday meal.
59 Paul Goldberger, "The Rise of the Private City," in *Breaking Away: The Future of Cities,* ed. J. Vitullo-Martin (New York: The Twentieth Century Fund Press, 1996), 146.
60 Fainstein, *The City Builders,* 245.
61 Hannigan, *Fantasy City,* 200.
62 Mike Davis, *City of Quartz: Excavating the Future in Los Angeles* (New York: Verso, 1990), 227.
63 Robert A. Baade, "Stadiums, Professional Sports and City Economies: An Analysis of the United States Experience," in *The Stadium and the City,* ed. J. Bole and O. Moen (Keele, Staffordshire: Keele University Press, 1995), 277-94.
64 Marc V. Levine, "Downtown Development as an Urban Growth Strategy: A Critical Appraisal of the Baltimore Renaissance," *Journal of Urban Affairs* 9 (1987): 103-23.
65 Robert Perry, *Galt, U.S.A.: The American Presence in a Canadian City* (Toronto: Maclean-Hunter, 1971), 65.
66 McKeough's comments are cited in James M. Cameron and Ronald Bordessa, *Wonderland through the Looking Glass: Politics, Culture and Planning in International Recreation* (Maple, ON: Belston, 1981), 56.
67 Cameron and Bordessa, *Wonderland through the Looking Glass,* 120.
68 David Lasker, "A Virtual Disney World Close to Home," *Globe & Mail,* 27 March 1999, C20.
69 David Y.H. Wu, "McDonald's in Taipei: Hamburgers, Betel Nuts, and National Identity," in *Golden Arches East: McDonald's in East Asia,* ed. J.L. Watson (Stanford, CA: Stanford University Press, 1997), 110-35.
70 David Akin, "We're Becoming Less like Americans: Poll," *National Post,* 21 June 2001, A8.
71 Stephen Fjellman, for example, argues that Frederick Jackson Turner's "frontier thesis" of 1893 is "enshrined at Walt Disney World." Here, space is depicted as the new frontier, the conquering of which will permit Americans "to retain the entrepreneurial individualism that is our characteristic right as Americans." Stephen M. Fjellman, *Vinyl Leaves: Walt Disney World and America* (Boulder, CO: Westview Press, 1992), 60.
72 See Rowland Lorimer and Jean McNulty, *Mass Communication in Canada* (Toronto: Oxford University Press, 1996), 194.
73 Paul Audley, *Canada's Cultural Industries: Broadcasting, Publishing, Records and Film* (Toronto: Lorimer, 1983), 320-1.
74 David Taras, "Defending the Cultural Frontier: Canadian Television and Continental Integration, " in *Seeing Ourselves: Media Power and Policy in Canada,* ed. David Taras and Helen Holmes (Toronto: Harcourt Brace Jovanovich Canada, 1992), 178-82.
75 Marc Raboy, *Missed Opportunities: The Story of Canada's Broadcasting Policy* (Montreal: McGill-Queen's University Press, 1990), 250.

76 Ted Magder, "Franchising the Candy Store: Split-run Magazines and a New International Regime for Trade in Culture," *Canadian-American Public Policy* 3 (April 1998): 47.
77 Mark Rosentraub, *Major League Losers: The Real Cost of Sports and Who's Paying For It* (New York: Basic Books, 1999).
78 Maurice Roche, *Mega-events and Modernity: Olympics and Expos in the Growth of Global Culture* (London and New York: Routledge, 2000), 233.
79 Scott Cummings, "Private Enterprise and Public Policy: Business Hegemony in the Metropolis," in *Business Elites and Urban Development: Case Studies and Critical Perspectives,* ed. S. Cummings (Albany, NY: State University of New York Press, 1988), 13.
80 Ibid., 3-21.
81 Olivier Courteaux, "The Inner City for Fun and Profit," *National Post,* 19 March 1999, B5.
82 See Scott Lash and John Urry, *Economies of Signs and Spaces* (London: Sage Publications, 1994).
83 Chris Cobb, "Pop Icons Bring Wealth into Canada," *National Post,* 21 June 2001, A8.

3
Transnationalism, Diasporic Communities, and Changing Identity: Implications for Canadian Citizenship Policy

Lloyd L. Wong

The processes of globalization and human migration are interconnected and implicate notions of belonging and citizenship. The dominant forms of citizenship and cultural identity that have been embedded in national categories and exclusive practices of identification are now being questioned.[1] This chapter follows this line of questioning by examining the impact of recent human migration on Canadian citizenship. While the migration of people dates back to the beginnings of recorded history, and Cameron and Stein take the position that globalization is centuries old (see Chapter 1 of this volume), the past one hundred years has been unique. Unlike previous centuries, the twentieth century saw a massive international and global migration of people, a situation which still holds true today. In contrast to the movement of capital across state boundaries, the movement of people is tightly regulated and controlled, to the extent that some scholars refer to this situation as "global apartheid"[2] and "closed worlds."[3] Others, such as Harvey, note that while state boundaries are not as porous for people as they are for capital, they are, however, porous enough.[4] This porousness has facilitated the recent creation of complex transnational and diasporic communities and, along with other movements of people in the world, it threatens the control of the modern nation-state. The globalization of economies and culture has created new conditions that are transforming identity and the institution of citizenship throughout the world. Nationalism and the nation-state are in crisis in the current global system, in which the nation is no longer the privileged site of mediation between the local and the global. However, with respect to citizenship and human migration, the nation-state continues to be the privileged site, albeit one that is under pressure. In the case of the Canadian state, the forces of globalization have produced a situation in which difficult choices are being made with respect to the future direction of both immigration and citizenship policy. Ultimately these choices are limited, at a practical level, by the ideological and political positions adopted by the state.

The concept of globalization itself is wide-ranging, but it encompasses three basic notions: globalization as transference, as transformation, and as transcendence.[5] Similar to the concept of "globalization," the concept of "transnationalism" is wide-ranging. One reason for this is that, historically, the term "transnationalism" has been used in distinct yet similar ways. In the political science literature, the term was first used in the 1920s, and contemporary usage refers to transnational economic and political actors on the world stage. In the 1970s literature, "transnationalism" was used to describe a breadth of activities that included social movements, economic relations, mass media, and migrants' ties to their homelands.[6] The political science literature refers to the politics of international relations and does not examine transnational relations at the social or cultural level, which have been the domain of anthropology and sociology. In recent anthropological literature, transnationalism has been theoretically framed in order to allow for comprehensive analyses and syntheses. Two such ways are (1) distinguishing transnationalism "from above" and "from below," and (2) conceptualizing transnationalism as transmigration.[7]

Transnationalism "from above" includes the macro-level structures and processes of capitalist classes, international and other powerful elites via multinational corporations, and other supranational organizations that produce homogenizing and elitist forces. Transnationalism "from below" includes the macro- and micro-level structures and processes of non-elites, which generate multiple and counter-hegemonic forces. They are micro in the sense that they are grounded in the daily lives and practices of ordinary people and include the development of cultural hybridity, multi-positional identities, and transnational business practices of migrant entrepreneurs.[8] The transnational and diasporic communities referred to later in this chapter are not monolithic. They are heterogeneous and include stratified class differences. They manifest transnationalism both "from above" and "from below," the latter being more common.

In this chapter, transnationalism is conceptualized as transmigration that contributes to the formation of transnational and diasporic communities as well as transnational social spaces. These transnational social spaces include people's sustained ties and social networks, along with their movements across the borders of nation-states.[9] Transmigrants retain ties to multiple societies and this constitutes a paradigm shift in the fields of international migration and ethnic and racial studies, a shift that is still in progress. In Canada, ethnic scholarship is now challenged by the transnationalism paradigm[10] and, in the context of globalization, the perspective of transnationalism has become a useful analytic model for explaining and understanding international migration. Transnationalism has become a way of life for many international migrants as the rapid transformation of travel and telecommunications technology has facilitated both the formation of transnational networks and the development and solidification of transnational and diasporic communities.

When globalization is used to refer to processes that first connect and integrate societies, the concept of transnationalism overlaps with it; the distinction is that transnational processes are more limited because they anchor in, as well as transcend, societies and nation-states. Kearney refers to these processes as "transtatal."[11] Hence, transnationalism is a subset of globalization. Appadurai's analysis of the global cultural economy identifies five overlapping and disjunctive dimensions of global cultural flow that he terms ethnoscapes, mediascapes, technoscapes, financescapes, and ideoscapes. Ethnoscapes refer to the global landscape of persons who make up the shifting world in which we live, and include tourists, immigrants, refugees, exiles, guest workers, and other moving groups and persons.[12] It is this global ethnoscape that contains transnational and diasporic communities.

The social policy implications of transnationalism for the Canadian state are enormous, as this phenomenon requires more flexible and inclusive forms of citizenship at a time when the state appears to be choosing policy headed in the opposite direction. The recently proposed Bill C-16 illustrates the Canadian state's response and resistance to transnationalism as the state attempted to forge a "thick" citizenship for Canada by using restrictive and punitive criteria. Before discussing Bill C-16, it is necessary to examine in greater detail transnational and diasporic communities and their relationship to more general and contemporary processes of globalization. Moreover, it is also necessary to examine the impact of transnationalism on identity, particularly in the realm of deterritorialization and changing conceptions of citizenship. These processes have profound implications for citizenship policy in the context of an increasingly supranational/postnational and deterritorializing world and the search by nation-states for social cohesion via common values, identity, and civic engagement.

Transnationalism and Diasporas

Transnationalism and Transnational Communities

Over thirty years ago, sociologist Anthony Richmond coined the term "transilience," which is still in use today.[13] This term originally referred to the exchanges of skilled and highly qualified migrants among advanced societies, and these migrants were hence referred to as "transilients." The term is now used more broadly to apply to a wide range of movers whose permanence in one locale is neither expected nor necessary. Transilients do not necessarily acculturate or integrate into the receiving society, but rather maintain close ties with family and friends; are aware of changing economic, political, and social conditions in their former country and elsewhere; and have high rates of re-migration and return.[14] Richmond's concept of transilience was the forerunner to the current 1990s conceptualization of the transnational migration or transmigration of people as part of the overall phenomenon of transnationalism.

In anthropology, Schiller, Basch, and Blanc-Szanton have been the leading proponents of the transnationalist perspective, and they have defined transnationalism as "a social process in which migrants establish social fields that cross geographic, cultural, and political borders. Immigrants are understood to be transmigrants when they have developed and continue to maintain multiple relations – familial, economic, social, organizational, religious, and political – that span borders."[15] More recently, they have argued that contemporary immigrants should not be characterized as the "uprooted" who have left behind a home and a country, as many of them maintain multiple linkages to their homeland. They state: "The popular image of immigrant is one of people who have come to stay, having uprooted themselves from their old society in order to make for themselves a new home and adopt a new country to which they will pledge allegiance ... Yet it has become increasingly obvious that our present conceptions of 'immigrant' and 'migrant,' anchored in the circumstances of earlier historic movements, no longer suffice. Today, immigrants develop networks, activities, patterns of living, and ideologies that span their home and the host society."[16]

Increasingly, immigrants have multiple interconnections that cut across international borders and public identities that are configured in relationship to more than one nation-state. In terms of human agency, these "migrants" are engaged in taking actions, making decisions, and developing identities through social networks that simultaneously connect them to two or more societies, and these practices are multistranded; thus these migrants are referred to as "transmigrants."[17] As such, transnational communities are those that span two or more nations. At the behavioural and structural levels, transmigrants' actions and identities are embedded in transnational social networks. This transnationalism can be contrasted to the older notion of sojourning, where people settle and become incorporated in the economy and political institutions, localities, and patterns of daily life of the country where they reside. Transmigrants are engaged "elsewhere" in the sense that they maintain connections, build institutions, conduct transactions, and influence local and national events in the countries from which they emigrated.[18] Thus transmigration creates transnational and diasporic communities that have multistranded social relations linking different societies. Scholars now face the challenge of reassessing their traditional notions of territorially based communities and singular societies and cultures. The nation is an imagined community; however, when the imagination moves beyond borders, transnational and diasporic communities are also imagined communities.

With emerging transnationalism, the current terminology, concepts, and theoretical perspectives used in social theories of migration are being reformulated and redefined. The immigration experience can no longer be safely ensconced in macroscopic generalizations in which emerging social differentiation is based on class, ethnicity, and gender.[19] This new transnational paradigm entails a shift from traditional terms such as "international migration," "home society," "settler society," "sending country," "receiving country," "push/pull," "immigrant," "migrant," and "temporary worker." This fundamental shift from *inter*national to *trans*national marks the new paradigm. These transnational communities are related to diasporas.

Diasporas and Diasporic Communities

Historically, "the Diaspora" referred specifically to Jews, their exile from their historic homeland, and their dispersion throughout many lands under conditions of oppression and moral degradation.[20] In the late twentieth century, however, the notion of "diaspora" was broadened and redefined to include many other groups. A little over a decade ago, Connor defined diaspora simply as "that segment of a people living outside the homeland."[21] Since then, several new and elaborate definitions of contemporary diaspora have been developed, many of which have been built upon previous definitions. For example, Safran argues for an extension of Connor's earlier working definition of diaspora, to include notions of collective memory, alienation, and commitment to an ancestral homeland.[22] Using such a definition, Safran notes that contemporary diasporas also include Armenian, Maghrebi, Turkish, Palestinian, Cuban, Greek, and Chinese. Cohen draws upon the classical tradition and Safran's insights to expand the definition to include (1) not just dispersal from a homeland but also expansion, which includes the search for work and trade; (2) ethnic solidarity; and (3) the possibility of a distinctive creative life in host pluralistic countries.[23] While Cohen posits nine common features of diasporas, he argues that no one diaspora will manifest all features. He notes that, today, at least thirty ethnic groups declare that they are diasporas and are recognized as such by others. Following Cohen's definition, Van Hear conceptualizes diasporas as populations that satisfy three minimal criteria: (1) the population is dispersed from a homeland to two or more other territories; (2) the presence abroad is enduring, although exile is not necessarily permanent, but may include movement between homeland and new host; and (3) some kind of exchange – social, economic, political, or cultural – occurs between or among the spatially separated populations constituting the diaspora.[24] This chapter adopts this general definition of diaspora, using the term to refer to any internationally dispersed ethnic group or community.

The analysis of specific cases of diasporas is emerging in various literatures. For example, literature on the Chinese diaspora is growing. Chan's recent work argues that, paradoxically, a rational family decision is made for dispersing the Chinese patrilineal family in order to preserve and strengthen the family in a resourceful and resilient way. He notes that "families split in order to be together translocally" and cites "astronaut families" of Hong Kong as a model. Moreover, Chan argues that these spatially dispersed families constitute strategic nodes and linkages of an ever-expanding transnational field in which a new Chinese identity is emerging.[25] The work of Ip, Wu, and Inglis in Australia points to a conceptualization of Taiwanese immigrants more as a diaspora than as migrants or immigrants, with the emergence of diasporic identities that are at once local and global, and encompass both "imagined" and "encountered" communities.[26]

Relationship between Transnational Communities and Diasporas

Considerable overlap exists between the concepts of "transnationalism" and "diaspora." Indeed, each word often takes adjectival form to describe the other. The concepts of "transnationalism" and "transnational communities" are broader and more inclusive ones than "diaspora" and "diasporic communities," which, as indicated above, have very specific criteria. As such, transnational communities encompass diasporas; however, not all transnational communities are diasporas.

To extend the Chinese example mentioned above, many Chinese businesspeople engage in hypermobility through transnational networks. Skeldon observes that Chinese transmigrants operate in transnational social networks that allow them to "flow" from one part of the system to another, depending on conditions of economic boom or recession, political liberalization or repression, in any part of that system.[27] Thus terms such as "new extended family," "diasporic families," and "trans-Pacific networks" are now used to discuss this flow along points in a network. As the links between nodes become established over time, social networks and fields develop.

Other scholars have made subtle distinctions between transnational communities and diasporas. For example, Faist notes that diasporas, consisting of first-generation refugees, represent a very distinct form of transnational community and that diasporas do not necessarily need contemporary and concrete social ties, as memory of a homeland is a symbolic tie.[28] Since transnational communities is a broader concept, the question arises as to how transnationalism can be measured empirically.

The empirical measurement of transnationalism can include many factors. Van Hear suggests that transnationalism be measured by assessing the strength or weakness of a given population's commitment to its place of origin, to its current place of residence, and to others in the diaspora.[29] However, when various measurements are applied to any one specific transnational community, the evidence of commitment may be very mixed and allegiance may be very elastic. As well, specific measures, in and of themselves, may not necessarily provide an adequate measure of commitment. For example, citizenship status may have limited value as a measure in a situation where individuals are unable to exercise choice in attaining citizenship in the host nation. Moreover, as a result of the deterritorialization of identity and emergent multiple identities in transnational communities, citizenship status may not reflect loyalty and commitment. Some individuals in transnational communities may experience contradiction and disjuncture regarding loyalties. An example of this was the news reports in 1999, about some Canadians of Serbian origin who went to the Balkans to join the Serbian war effort against NATO forces and hence against other Canadians. The RCMP examined the legality of this alleged action, using the Foreign Enlistment Act and the Criminal Code; the latter considers such an action – assisting an enemy who is at war with Canada – to be "high treason."[30]

In summary, as people in transnational and diasporic communities operate in complex transnational social networks, they create and solidify multiple identities that are grounded in multiple societies, and they thus emerge with a singular hybridized transnational identity or separate multiple identities that link them simultaneously to several nations. This experience has important ramifications for identity. However, before examining the issue of social identity, a brief analysis of the emergent immigrant and ethnic populations in Canada is in order since Canada, along with Australia and the United States, has been a major "immigrant-receiving" country over the past thirty-five years.

The Changing Face of Canada: A Sociodemographic Profile and Evidence of Transnationalism

Canada's population has always been diverse, so the face of Canada is actually changing from diversity to greater diversity. However, it was not until the late 1960s, when fundamental changes were effected in Canadian immigration policy, that the Canadian population became noticeably and substantially non-White and particularly non-British and non-French. In 1962, racist criteria for selection of immigrants were removed from Canadian immigration policy, and in 1967, meritocratic criteria (such as the points system) were introduced. A major consequence of these changes was the decrease, from the 1960s to the 1990s, of the proportion of immigrants from Europe and the United States and an increase of immigrants from Asia, Africa, Central and South America, and the Caribbean (see Table 1). Immigrants from these latter areas increased from 14 percent of all immigrants in 1965 to 77 percent in 1999. Immigrants from the United Kingdom constituted 31 percent of all immigrants in 1956 and by 1999 constituted only 2 percent (see Table 2). In 1956, the top ten origin countries of immigrants were European ones and the United States; these countries were the original homelands of the vast majority of immigrants (87 percent). By 1999, very few of the top ten countries of origin of immigrants to Canada were European, with the United Kingdom and the United States combining to account for only 5 percent of immigration. Most of the top ten were Asian countries and, moreover, the top ten countries constituted only 51 percent of all origin countries, indicating the increasing diversity of origin countries. Correspondingly, the Canadian population has changed dramatically with respect to ethnic origin. In 1941, the non-British and non-French population constituted only 20 percent of the Canadian population, but by the 1990s, it constituted 31 percent, or almost one-third.[31] These figures must be considered in the context of the fact that "other" ethnic origins include growing numbers of recent immigrants who are "people of colour" and live primarily in Canada's larger urban centres. Thus greater ethnic diversification has taken place in the larger Canadian cities than in other parts of Canada.

For example, the Greater Vancouver Area has experienced tremendous ethnic population diversification over the last three decades. In terms of ethnic origin, Chinese now make up 25 percent of Vancouver's population and 50 percent of the city of Richmond, which is adjacent to and south of Vancouver. In the early and mid-1990s, approximately one-third of the Chinese immigrants from Hong Kong were coming to Canada as business immigrants under the "Independent Class" of the Canadian immigration policy. Most of these immigrants settled in larger metropolitan areas such as Toronto and Vancouver. The following two case descriptions illustrate these immigrants' transnational practices and social identity.

Case 1: Mr. X

Mr. X is a recent immigrant who came to Canada in 1993 under Canada's Business Immigration Program. He has good reading and writing skills in English, but his conversation skills are poor. He is in his late forties and lives in Canada with his wife and two children. His mother, two sisters, and brother live in Hong Kong. He communicates with them approximately two to three times a month and visits them in Hong Kong several times a year, each visit approximately one month in duration. While in Hong Kong visiting his family, he also conducts business.

Mr. X is a manufacturer of traditional Chinese furniture and also does wood carving for traditional Chinese interiors. He has thirty people working for him in his factory in Hong Kong, which is a family-run business originally started by his father and currently being managed by his brother. While maintaining and overseeing his business operations in Hong Kong, Mr. X has opened up a small Chinese furniture-assembling factory in Canada; it employs two full-time workers and some casual help. He also has a furniture retail store in Vancouver that employs two full-time workers, one of whom is his wife. Furthermore, he is involved in renovations and has hired craftsmen to take on some interior decoration jobs. His clients are primarily from the Chinese transnational community. Mr. X is involved in manufacturing, wholesale, and retail business activities, and he communicates with his business associates in Hong Kong several times each month.

Mr. X has found a niche in the market largely because his skills are very specialized and he has few competitors in Vancouver. He is slowly building up a reputation locally so that Asian restaurants, Chinese temples, and Asia-related institutions use his service and buy furniture from him. He has built a private Buddhist temple for a Hong Kong businessman and helped decorate a postsecondary institution in Vancouver.

Mr. X's aim is not to limit his business to the Asian market. He hopes to open up one more retail store and to introduce Asian furniture to non-Asians. Since he personally designs his furniture, he is hoping to modify Chinese furniture to suit Western tastes. To have the capital he needs to expand his business, he is going to transfer to Canada part of the profits he earns in Asia.

To oversee his business on both sides of the Pacific, Mr. X spends three months per year in Asia and the rest of the time in Vancouver. His wife takes over the operation of his Vancouver business while he is away and (as mentioned above) his brother in Hong Kong takes care of the factory there when he is in Vancouver.

With respect to Mr. X's social identity, he has a strong transnational attitude. He is prepared to go wherever his business takes him, and he does not feel very strongly about his own identity as a Hong Kong Chinese or as a Canadian Chinese. In that sense, he has a cosmopolitan identity. He still has friends in Hong Kong and stays in touch with them two to three times a year when he is not in Hong Kong. The issue of national identity is not a very important one to him.

Case 2: Mr. Y

Mr. Y is also a recent immigrant who came to Canada in 1993 under Canada's Business Immigration Program. He is in his mid-forties and lives in Canada with his wife and one young child. His parents and sister live in Hong Kong, and he communicates with them approximately twice a

Table 1

World area of origin of immigrants to Canada, 1956-99

	Year (%)					
Region of origin	1956	1965	1975	1985	1995	1999
Northern Europe, Great Britain, United States, Australia, and New Zealand	71.1	55.9	38.0	19.6	10.3	23.4**
Southern and Eastern Europe	24.1	30.1	12.7	11.3	12.3*	–
Africa, Asia, Central and South America, Caribbean, and other	4.8	14.0	49.3	69.1	77.4	76.6
Total	100.0	100.0	100.0	100.0	100.0	100.0
Total number	164,857	146,758	187,881	84,302	212,504	189,816

*This percentage is higher than expected due to a large number of refugees (5,964) from Bosnia-Hercegovina.

**Includes Southern and Eastern Europe

Sources: Citizenship and Immigration, *1956 Immigration Statistics* (Ottawa: Author, 1957), 15; Citizenship and Immigration, *1965 Immigration Statistics* (Ottawa: Author, 1965), 20; Citizenship and Immigration, *1995 Immigration Statistics* (Ottawa: Author, 1998), 32; Citizenship and Immigration, *Facts and Figures 1999* <www.cic.gc.ca/english/pub/facts99/index.html> (29 November 2001); Employment and Immigration, *1985 Immigration Statistics* (Ottawa: Employment and Immigration, 1987), 24; Manpower and Immigration, *1975 Immigration Statistics* (Ottawa: Manpower and Immigration, 1976), 9.

Table 2

Top ten countries of origin for immigrants to Canada, 1956-99

1956		1965		1975		1985		1995		1999	
Country	%	Country	%	Country	%	Country	%	Country	%	Country	%
Great Britain	31	Great Britain	27	Great Britain	19	Vietnam	12	Hong Kong	15	China (PRC)	15
Italy	17	Italy	18	United States	11	Hong Kong	9	India	8	India	9
Germany	16	Germany	12	Hong Kong	6	United States	8	Philippines	7	Pakistan	5
United States	6	United States	10	India	5	Great Britain	5	China (PRC)	6	Philippines	5
Netherlands	5	Portugal	4	Portugal	4	India	5	Sri Lanka	4	Korea (Rep.)	4
Greece	3	Greece	4	Jamaica	4	Poland	4	Taiwan	4	Iran	3
Austria	3	France	4	Philippines	4	Philippines	4	Bosnia-Hercegovina	3	United States	3
Hungary	2	Hong Kong	3	Italy	4	Jamaica	4	Great Britain	3	Taiwan	3
France	2	Netherlands	2	Guyana	2	El Salvador	3	United States	2	Sri Lanka	2
Denmark	2	India	2	South Korea	2	Guyana	3	Pakistan	2	Great Britain	2
Top ten	87	Top ten	86	Top ten	61	Top ten	57	Top ten	54	Top ten	51
Other	13	Other	14	Other	39	Other	43	Other	46	Other	49
Total	100	Total	100	Total	100	Total	100	Total	100	Total	100
(N)	164,857	(N)	146,758	(N)	187,881	(N)	84,302	(N)	212,504	(N)	189,816

Sources: Citizenship and Immigration, *1956 Immigration Statistics* (Ottawa: Author, 1957), 15; Citizenship and Immigration, *1965 Immigration Statistics* (Ottawa: Author, 1965), 20; Citizenship and Immigration, *1995 Immigration Statistics* (Ottawa: Author, 1998), x; Citizenship and Immigration, *Facts and Figures 1999* <www.cic.gc.ca/english/pub/facts99/index.html> (29 November 2001); Employment and Immigration, *1985 Immigration Statistics* (Ottawa: Employment and Immigration, 1987), xi; Manpower and Immigration, *1975 Immigration Statistics* (Ottawa: Manpower and Immigration, 1976), 8-10.

month while he is in Canada and visits them in Hong Kong as often as five times a year. While in Hong Kong spending time with his family, he also conducts business and visits his friends.

Mr. Y is a watch manufacturer. His factory in Hong Kong employs sixty people and his products are mainly exported to North America. After immigrating to Canada, he set up a retail shop selling watches as well as a design centre in Vancouver, which employs eight to nine full-time workers. He hopes to open more retail shops in different parts of Vancouver. He is interested in introducing a greater variety of watches, in terms of price range and style, to the Canadian market. Hence, his client base is mainly Caucasians, only 10 percent of his clients being Chinese. He also finds it cheaper to set up a design centre in Canada, since the cost of hiring professionals and renting office space in Hong Kong is very high. Furthermore, he likes the fact that his employees are more stable and dependable in Canada, as they don't need to "job-hop" in order to get a higher salary. Mr. Y also set up a design centre in Vancouver to fulfil the requirements of the Business Immigration Program. The BC Business Immigration Branch has encouraged "research and development" types of businesses, so Mr. Y decided to set up his design centre in Vancouver to facilitate his permanent residency status. An additional benefit of being in Vancouver is the fact that he is able to obtain new design ideas and an understanding of the North American market.

Mr. Y spends about five months each year in Hong Kong, each visit approximately one month in duration, before returning to Canada. He also spends time attending trade shows in Europe. He keeps in touch with his businesses both in Hong Kong and in Vancouver by phone and by fax. He is in contact with his business associates about twice a week. In order to keep his business running smoothly in Hong Kong when he is away, he belongs to an international management system. Mr. Y mentioned that setting up an office in Vancouver actually facilitates his communication with his clients in North America and makes his operation more efficient. These effects are largely due to the time difference between Hong Kong and Vancouver, which makes it possible for him to talk to importers in North America during the day and to give instructions to his office in Hong Kong at night (which is daytime there). His office can give him an answer that he can in turn share with the importers the next morning.

Mr. Y does not consider himself to be a Canadian, but rather still regards himself as a Hong Kong Chinese despite the fact that his business operations are very transnational in nature. It is likely that he and his family may move back to Hong Kong in the near future.[32]

These descriptions illuminate the nature of these two immigrants' transnationalism and provide some clues to their emergent identities. It must be remembered that not all contemporary diasporic communities experience transnationalism in the same way, and that what has been provided here is only an example of some aspects of the Chinese diasporic experience.

Recent research on Chinese immigrant entrepreneurs has established empirical evidence that they have extensive transnational social fields that have family, personal, ethnic, and business dimensions.[33] These entrepreneurs, as well as many non-entrepreneur Chinese immigrants, are engaged extensively in the practice of transnationalism and transmigration, facilitated by communications technology and jet travel. The enabling technology includes the Internet, electronic mail, faxes, and long-distance telephone calls, all of which are relatively inexpensive. Hutton's study of the metropolitan transformation of Vancouver, due to international migration, provides data on the growth of Asia Pacific passenger traffic for Vancouver International Airport. From 1990 to 1995, the total number of passengers for the Asia Pacific region increased from 790,000 to 1,590,000, which is an increase of over 100 percent over a five-year period.[34] As well, his data show that Vancouver's network of air connections with principal Asia-Pacific gateway cities includes eleven cities, nine airlines, and seventy-two direct flights per week, of which twenty-three are to Hong Kong.[35] Vancouver International Airport also has direct air connections to major US and European cities such as New York, London, and Paris, connections that facilitate transnationalism and transmigration.

In summary, the rapid diversification of the Canadian population over the last thirty years has solidified a multi-ethnic and multicultural society. This transformation, combined with the forces of economic and cultural globalization, has contributed to the development of diasporic and transnational communities. These communities are the logical outgrowths of multiculturalism as acceptance and promotion of cultural differences encourage and sustain linkages to places of origin. These linkages have important implications for identity.

The Deterritorialization of Social Identity

The literature on globalization is pervaded by a concern with how production, consumption, communities, politics, and identities become detached from local places. The term "deterritorialization" is used to describe such processes.[36] The continuing development and advancement of microchip technology contributes to the disembedding of social relations and the compression of time and space, which promotes deterritorialization. However, deterritorialization must be contextualized within specific processes and different levels of analysis. For example, at the level of the nation-state, the social process of deterritorialization might involve the state continuing to make claims and exercise influence on emigrants who have left its national territory. Another example is at the level of the individual, for whom the social process of deterritorialization might involve identity formation and activism through "communities of interests," rather than place communities, via the Internet and the World Wide Web, as Deibert discusses in Chapter 4.

While globalization has not significantly altered national territory in terms of geography, it is having pronounced effects on the territoriality of nation-states in terms of institutional practices. As Sassen points out, "Economic globalization entails a set of practices which destabilizes another set of practices, namely some of the practices that came to constitute national state sovereignty."[37] The assumed one-to-one relationship of state and territory is increasingly being questioned and challenged in a context of deterritorialization. As Appadurai points out, with increasing movements of people, flows of legal and illegal commodities, and massive movements of arms across state borders, states are left with attempting to monopolize the idea of territory as the diacritic of sovereignty.[38] In the global market for "loyalties," nation-states do not compete very well. Furthermore, the state is now also a competitor in the "legitimacy" marketplace, and it has to justify what it stands for within the context of deterritorialization.[39]

Albrow has argued that social activities that transpire in any one given locale may be disconnected from those in another, but that they also contribute to parts of social worlds that may extend beyond localities and the national level.[40] These include not only the more obvious economic linkages, but equally kin, friendship, and special interest relationships. These linkages have been affected by the recent shift in how time and space are constructed. They can all be sustained actively at a distance via recent developments in communications technology and inexpensive transportation – developments that result in space-time compression and time-space distanciation. The latter constitutes the stretching of social systems across time and space on the basis of social and system integration. Giddens uses the concept of "disembedding of social systems from the local context" to describe how organizations and networks connect the local and global in ways that were not possible in traditional, geographically bound communities.[41]

The deterritorialization and the delinking of community and identity from place opens up the possibility of new theoretical developments; but at the same time, recognition of the importance of place, or in some other cases, at least a geographic contextualization in transnational discourse, must continue.[42] The notion of deterritorialization need not be perceived as excluding or negating local "place" or territory, but rather as relativizing or decentring it. In this sense, it shifts the balance from solely territorially defined politics to non-territorial forms of organization and identity.[43] The terms "translocalities" and "multilocationality" have emerged to indicate a local embeddedness or "rootedness" to transnational processes. In other words, these processes embody culturally heterogeneous places that are largely divorced from their national contexts and that straddle formal political borders.[44] Thus transnational and diasporic identity formation illustrate the fact that identity is not singular, but rather plural and always evolving. The ethnoscape is decentred and abstract, but can situate actors within specific networks and social constructions. As such, ethnography has the task of determining the local place as lived experience in a globalized, deterritorialized world. Appadurai perceives a need to reconceptualize the "landscapes of group identity" where "groups are no longer tightly territorialized, spatially bounded, historically unselfconscious, or culturally homogeneous."[45] Processes of transnationalism and globalization are likely to give new significance and meaning to the notion of ethnicity rather than abate its importance. Within transnational and diasporic communities, a deterritorialization of ethnicity, particularly among refugees and other reactive migrants, has occurred.

In summary, deterritorialized social identities provide a challenge for nation-states, as transnational and diasporic communities are primarily communities of interest. Globalization involves a relativization and destabilization of old identities and the creation of new, hybrid entities that include transnational and diasporic communities. The deterritorialization of social identity challenges the nation-state's claim of making exclusive citizenship a defining focus of allegiance and fidelity, in contrast to the reality of overlapping, permeable, and multiple forms of identity.[46] Thus deterritorialization has implications for national conceptions of citizenship.

Changing Conceptions of Citizenship

Conceptions of citizenship are subject to change because citizenship is a legal, social, and ideological construction. Historically, it has been linked with the development and evolution of nation-states. While the 1648 Westphalian peace settlements established the concept of the nation-state, based on sovereignty of territory, now territory is the site of the crisis of sovereignty in a transnational world. The deterritorialization of identity within transnational and diasporic communities threaten the modern nation-state's conception of citizenship because citizenship has been circumscribed in national arenas. People in transnational communities are engaged in multiple places and their activities cross social, cultural, and territorial boundaries, thus mediating a transformation of citizenship. This transformation suggests that citizenship may transcend national boundaries in transnational communities made up of people with multiple and diverse identities that affect their sense of belonging and attachment to an "imagined national community."

Hammar observes that membership in a nation and membership in a state are not identical, and calls into question the premise that a territory necessarily constitutes or defines a people, as is supposed in a nation-state.[47] Furthermore, Jacobson notes, "Under the impact of transnational migrations, the nation-state is being 'unpacked.' Community, polity, and territory are becoming, rather than coextensive, discrete if overlapping spheres. Regional and transnational political institutions, transnational, subnational, and diasporic communities, and the state itself, now more an administrative entity that is increasingly being stripped of its primordial quality, occupy different (if linked and partly shared) spaces. Identities are being deterritorialized."[48] As economic and cultural globalization develop, the relationship between territorial nation-states and citizenship must be re-examined as deterritorialization of social identity increases and individuals develop social ties and memberships to multiple communities. In a world with significant transient populations of transnational and diasporic communities, either the conceptualizations of membership and citizenship have to be reformed or the very notion of the nation-state will have to be re-thought.[49]

The notion of citizenship has recently re-emerged as a prime area of investigation.[50] In the 1950s and 1960s, the issue of citizenship, as exemplified by the work of T.H. Marshall, revolved around social inequality and social justice with respect to the legal, social, and political rights of the disadvantaged in society. Current issues regarding citizenship now include questions of how citizens view and fulfil their responsibilities and roles as citizens in light of competing forms of national, regional, ethnic, or religious identities. As well, current conceptions of citizenship have highlighted the notion of "citizenship as social membership," extending beyond formal obligations that are legally defined. Thus theories and models of contemporary citizenship incorporate both citizenship-as-legal-status and citizenship-as-desirable-activity, though the two are sometimes conflated.

Delanty conceptualizes four models of citizenship, in which it is defined by rights, duties, participation, and identity (the latter two give citizenship a substantive [non-legal] dimension).[51] The emphasis here will be on the "identity" dimension of citizenship. In a recent review of citizenship theory, Kymlicka and Norman call for a theory of citizenship that focuses on civic virtues and citizenship identity.[52] Citizenship cannot be solely and strictly conceived as a legal status formulated by a nation-state. Transmigrants are de facto citizens of more than one nation-state. The traditional conception of citizenship as a singular loyalty is diminishing as the moral tie between land and people weakens.

Historically, citizenship has been defined in many ways outside of the modern nation-state (from city-states to empires) with its dual or plural structures of membership, legal identity, and rights. Hence, it is really definable in terms of the existence of a political community, civil society, and public sphere, and not as coterminous with a nation-state. This discrepancy has led to the "postnational problematic," in which the study of citizenship, with emphasis on the social formations of rights, obligations, membership, and identity, cannot be comprehensive or credible if it restricts itself to nation-statist assumptions.[53] This problematic has a research agenda that includes rights, membership, and identity of migrants, immigrants, transmigrants, and those in diasporic communities; it is most developed in the case of Europe.

European Postnational Citizenship

Tambini points out that the economic and cultural structures upon which national citizenship depend have been undermined, resulting in its decline. The processes contributing to this decline include economic globalization, cultural denationalization, migration, and the transnationalization of institutions.[54] With respect to migration, the existence of post-Second World War *Gastarbeiter* (guestworkers) in Western Europe contributed to the development of marginal and marginalized groups referred to as "denizens" and "interstate societies." These groups transcended the limits of the nation-state and had memberships in multiple societies as a result of European migration. The existence of millions of denizens in Europe, combined with the European Union's decision to allow member citizens freedom of movement, contributed to the beginnings of a redefinition of citizenship: from a national identity to a new form within a broader European context. In many European countries, uncertain relationships exist between nationality and citizenship, particularly with respect to immigrants and denizens and questions about integration and social cohesion. Is a postnational European citizenship possible?

Over a decade ago, scholars such as Brubaker were noting that classical models of citizenship needed to be modified.[55] Bauböck revisited the relationship between citizenship and territorially bounded states, and called for a conceptualization of citizenship that is transnational and that recognizes membership in multiple communities.[56] Thus the need to develop a postnational perspective on citizenship was recognized in the early 1990s, and many scholars have since adopted the theme of "deterritorialization of citizenship" in Europe.[57]

A new type of citizenship is emerging in the European Union. It is neither national nor cosmopolitan, but rather multiple in terms of identities, rights, and obligations, and expressed and structured through increasingly complex community institutions, states, national and transnational voluntary associations, regions, and alliances of regions. Soysal advocates a "post-national membership" model of citizenship and compares it to the classical model of national citizenship.[58] Her analysis moves beyond the traditional and classical understanding of citizenship as belonging to a nation and challenges the traditional assumption that national citizenship is a precondition of membership in a polity. This model is based more on human rights than on territorial considerations and supersedes the national citizenship model that was prevalent from the nineteenth to the mid-twentieth century. The source of legitimacy in the postnational model is the transnational community, and Soysal points to the growing number of dual nationality acquisitions as a formalization of the fluidity and multiplicity of postnational membership.[59]

In contrast to Soysal's emphasis on rights, Delanty notes the emergence of a communitarian ideology of European cultural identity and argues that a new kind of citizenship, focused less on rights and more on identity, is supplementing the formal postnational citizenship. He argues further that the substantive dimension of citizenship needs to be recombined with the formal dimension and that the core of postnational citizenship is the substantive concern for participation and multi-identification. Delanty suggests that the theorizing of citizenship must go beyond the spatial, national domain to include multiple layers on the regional, national, and supranational levels.[60]

Very recent work by Kastoryano, on conceptualizing citizenship under Maastricht, concludes that citizenship is "extraterritorial." Kastoryano points out that, according to Article 8 of the Maastricht Treaty, any individual who holds the nationality of a member state is a "citizen of the [European] Union," which is a projection of citizenship in relation to nationality worked out within the framework of nation-states.[61] This projection implies that citizenship is extraterritorial. According to the Maastricht Treaty, however, "citizens of the Union" are granted local voting rights on the basis of residence. Thus they have multiple belongings and allegiances that are a challenge to the unitarian and territorial nation-state. These multiple belongings and networks link home country to country of residence and create a broader web of European space. This space has diminishing internal frontiers and borders because of the freer movement of goods, property, and capital, and the adoption of a common currency. These complex interactions facilitate a new conceptualization of citizenship. The emergence of transnational solidarity networks among immigrants raises the question of the link between participation and citizenship, nationality and identity, politics and culture, both within the nation-state and in the European Union, the latter of which has been described by Castells as a "network state."[62] Transnational networks, like the general processes of globalization, provide challenges to the nation-state as they reconfigure political structures and the balance between nation and state. The state is considered as the driving force behind the construction of global structures and the nation as a resource for political action.[63] The emergence of transnational communities in the European Union results in a growing deterritorialization of identity and extraterritorialization of citizenship, which is legally prescribed by the Maastricht Treaty.[64] This deterritorialization raises the question of how national citizenship is accounted for in the postnational framework. The empirical evidence still shows that the nation-states remain the driving force of the European Union, despite the fact they have submitted to supranational norms, and remain the basis for transnational enterprise. Thus a "European" identity does not exist at this point in time; however, the possibility of one cannot not be ruled out. Such an identity could be socially constructed through a European identity project.[65]

The postnational model presents an oppositional conceptualization to the national citizenship model. Transnational structures in Europe are viewed as having transcended the power and influence of individual nation-states. To that extent, EU citizenship has the potential, at least, to be a new institution that delinks citizenship from nationality and territory and includes transmigrants and transnational and diasporic communities. While to some degree this new and fresh model represents aspects of the social reality of transnational diasporic communities, it nevertheless must still account for the continued power and importance of the nation-state. The nation-state is far from finished; however, it no longer has a monopoly of power within the politics of globalization.[66] While debates and theorizing about the postnational model are ongoing, the logical extension of this model is the notion of global citizenship and global/world governance.

Global Citizenship?

Citizenship is principally a modern, Western invention and, with economic and cultural globalization, the sociology of citizenship is being radically rethought.[67] If citizenship is understood to be both formal (as a legal status) and substantive (as a set of attitudes, relationships, and expectations), then a territorial limitation and condition is not imperative. This raises the question of the feasibility of the notion of global citizenship.

Only a decade ago, Turner's writings about the globalization of citizenship stated that the concept of global citizenship was premature.[68] The conceptual apparatus is now arguably in place. Turner suggested that one possible line of theoretical development of the notion of citizenship is "global citizenship," conceptualized as the political counterpart of the world economy. Falk's pioneering work shows that the making of global citizenship is an emergent possibility.[69] He argues for humane governance based on comprehensive human rights that are a result of transnational and grassroot democratic forces, and further suggests that the transition to humane global governance involves a non-territorial conception of identity and community.[70] More recently, Habermas has suggested that the notion of world citizenship is "no longer merely a phantom," although its achievement is still very far away.[71] In this sense, state citizenship and world citizenship are now on a continuum that is showing itself in outline form. While a world state is extremely remote, a global civil society is now gradually emerging, and this will impact on current conceptions of citizenship.[72] Within nations, the struggle for citizenship is, first and foremost, for civil, followed by political and social, citizenship. Therefore, at a global level, the rights and entitlements of all human beings are transcending the domain of nation-states, and this is likely the beginning of a global civil society and global governance. Drainville sees this development as an important moment in the history of organized capitalism, and argues that these forms of society and power are created with the aim of preserving existing order in a globalizing world of transnational capital. For other scholars, the political dimensions are primary and the economic secondary.[73] No particular model of global governance is dominant, although the general tone of scholars is inclusive, participatory (democratic), and fosters global citizenship.[74] Thus global governance contributes to, and reflects the making of, global civil society in a post-Westphalian world order where, in the context of deterritorialization, nation-states are increasingly losing their control over the destinies of individuals. Politics itself thus has increasingly global dimensions, one of which suggests a rethinking of democracy as a new cosmopolitan order of global governance.[75]

In summary, the world has increasing numbers of people who have homes away from home and who have multiple identities. The preference of such transnationals is often for the retention of the culture of their homelands while they also seek the right of a national citizenship. The trends discussed above, along with this increasing transnationalism, have implications for the immigration and citizenship policies of nation-states.

Policy Implications for Canadian Citizenship

Historically, nation-states have attempted to make exclusive citizenship a sine qua non. As Cohen notes, however, "The world is simply not like that any more; the scope for multiple affiliations and associations that has opened up outside and beyond the nation-state has also allowed a diasporic allegiance to become both more open and acceptable. There is no longer any ... coincidence between social and national identities. What nineteenth-century nationalists wanted was a 'space' for each 'race,' a territorialization of each social identity. What they have got instead is a chain of cosmopolitan cities and an increasing proliferation of subnational and transnational identities that cannot easily be contained in the nation-state system."[76]

The Canadian state is having difficulty containing the increasing proliferation of subnational and transnational identities within its population. This is due to Canada's historical and contemporary reliance on immigration for nation building and economic growth, as well as its implementation of a non-racist immigration policy in the 1960s. However, the state certainly governs and intervenes through its immigration and citizenship policies and, as will be shown, it is choosing to forge a citizenship policy that resists the transnational practices of recent immigrants.

Citizenship in Canada is currently being redefined as the process of globalization produces pressure to reconfigure the balance of responsibilities within the triangular relationship of states, markets, and communities.[77] The Canadian state's citizenship regime is attempting to reverse what it believes is a diminishment of authority over citizenship, using dimensions of territory and reinforcing a pan-Canadian citizenship regime.

Nation building in Canada has always involved immigration and, over the past fifty years, has come to involve citizenship. One fairly general view of nation building is that it attempts, through a set of historical and affective processes, to link together disparate and/or heterogeneous populations in order to create loyalties to, and identification with, a central state apparatus and institutional structure.[78] Thus policies on citizenship attempt to create the social conditions whereby diverse populations are able to identify as "one" within the nation-state. This entails an affective political process that includes attending citizenship classes, taking the citizenship test, taking the oath of citizenship, and receiving the Canadian citizenship certificate.

Prior to 1947, those living in Canada were British subjects, not Canadian citizens, as the concept of "Canadian citizenship" did not yet exist. On 1 January 1947, the first Canadian Citizenship Act came into effect and officially established a unique Canadian identity, both within Canada and internationally, and brought, among other things, the Canadian passport. This citizenship legislation lasted thirty years, until 1977, before it was revised. In 1999, another initiative to revise citizenship policy was introduced, but the proposed legislation (Bill C-16) expired before being passed into law, because of the November 2000 federal general election. The Canadian government's current plan is to re-introduce this initiative for new citizenship legislation sometime in 2002. The reasons that the Canadian government provided for the necessity of revisions back in 1977 are similar to the ones provided in 1999. That is, revisions were (and are) deemed necessary in order to reflect a growing and changing society that has access to new technologies, improved communication, and increased personal freedoms.

It is clear that the Canadian state is struggling with changing conceptions of citizenship in a globalizing world and is attempting to redefine citizenship in a way that maintains the autonomy and preservation of the Canadian nation-state. The former minister of Citizenship and Immigration, Lucienne Robillard, in her introduction of the proposed Citizenship of Canada Act for its second reading in the Canadian House of Commons, expressed the government's concern to preserve the relationship between citizenship and the nation-state. She described Canadian citizenship as "one of the world's most respected citizenships," as "the very foundation of the Canadian identity," and as "the common denominator that unites us from coast to coast."[79] At the same time, the government specified that revisions in legislation were necessary to clean up inconsistencies and some fundamental provisions that are unclear and open to interpretation by the courts. Politically, the current legislation is a liability for the government, as it is perceived (by many Canadians and by the Opposition) to be open to abuse by people seeking Canadian citizenship.[80] The federal government thought that the recently proposed act (Bill C-16) would correct these inconsistencies and clarify ambiguous provisions; but, more importantly, it believed (and continues to believe) that the value of Canadian citizenship would be strengthened under a more modern act and a new legislative framework. As noted earlier, citizenship is an ideological construction, and as Labelle and Midy have pointed out, the Canadian government is active on an ideological front, seeking to define, enhance, and promote Canadian citizenship along with its underlying values and obligations.[81]

Transnationalism and the Recently Proposed Bill C-16: An Act Respecting Canadian Citizenship

Table 3 summarizes the major sections of Bill C-16 – the recently proposed Citizenship of Canada Act – that relate to the issue of globalization and transnationalism. The following sections discuss these issues in greater detail.

Children Born in Canada: Questioning Birthright

Bill C-16 proposes no change in the access to Canadian citizenship by birthright. However, during the drafting of the bill, in the spring of 1998, serious disagreement arose among Liberal cabinet ministers and backbenchers regarding whether Canada should reconsider automatically giving citizenship to everyone born in the country.[82] Former minister Lucienne Robillard floated a proposal that Canada reconsider giving citizenship on the basis of birthright. This was a reaction to an Ontario court decision quashing deportation of a Toronto mother on the grounds that it violated the rights of her two Canadian-born children. In the end, Minister Robillard decided against abolishing an automatic right of citizenship for children born to parents without status in the country. Taking away this right would have meant putting children in a situation of being stateless in Canada, which the minister was not prepared to do. As transnational communities become established in Canada and elsewhere, legal and illegal movements of people between countries for purposes of work and leisure will increase. Citizenship via birthright need not be viewed in a negative light; the minister's recognition of this fact was the impetus for reconsideration of the issue.

Limiting the Transmission of Citizenship

Currently, children born abroad of a Canadian parent automatically acquire Canadian citizenship at birth. All generations beyond the first generation of Canadians born abroad also acquire Canadian citizenship at birth but lose their citizenship status at age twenty-eight unless they apply to retain it. In order to qualify for retention, one year of residence in Canada prior to application is required. In Bill C-16, no change is proposed to this system as it pertains to the first and second generations of children born abroad to a Canadian parent, as they would automatically acquire Canadian citizenship. For the second and subsequent generations born abroad, the proposed policy also remains the same with respect to their automatically acquiring citizenship at birth and being required to apply to retain it by age twenty-eight. However, according to the proposed residency requirement, members of these later generations would have to be "physically present" in Canada for at least three of the five years preceding the application before age twenty-eight. The residency requirement is thus tripled and the requirement of physical presence in Canada added. Moreover, the third generation and beyond would no longer have any claim to Canadian citizenship, which would thus limit its transmission to the second generation only. Members of this and subsequent generations would have to meet regular immigration requirements first and then the normal requirements of citizenship, just like any other immigrant to Canada. In its restriction of citizenship, this proposal reflects the state's desire for reterritorialization and is a reaction against emergent transnational, intergenerational networks of Canadian citizens in transnational communities.

Residency Requirements: The Quest for Reterritorialization

Currently, a permanent resident must reside in Canada for at least three years within a four-year period preceding his or her application for citizenship. However, the courts have offered diverse interpretations of what constitutes "residence" in Canada. Many judges believe that it is the "quality of attachment to Canada" that determines residency and not just the number of days a person is physically present in the country. For example, Federal Court judge Jean-Eudes Dube recently wrote, "Residency in Canada for the purposes of citizenship does not imply full-time

Table 3

Comparison of current and recently proposed Canadian citizenship policies on issues relating to transnationalism

Current policy (C-29)	Recently proposed policy (C-16)
Citizenship by birth All children born in Canada	**Citizenship by birth** All children born in Canada[1]
Children born abroad of a Canadian parent, for all generations beyond the first. Lose citizenship at age 28 if they do not register to retain it, which requires one year of residence in Canada prior to application.	Children born abroad of a Canadian parent, only for the first generation. Members of second generation will lose citizenship at age 28 if they do not register to retain it, which requires three years of physical presence in Canada within five years prior to application. Third generation has *no* claim to Canadian citizenship.
Citizenship by naturalization At least three years of residence in Canada within the four years prior to date of application.[2]	**Citizenship by naturalization** At least three years (1,095 days) of *physical presence* in Canada within the six years prior to date of application.[3]
Adequate knowledge of Canada and of the responsibilites and privileges of citizenship. Applicants may answer knowledge questions through an interpreter.	Adequate knowledge of Canada and of the responsibilites and privileges of citizenship and ability to communicate this knowledge in one of the two official languages *without* an interpreter.

Dual and multiple citizenship	**Dual and multiple citizenship**
Allowed	Allowed[4]
Oath	**Oath**
I swear (or affirm) that I will be faithful and bear true allegiance to Her Majesty Queen Elizabeth the Second, Queen of Canada, Her Heirs and Successors, and that will faithfully observe the laws of Canada and fulfil my duties as a Canadian citizen.	From this day forward, I pledge my loyalty and allegiance to Canada and Her Majesty Elizabeth the Second, Queen of Canada. I promise to respect our country's rights and freedoms, to defend our democratic values, to faithfully observe our laws and fulfil my duties and obligations as a Canadian citizen.

1 Members of the Liberal government disagreed whether this should be changed.

2 The Federal Court has interpreted residence as not necessarily requiring physical presence in Canada. It can include having ties to Canada through owning a home, paying taxes, and having immediate family members who reside in Canada. Applicants are also able to count time in Canada prior to permanent resident status, at a rate of 0.5 for every day.

3 This criterion strictly and narrowly defines residence as physical presence in Canada. Applicants cannot count time in Canada prior to permanent resident status. The original bill was more restrictive in its requirement of three years within the last five, but this was changed to six by the House of Commons Standing Committee on Citizenship and Immigration in their Second Report, 13 May 1999.

4 Countries that allow dual citizenship include Argentina, Brazil, Egypt, France, Great Britain, Iran, Italy, Jamaica, New Zealand, South Africa, and the United States. Countries that do not allow dual citizenship include Australia, Germany, India, Japan, Poland, Russia, and Sweden.

physical presence."[83] The quality of attachment to Canada has been measured by the criteria of owning a home in Canada, having a home address, having a Canadian bank account, paying Canadian taxes, and having family members in Canada. Bill C-16 stipulates that a permanent resident must have accumulated at least three years (1,095 days) of physical residence in Canada within a six-year period preceding application for citizenship. While the three-year time period remains the same and the base period increases from four to six years, the major change is the strict and narrow interpretation of permanent residence as physical presence in Canada. The government has stipulated that applicants would be responsible for proving their physical presence in Canada by providing official documents such as students' school records; affidavits or letters from employers, landlords, and neighbours; stamps in passports; and the like. Andrew Telegdi, former parliamentary secretary to the minister of citizenship and immigration, defended the new residency requirements, stating, "These new requirements have been established because we strongly believe that to preserve the value of citizenship we must ensure that all people who are Canadian citizens develop and maintain real links with Canada."[84]

This proposed change was (and continues to be) a very contentious one in a globalized, deterritorialized world characterized by processes of time-space distanciation, space-time compression, and the disembedding of social relations. The proposed legislation is much more severe than the current legislation, which is flexible and open to interpretation. In essence, it constitutes reterritorialization in the face of the deterritorialization of citizenship and identity. As a result of globalization, the role of territory in defining a people (as in the nation-state) is diminishing, and the idea that land and people are tightly bound together in a unitary state is now becoming more tenuous.[85] Hence, the Canadian state is resisting these changes and trying to re-establish territory as the basis of citizenship.

This proposed requirement in Bill C-16 also reflects the government's desire for potential citizens to demonstrate their attachment to Canada by making Canada their residence or home, thus assuming that home is where you must spend most of your time. This raises several questions from a transnationalist perspective. Can one not have Canada as a home and also have a "home away from home"? And why, in any case, does one need to spend most of one's time at home? Another rationale expressed by the government is, "The intent is that individuals should be familiar with Canadian way of life before they're admitted as citizens. And the only way to do that is to be here."[86] This prompts the question, "What is the Canadian way of life?" and is reminiscent of a question popular thirty years ago: "What is Canadian culture?"

This proposed "physical presence" residency requirement would land-lock people into Canada in an age of globalization. It is contrary to the trend of transnationalism and would have a restrictive effect on transmigrants, particularly business immigrants who have small or large transnational businesses. As well, this requirement would affect young immigrants whose career paths take them abroad for work, study, and travel. The current policy, which has a more flexible, discretionary, and interpretative residency requirement, is much more suited to the realities of globality than the proposed one, which is rigid, narrow, and physically restrictive.

Knowledge of Canada: Practising Cultural Fundamentalism

The current policy requires potential citizens to demonstrate an adequate knowledge of Canada and of the responsibilities and privileges of citizenship through a test of knowledge that allows for the use of an interpreter. The recently proposed policy also requires the same demonstration, but it has to be in English or French *without* an interpreter. This new requirement that knowledge of Canada be demonstrated through communication in an official language is also a form of cultural fundamentalism that establishes language as a cultural criterion for citizenship. In one sense, this proposal establishes linguistic compliance as a requirement for citizenship in a contemporary democratic society. In another sense, it represents an issue of governmentality or a way of framing governance that is mediated by notions of an imagined Canadian community that speaks English and French. That is, one is not really Canadian if one does not speak English or French.

Dual and Multiple Citizenship: An Uneasy and Questioned Paradox

Legalization of dual and multiple citizenship is really the institutionalization of the transnational ties people have. Canada has allowed dual and multiple citizenship since 1977, and it is possible not only to have two or more citizenships at the same time but also to have them for an indefinite time. However, dual and multiple citizenship have generated a sense of unease among some government officials. In the mid-1990s, the Standing Committee of Citizenship and Immigration Canada recommended that Canadians who hold dual citizenship accord precedence to their Canadian citizenship and, moreover, recommended that a condition of obtaining Canadian citizenship be the acknowledgment of this principle by immigrants who choose to seek citizenship via naturalization.[87] In the recently proposed legislation of Bill C-16, dual and multiple citizenship continues to be allowed, although a few years ago, in the formative stages of this legislation, this aspect was questioned in a proposal put forth by the Department of Citizenship and Immigration. While the seriousness of the state's intention to eliminate dual/multiple citizenship is unclear, the fact that it was raised publicly was perhaps a reminder to the people of Quebec of a potential cost of separation. Also important, though, is the fact that the Canadian government's publication material on dual and multiple citizenship devotes minimal space to noting the advantages of dual and multiple citizenship and significantly more space to pointing out its disadvantages.[88]

The evidence suggests that the Canadian state reluctantly continues to allow for dual and multiple citizenship. Why is this the case and why does dual citizenship present challenges to the state? The government assumes that the greater the level of transnationalism in an individual's life, the greater the ambivalence, divergence, and perhaps contrariety with Canada. Some native-born Canadians react to dual status by questioning the loyalty and allegiance of immigrants who retain such strong transnational ties and belong to transnational communities. Thus dual citizenship is seen by many to "devalue" citizenship and to hinder immigrant adaptation and integration. This unease is more likely to be felt by long-term and native-born residents than by immigrants themselves. Furthermore, recent theorizing in the United States, from the Carnegie Endowment for International Peace, suggests that, far from acting as a hindrance to adaptation, dual citizenship may actually help to facilitate the cultural and political incorporation of new immigrants who would otherwise fail to naturalize and would remain politically and culturally isolated.[89]

Another concern regarding plural citizenship relates to the issue of divided national allegiances, loyalty, and patriotism. The Canadian state questions whether it can trust in the loyalty of those who belong to transnational communities and have plural citizenship. With the exception of war and military service, many of the important issues, such as legal culpability and taxation, can be effectively resolved through bilateral and international treaties and agreements, so the issue of loyalty is not so much material or even electoral, but rather symbolic.[90]

Oath: Swearing Loyalty and Allegiance

The recently proposed oath requires the swearing of allegiance first and foremost to Canada (see Table 3). It places more emphasis on rights and freedoms, democratic values, laws, and obligations than the current oath. It also retains the requirement of swearing loyalty and allegiance to the Queen of Canada, Her Majesty Elizabeth the Second. This is problematic for many Québécois, First Nations, and those in transnational, diasporic communities. While the swearing of loyalty and allegiance to a queen who lives overseas in a foreign country may seem strange and be confusing for some transmigrants, this irony perhaps illustrates transnationalism itself. At a symbolic level, the oath is a declaration created by the state to reflect a commitment to shared values. The oath and the section of the Citizenship of Canada Act on "knowledge of Canada" are really references to values. As journalist Gagnon has noted, "Ms Robillard wants the future citizens to 'know Canada, share its values and develop a sense of belonging' ... What do private feelings have to do with citizenship? We should require future citizens to obey our laws, follow our main social codes and support themselves. Period ... As for the 'values' well, the fact is that Canadians don't share common values. Some don't even believe in democracy, which is okay in a democracy. And what are Canadian values?"[91] Gagnon is clearly questioning Robillard's "thick" conception of citizenship as encompassing shared values and identity.

In summary, many of the major proposed revisions and policies in Bill C-16 run counter to the trends of transnationalism, deterritorialization of identity, and emergent transnational practices. These proposed revisions include (1) the limitation of the transmission of citizenship to the second generation; (2) strict physical residency requirements; (3) knowledge of Canada as demonstrated through English or French language proficiency; and (4) changes to the oath. These proposed changes to the Citizenship Act illustrate the Canadian state's attempt to re-establish its authority over a "thinning" citizenship by layering up to a "thicker" form of citizenship. This process includes specific revisions and policies stipulating reterritorialization, limiting generational transmission of citizenship, and asserting cultural dominance and fundamentalism via language requirements. As well, the open and public discussions that took place when the bill was introduced – in which birthright and dual citizenship were questioned – are further illustrations of the state's desire for layering up to a "thicker" citizenship. These proposed changes illustrate the state's fear of diversity and desire for territorial fixity in its attempt to homogenize the citizenry of Canada. The changes move toward the neoconservative and ultranationalist views of immigrants and immigration as threats to social cohesion in Canada.

While the above has shown the incongruence between emergent trends of transnationalism and recently proposed Canadian citizenship policy, the challenge now is to determine what changes are appropriate and needed in citizenship policy. At the risk of oversimplifying, citizenship can arguably be conceptualized and understood in the binary fashion alluded to earlier:

- *Thick citizenship,* characterized by a set of common values and a shared cultural identity, producing a substantive national identity and social cohesion based on homogeneity.
- *Thin citizenship,* characterized by minimal shared values and cultural identity, producing a society based on civic participation, human rights, and rule of law, with recognition of difference and diversity.

These recently proposed revisions to Canadian citizenship policy represent the Canadian state's attempt to forge a "thicker" citizenship by tightening the rules and making them more restrictive. These measures are punitive rather than affective and do not recognize difference and diversity. They indicate that the Canadian state is choosing to revert, in perhaps nostalgic fashion, to older and traditional conceptions of national citizenship. This shift goes against the trend toward liberalized citizenship regimes in Western immigrant-receiving countries and, more recently, in Europe.[92] The choice of a "thin but strong" citizenship, more attuned to the realities of transnational and diasporic communities, has not been made officially, but in a number of respects it is widely practised. This disparity between law and reality results in ambiguous situations that cause problems for many immigrants in transnational communities.

Kymlicka and Norman point to an increasing number of theorists who argue that citizenship must take group differences into account.[93] They feel that a conception of "differentiated citizenship" is needed, according to which members of certain groups would be incorporated into the political community not only as individuals but also through the group, their rights depending in part on their group membership. These demands for differentiated citizenship pose a serious challenge to the prevailing conception of citizenship, as many people regard the idea of group-differentiated citizenship as a contradiction in terms. The orthodox position views citizenship as a matter of treating people as individuals with equal rights under the law. A differentiated citizenship, as opposed to a common citizenship, is therefore a radical development in citizenship theory.

Kymlicka further suggests that the state establish certain group-specific rights or "special status" for minorities; thus a multicultural citizenship would be differentiated and would encompass both individual and group-specific rights.[94] Kymlicka and Norman's discussion is of small "c" citizenship and it would be provocative to apply these ideas to the Citizenship Act itself. It is feasible to consider a differentiated and "thinner" act, which would contain "special status" provisions for those in transnational and diasporic communities as well as more flexible citizenship requirements, which recognize diversity.

Searching for Social Cohesion via Common Values and Identity: The Research Questions

Why the Search?

In a postmodern world, where globalization produces tendencies toward deterritorialization, hybridization, disjuncture, and fragmentation, it is no surprise that the Canadian state has placed an emphasis on common values, identity, and social cohesion, the latter quality being the focus of social policy initiatives and research funding. This focus has given the term "social cohesion" currency in state-funded academic and policy-oriented research.

In other parts of the world, the value attached to citizenship has been declining, particularly in Europe and the United States.[95] This may also be the case in Canada, although rates of naturalization have remained high. While rates of naturalization are often used as a measure of the value of citizenship among immigrants, the reasons for seeking naturalization may have changed for many immigrants, particularly those in transnational and diasporic communities. Cohen suggests that the strong cultural bonds of language and religion and a sense of common history and fate impregnate transnational relationships, giving them affective and intimate qualities that formal citizenship in a nation-state cannot.[96] Thus transmigrants may use the nation-state instrumentally – practising "instrumental citizenship"[97] – rather than revering it affectively. Scholars have also referred to this as "self-centred citizenship"[98] and "flexible citizenship."[99] Rosenau describes "self-centred citizenship" as a situation in which individuals have a high priority of attachment to self and a low priority of attachment to society; he argues that this form is becoming more common with the increase in global turbulence and the weakening of governments.[100] Rosenau points out that many are compelled to practise self-centred citizenship by default, for while they may be inclined to care about the larger society, they are confused about where and how they fit within it. Rosenau calls those whose political homes have been transformed by globalization "jet-set riders," and argues that their attachment to national communities becomes less salient as they focus on concerns beyond national boundaries.[101] Ong coined the term "flexible citizenship" to describe the activities of overseas Chinese in the 1990s and their opportunistic search for citizenship abroad. Overseas citizenship gave these transnationals flexibility in their accumulation of capital, while nation-states linked immigration policy with the transfer of capital. This resulted in a commodification of citizenship. Yet identity is an important constituent part of citizenship. Further research is needed in order to understand the relationship between a person's citizenship and his or her national identity.

Related to this issue is the question of whether or not dual and multiple citizenship are forms of instrumental and flexible citizenship. Research is also needed into how Canadian economic and cultural globalization affects transmigrants' citizenship statuses and the value they place on citizenship. The Canadian government perceives that devaluation and commodification of Canadian citizenship has occurred, and its counter-response, to re-emphasize the value of Canadian citizenship, has been policy initiatives such as Bill C-16. The following quotations from Citizenship and Immigration Canada (CIC); former minister of citizenship and immigration

Lucienne Robillard; and Andrew Telegdi, former parliamentary secretary to the minister of citizenship and immigration, illustrate the government's response:

> *CIC:* Strengthening the Value of Canadian Citizenship: The Government of Canada's Plan for Modernizing the *Citizenship Act.*[102]

> *Robillard:* If being a Canadian is to mean something, we have to have some rules here.[103]

> *Telegdi:* It is also important that we include changes to strengthen the value of Canadian citizenship ... The new act is a step in the right direction for all of us since it helps to promote the great value of Canadian citizenship. This is important for those of us who already possess this valuable asset. It is just as important for those who want to become Canadian citizens.[104]

This re-valuation of citizenship by the state is clearly an attempt to enhance social cohesion in Canada through an integration of the entire population into shared values. However, are shared values really the key to social cohesion?

Shared Values

Little research has been done into what values are shared among the Canadian population, and it is clear that many values are not shared or common. Jenson's mapping of social cohesion addresses the question of values by identifying the following research questions: What are the consequences, if any, of existing differences in values? Which differences matter and which are the inevitable – even desirable – manifestation of Canada's multinational and polyethnic history?[105] These questions need to be answered in Canadian empirical social science research.

At the "Policy Research: Creating Linkages" conference, held in Ottawa in 1998, Nevitte discussed "clashes over values" and their impact on social cohesion.[106] Kymlicka disagreed with Nevitte's notion of "clashes over values," and questioned the need to have shared values. He argued that the key to social cohesion is not shared values, but rather identities. That is, people can have differing identities despite shared values.

Identity

Kymlicka contends that identity is the real basis of social unity and cohesion and that it is important to have a shared citizenship identity that will supersede rival national identities in a multi-nation-state.[107] If identity is the key, then two fundamental questions arise:

1 Where will shared identity come from?
2 In what ways will shared identity be achieved?

Kymlicka's answer to the first question is "history" and participation in Webber's "the Canadian conversation," which is a uniquely Canadian discourse with distinctive vernaculars.[108] Thus it is argued that if diverse groups grow up listening to a national "conversation," it becomes a part of their identities. Kymlicka states, "The fact is that Canadians have exhibited a desire to continue the national conversation. Canadians identify enough with each other, and with our shared history, to find the prospect of stopping the conversation unacceptable."[109] This claim needs empirical investigation, particularly with regard to recent immigrants and transnational communities. An important research question is whether the reterritorializing thrust of the citizenship policy would ensure citizens' understanding of history and participation in "the Canadian conversation." For example, are recent immigrants and transmigrants really interested enough in the game of hockey – supposedly Canada's game and pastime – to engage in this aspect of the Canadian conversation?

The second question about shared identity is even more difficult to answer. Kymlicka and Norman phrase it in greater detail: "How can we construct a common identity in a country where people not only belong to separate political communities but also belong in different ways – that is, some are incorporated as individuals and others through membership in a group?"[110] Kymlicka's emphasis on identity has also influenced Jenson's mapping of social cohesion research in Canada. Jenson has identified a research agenda that includes questions pertinent to the issue of transnationalism and citizenship: "Where does a collective national identity – a sense of belonging – come from? Is social capital – that is, trusting connectedness – the key, or is commitment to an "imagined community" with common political projects? Can citizens' identities be both varied and multiple without threatening social cohesion, or is adherence to a single national vision necessary?"[111] As well, Kymlicka recently posed the following question: "Have they [immigrants] adopted a Canadian identity or held onto an ancestral identity?"[112] Given the existence of transnationalism and diasporic communities, this question is dated. For an increasing number of immigrants, it is no longer a question of having identity with either Canada or an ancestral nation. Instead they have multiple or transnational identities.

In both O'Connor's and Jenson's work on mapping social cohesion, the concept of "social capital" emerges as an important one for social cohesion.[113] Regardless of how "social capital" is defined, for members of transnational communities and diasporas, the context of much of their social capital is *transnational*. This fact brings into question the relationship of social capital to social cohesion. For example, when individuals and households are embedded in transnational social networks, how does this form of social capital facilitate or enhance social cohesion in Canada? What are the implications of these cross-national linkages for civic engagement in Canada?

Searching for Social Cohesion via Civic Engagement

The research questions surrounding common values and identity provide for politically crucial research and debate. Given the diversity of the Canadian population, the search for Canadian common values and a Canadian identity may be extremely long at best and futile at worst. At some point, assuming the best, these common values and identity may be found; then, the layering up to a "thick" citizenship will be possible through citizenship education rather than the restrictive and punitive measures of citizenship policy. However, if we assume that these qualities do not exist, then the question becomes, "Can we construct a 'thin but strong' citizenship that facilitates social cohesion?" Recent research on civic engagement as social capital suggests that the answer is yes, provided that the notion of community is reconceptualized. The primary research question now becomes, "How can civic engagement be encouraged?"

Recent work by Frideres suggests that a positive identification with governing bodies enriches the practice of citizenship and that "community as a place" (the traditional, geographically bound community) is disappearing and being replaced by "community as space." This shift means that a reconceptualization of "community" must take place. Steps taken, via civic engagement, will acknowledge this new conceptualization.[114]

If community is no longer thought of as "place" but rather as "space," the integration of transnational and diasporic communities into Canadian society becomes much easier. A "thin but strong" citizenship would then emphasize the *quality* of civic engagement rather than the *quantity* of time spent physically present in Canada or the avowed allegiance and loyalty to Canada. While this civic engagement would be recognized by the Canadian state as "local," it would also simultaneously be "translocal," "multilocal," or "glocal."

At this point, the question, "How can civic engagement be encouraged?" is not easily answered. While it is premature and not in the scope of this chapter to speculate on the answers to this question, it is important to note that the state cannot impose civic engagement, but only encourage it. As Cairns has suggested in his discussion of Canadian citizenship, the modern state cannot use coercion to produce the behaviour it requires of its citizens.[115]

Conclusion

As Franklyn Griffiths recently pointed out, "The thought of a distinct 'national culture' ... is no longer viable, if ever it was ... To underwrite the project of a national culture for purposes of unity, identity, social cohesion, civility, or whatever, is to be misguided ... In an era when international relations among states are being displaced, but by no means replaced, by transnational relationships among populations, a society of ethnic, social, and elective diversity is an asset and not a liability. Those in Ottawa who may be doing so should stop worrying about 'cultural pastiche.'"[116] As the social forces of globalization and transnationalism now, more than ever, challenge the Canadian state as a definer of citizenship, the Canadian state's response need not be resistance by imposing a thick and exclusive citizenship, rooted in the soil, and in language, allegiance, and loyalty. This approach is in direct contradiction to the realities of deterritorialized transnational and diasporic communities and their participants' transmigration, multiple and transnational identities, and changing conceptions of citizenship. It is possible and more realistic for the Canadian state to choose a "thin but strong" and inclusive definition of citizenship that harmonizes with other Canadian social policies and provides for a "differentiated and multicultural citizenship." This new conceptualization would emphasize a qualitative form of civic engagement and social capital while acknowledging that, for many landed immigrants and Canadian citizens, the models of assimilation and acculturation are no longer valid and have been replaced by transnationalism and diaspora. This approach to citizenship would also recognize the deterritorialized and multiple identities of transmigrants and acknowledge a new perception of community.

Notes

1 N. Papastergiadis, *The Turbulence of Migration* (Cambridge: Polity Press, 2000), 2.

2 A.H. Richmond, *Global Apartheid: Refugees, Racism, and the New World Order* (Toronto: Oxford University Press, 1994), xv, 115.

3 P. Hirst and G. Thompson, *Globalization in Question* (Cambridge: Polity Press, 1996), 181.

4 D. Harvey, "Globalization in Question," *Rethinking Marxism* 8, 4 (1995): 1-17.

5 J. Bartelson, "Three Concepts of Globalization," *International Sociology* 15, 2 (2000): 180-96.

6 S. Mahler, "Theoretical and Empirical Contributions toward a Research Agenda for Transnationalism," in *Transnationalism from Below,* ed. M. Smith and L. Guarnizo (New Brunswick, NJ: Transaction, 1998), 66.

7 Ibid., 66, 73.

8 Ibid., 67; L. Guarnizo and M. Smith, "The Locations of Transnationalism," in *Transnationalism from Below,* ed. M. Smith and L. Guarnizo (New Brunswick, NJ: Transaction, 1998), 5.

9 T. Faist, "Transnationalization in International Migration: Implications for the Study of Citizenship and Culture," *Ethnic and Racial Studies* 23, 2 (2000): 189.

10 D. Winland, "'Our Home and Native Land'? Canadian Ethnic Scholarship and the Challenge of Transnationalism," *Canadian Review of Sociology and Anthropology* 35, 4 (1998): 555-78.

11 M. Kearney, "The Local and the Global: The Anthropology of Globalization and Transnationalism," *Annual Review of Anthropology* 24 (1995): 548.

12 Arjun Appadurai, "Disjuncture and Difference in the Global Cultural Economy," in *Global Culture: Nationalism, Globalization, and Modernity,* ed. M. Featherstone (London: Sage Publications, 1990), 296-7.

13 A.H. Richmond, "Sociology of Migration in Industrial and Post-Industrial Societies," in *Migration: Sociological Studies 2,* ed. J. Jackson (London: Cambridge University Press, 1969), 238-81.

14 A.H. Richmond, "Sociological Theories of International Migration: The Case of Refugees," *Current Sociology* 36, 2 (1988): 12; A.H. Richmond, *Immigration and Ethnic Conflict* (London: MacMillan Press, 1988), 2; and A.H. Richmond, *Global Apartheid: Refugees, Racism, and the New World Order* (Toronto: Oxford University Press, 1994), 51, 69.

15 N. Schiller, L. Basch, and C. Blanc-Szanton, *Towards a Transnational Perspective on Migration* (New York: The New York Academy of Sciences, 1992), ix.

16 L. Basch, N. Schiller, and C. Blanc, *Nations Unbound* (Langhorne, PA: Gordon and Breach, 1994), 4.

17 Schiller, Basch, and Blanc-Szanton, *Towards a Transnational Perspective on Migration,* ix; and C. Blanc-Szanton, L. Basch, and N. Schiller, "Transnationalism, Nation-States, and Culture," *Current Anthropology* 36, 4 (1995): 684.

18 N. Schiller, L. Basch, and C. Blanc-Szanton, "From Immigrant to Transmigrant: Theorizing Transnational Migration," *Anthropological Quarterly* 68, 1 (1995): 48.

19 J. Lie, "From International Migration to Transnational Diaspora," *Contemporary Sociology* 24, 4 (1995): 305.

20 W. Safran, "Diasporas in Modern Societies: Myths of Homeland and Return," *Diaspora* 1, 1 (1991): 83.

21 W. Connor, "The Impact of Homelands upon Diasporas," in *Modern Diasporas in International Politics,* ed. G. Sheffer (London: Croom Helm, 1986), 16.

22 Safran, "Diasporas in Modern Societies," 83-4.

23 Robin Cohen, "Diaspora and the Nation-State," *International Affairs* 72, 3 (1996): 515; Robin Cohen, *Global Diasporas* (Seattle: University of Washington Press, 1997), 26.

24 N. Van Hear, *New Diasporas* (Seattle: University of Washington Press, 1998), 6.

25 K.B. Chan, "A Family Affair: Migration, Dispersal, and the Emergent Identity of the Chinese Cosmopolitan," *Diaspora* 6, 2 (1997): 195.

26 D. Ip, C. Wu, and C. Inglis, "Settlement Experiences of Taiwanese Immigrants in Australia," *Asian Studies Review* 22, 1 (1998): 93.

27 Skeldon, "Emigration from Hong Kong, 1945-1994: The Demographic Lead-up to 1997," in *Emigration from Hong Kong: Tendencies and Impacts,* ed. R. Skeldon (Hong Kong: Chinese University Press, 1995), 72.

28 T. Faist, "Cumulative Causation in Transnational Social Spaces: The German-Turkish Example" (paper presented at the International Sociological Association's meeting on "Inclusion and Exclusion: International Migrants and Refugees in Europe and North America," New School for Social Research, New York, NY, 5-7 June 1997), 12-13.

29 Van Hear, *New Diasporas,* 242-4.

30 M. Jimenez, "It's Illegal for Canadians to Fight against Canada – RCMP Studying How Law Deals with Dual-Loyalty Issues," *National Post,* 28 April 1999, A10.

31 L. Dreidger, *Multi-Ethnic Canada* (Toronto: Oxford University Press, 1996), 62, 69.

32 The descriptions of Mr. X and Mr. Y are extracted from raw data from the author's previous SSHRCC-funded research.

33 See L. Wong, "Globalization and Transnational Migration," *International Sociology* 12, 3 (1997): 329-51; and L. Wong and M. Ng, "Chinese Immigrant Entrepreneurs in Vancouver: A Case Study of Ethnic Business Development," *Canadian Ethnic Studies* 30, 1 (1998): 64-85.

34 T. Hutton, "International Immigration as a Dynamic of Metropolitan Transformation:

The Case of Vancouver," in *The Silent Debate: Asian Immigration and Racism in Canada,* ed. E. Laquian, A. Laquian, and T. McGee (Vancouver: Institute of Asian Research, 1998), 292.
35 Ibid., 293.
36 Kearney, "The Local and the Global," 552.
37 S. Sassen, "Territory and Territoriality in the Global Economy," *International Sociology* 15, 2 (2000): 374.
38 Arjun Appadurai, "Sovereignty without Territoriality," in *The Geography of Identity,* ed. P. Yaeger (Ann Arbor: The University of Michigan Press, 1996), 48.
39 I owe this point to David Cameron (personal communication, 13 May 1999).
40 M. Albrow, *The Global Age* (Cambridge: Polity Press, 1996), 156.
41 A. Giddens, *The Consequences of Modernity* (Cambridge: Polity Press, 1990), 20-9.
42 See K. Mitchell, "Transnational Discourse: Bringing Geography Back In," *Antipode* 29, 2 (1997): 101-14.
43 D. Jacobson, "New Frontiers: Territory, Social Spaces, and the State," *Sociological Forum* 12, 1 (1997): 122.
44 J. Hyndman, "Border Crossings," *Antipode* 29, 2 (1997): 153.
45 Arjun Appadurai, *Modernity at Large* (Minneapolis: University of Minnesota Press, 1996), 48.
46 Cohen, *Global Diasporas,* 157.
47 As cited in Jacobson, "New Frontiers," 122.
48 Jacobson "New Frontiers," 122.
49 Van Hear, *New Diasporas,* 263.
50 See V. Bader, "The Cultural Conditions of Transnational Citizenship," *Political Theory* 25, 6 (1997): 717-813; W. Kymlicka, and W. Norman, "Return of the Citizen: A Survey of Recent Work of Citizenship Theory," *Ethics* 104 (1994): 352-81; M. Roche, "Citizenship and Modernity," *British Journal of Sociology* 46, 4 (1995): 715-33; B. Turner, "Contemporary Problems in the Theory of Citizenship," in *Citizenship and Social Theory,* ed. B. Turner (London: Sage Publications, 1993), 1-18; and B. Turner, "Outline of a Theory of Citizenship," *Sociology* 24, 2 (1990): 189-217.
51 G. Delanty, "Models of Citizenship: Defining European Identity and Citizenship," *Citizenship Studies* 1, 3 (1997): 285-303.
52 Kymlicka and Norman, "Return of the Citizen," 353.
53 Roche, "Citizenship and Modernity," 717.
54 D. Tambini, "Post-National Citizenship," *Ethnic and Racial Studies,* 24, 2 (2001): 198.
55 W. Brubaker, *Immigration and the Politics of Citizenship in Europe and North America* (New York: University Press of America, 1989).
56 R. Bauböck, *Transnational Citizenship* (Aldershot, UK: Edward Elgar, 1994).
57 D. Jacobson, *Rights Across Borders: Immigration and the Decline of Citizenship* (Baltimore: Johns Hopkins University Press, 1996); E. Meehan, *Citizenship and the European Community* (London: Sage Publications, 1993); T.K. Oommen, *Citizenship, Nationality and Ethnicity* (Cambridge: Polity Press, 1997); M. Roche, "Citizenship and Modernity," *British Journal of Sociology* 46, 4 (1995): 715-33; Y. Soysal, *Limits of Citizenship: Migrants and Postnational Membership in Europe* (Chicago: University of Chicago Press, 1994); and A. Weale, "Citizenship beyond Borders," in *The Frontiers of Citizenship,* ed. U. Vogel and M. Moran (New York: St. Martin's Press, 1991), 155-65.
58 Soysal, *Limits of Citizenship,* 140.
59 Ibid., 141.
60 Delanty, "Models of Citizenship," 292, 299.
61 R. Kastoryano, "Transnational Participation and Citizenship," *Transnational Communities Working Papers Series,* WPTC 98-12, December 1998, <www.transcomm.ox.ac.uk/working_papers.htm> (28 November 2001).
62 M. Castells, *End of Millennium* (Oxford: Blackwell, 1998), 311.
63 Kastoryano, "Transnational Participation and Citizenship," 4.
64 Ibid., 13.
65 Castells, *End of Millennium,* 333.
66 R. Holton, *Globalization and the Nation-State* (New York: St. Martin's Press, 1998), 107.
67 R. Cohen and P. Kennedy, *Global Sociology* (London: MacMillan Press, 2000), 82-3.

68 B. Turner, "Outline of a Theory of Citizenship," *Sociology* 24, 2 (1990): 211-13.
69 R. Falk, "The Making of Global Citizenship," in *Global Visions: Beyond the New World Order,* ed. J. Brecher, J. Childs, and J. Cutler (Boston: South End Press, 1993), 39-50.
70 R. Falk, *On Humane Governance* (Cambridge: Polity Press, 1995), 15, 95.
71 J. Habermas, "Citizenship and National Identity: Some Reflections on the Future of Europe," in *Theorizing Citizenship,* ed. R. Beiner (Albany: State University of New York Press, 1995), 279; J. Habermas, *Between Facts and Norms: Contributions to a Discourse Theory of Law and Democracy* (Cambridge: Polity Press, 1996), 515.
72 T.K. Oommen, *Citizenship, Nationality and Ethnicity,* 227.
73 A. Drainville, "The Fetishism of Global Civil Society: Global Governance, Transnational Urbanism and Sustainable Capitalism in the World Economy," in *Transnationalism from Below,* ed. M. Smith and L. Guarnizo (New Brunswick, NJ: Transaction, 1998), 37-59.
74 Commission on Global Governance, *Our Global Neighborhood* (Oxford: Oxford University Press, 1995), 5.
75 D. Held, "Democracy: From City-States to a Cosmopolitan Order?" *Political Studies* 40, special issue (1992): 10-39; D. Held, "Democracy and the New International Order," in *Cosmopolitan Democracy,* ed. D. Archibugi and D. Held (Cambridge: Polity Press, 1995), 96-120; and D. Held, *Democracy and the Global Order: From the Modern State to Cosmopolitan Governance* (Stanford, CA: Stanford University Press, 1995).
76 Cohen, *Global Diasporas,* 174-5.
77 J. Jenson, "Fated to Live in Interesting Times: Canada's Changing Citizenship Regimes," *Canadian Journal of Political Science* 30, 4 (1997): 628.
78 N. Schiller and G. Fouron, "Transnational Lives and National Identities: The Identity Politics of Haitian Immigrants," in *Transnationalism from Below,* ed. Smith and Guarnizo, 132.
79 L. Robillard, "Speech to the House of Commons," 3 February 1999, *Hansard,* no. 173 [online], <www.parl.gc.ca> (4 April 1999).
80 Citizenship and Immigration Canada, "Citizenship of Canada Act. Strengthening the Value of Canadian Citizenship: The Government of Canada's Plan for Modernizing the *Citizenship Act,*" November 1999, <www.cic.ci.gc> (25 January 2002), under "Publications," "Policy and Legislation."
81 M. Labelle and F. Midy, "Re-reading Citizenship and the Transnational Practices of Immigrants," *Journal of Ethnic and Migration Studies* 25, 2 (1999): 213.
82 A. Thompson, "Liberals Split on Birthright Proposal," *Toronto Star,* 14 May 1998, Migration Network E-mail listserv.
83 A. Duffy, "Citizenship Rulings a 'Sorry Mess,' Lawyer Says: Contradictory Judgments," 9 April 1999, <www.fact.on.ca> (27 November 2001).
84 A. Telegdi, "Speech to the House of Commons," 5 February 1999, *Hansard,* no. 175 [online], <www.parl.gc.ca> (4 April 1999).
85 D. Jacobson, "New Frontiers: Territory, Social Spaces, and the State," *Sociological Forum* 12, 1 (1997): 122.
86 B. Laghi, "Ottawa to Tighten Citizenship Rules," *Globe & Mail,* 13 November 1998, A1, A8.
87 Labelle and Midy, "Re-reading Citizenship," 219.
88 Citizenship and Immigration Canada, *Dual Citizenship,* Cat. no. Ci52-6/1998 (Ottawa: Public Works and Government Services Canada, 1998), <www.cic.gc.ca> (25 January 2002), under "Citizenship," "Canadian Citizenship."
89 P. Spiro, "Embracing Dual Nationality," Carnegie Endowment for International Peace – International Migration Policy, <www.ceip.org> (26 October 1999).
90 T. Aleinikoff, "After Nationality, Then What?" *Research Perspectives on Migration* 2, 2 (1999): 15.
91 L. Gagnon, "Citizenship Rules for Homebodies," *Globe & Mail,* 19 December 1998, D3.
92 C. Joppke, "How Immigration Is Changing Citizenship," *Ethnic and Racial Studies* 22, 4 (1999): 645.
93 Kymlicka and Norman, "Return of the Citizen," 369-70.
94 Kymlicka, as cited in M. Martiniello, "Citizenship, Ethnicity, and Multiculturalism: Post-National Membership between Utopia and Reality," *Ethnic and Racial Studies* 20, 3 (1997): 637.

95 D. Jacobson, *Rights across Borders,* 125.
96 Cohen, "Diaspora and the Nation-State," 517.
97 D. Ip, C. Inglis, and C. Wu, "Concepts of Citizenship and Identity among Recent Asian Immigrants in Australia," *Asian and Pacific Migration Journal* 6, 3-4 (1997): 363-84.
98 J. Rosenau, "Citizenship without Moorings: American Responses to a Turbulent World," in *Citizenship and National Identity: From Colonialism to Globalization,* ed. T. Oommen (New Delhi: Sage Publications, 1997), 227-60.
99 A. Ong, "On Edge of Empires: Flexible Citizenship among Chinese in Diaspora," *Positions* 1, 3 (1993): 745-78.
100 Rosenau, "Citizenship without Moorings," 230, 234-5.
101 Ibid., 236.
102 Citizenship and Immigration Canada, "Citizenship of Canada Act. Strengthening the Value of Canadian Citizenship," <www.cic.gc.ca> (10 December 1998).
103 A. Hanes, "Allegiance Oath Keeps Reference to Queen," *Ottawa Citizen,* 8 December 1998, <www.ottawacitizen.com> (20 December 1998).
104 Telegdi, "Speech to the House of Commons," 5 February 1999.
105 J. Jenson, *Mapping Social Cohesion: The State of Canadian Research,* Canadian Policy Research Networks Study no. F-03. (Ottawa: Renouf, 1998), 32.
106 N. Nevitte, "Canadian Values: Evolution or Revolution?" (paper presented at the "Policy Research: Creating Linkages" conference, Ottawa, 1-2 October 1998).
107 W. Kymlicka, *Finding Our Way: Rethinking Ethnocultural Relations in Canada* (Toronto: Oxford University Press, 1998), 173.
108 Ibid., 175.
109 Ibid., 177.
110 Kymlicka and Norman, "Return of the Citizen," 377.
111 Jenson, *Mapping Social Cohesion,* 35-6.
112 As cited in K. Schwinghamer and P. Berkowitz, "New Ways of Seeing," *University Affairs* 40, 2 (1999): 7.
113 P. O'Connor, *Mapping Social Cohesion,* Canadian Policy Research Networks Discussion Paper no. F/01 (Ottawa: Canadian Policy Research Networks, 1998), 3-8; and Jenson, *Mapping Social Cohesion,* 26-35.
114 J. Frideres, "Civic Participation, Awareness, Knowledge and Skills," in *Immigrants and Civic Participation: Contemporary Policy and Research Issues,* ed. Canadian Heritage (Ottawa: Canadian Heritage Multiculturalism, 1997), 40.
115 A. Cairns, "The Fragmentation of Canadian Citizenship," in *Belonging: The Meaning and Future of Canadian Citizenship,* ed. W. Kaplan (Montreal: McGill-Queen's University Press, 1993), 182.
116 F. Griffiths, "The Culture of Change," (paper presented at the "Analysing the Trends: National Policy Research" conference, Ottawa, 25-6 November 1999), 10.

4
Civil Society Activism on the World Wide Web: The Case of the Anti-MAI Lobby

Ronald J. Deibert

Over the course of the twentieth century, and at an accelerating pace over the last several decades, new information and communication technologies have fuelled numerous interrelated globalization processes.[1] To date, the prime beneficiaries of these new technologies have been global market forces, such as transnational corporations and global financial services. With the ability to move information rapidly around the planet, these global market forces have created a web of constraints that structures the policy options available to states, particularly in the macroeconomic policy area, thus shifting world order in a decidedly neoliberal direction.[2]

Although the identity of the immediate "winners" is clear, some have argued that these same technologies also offer the potential for citizen networks to flourish, perhaps even to such an extent as to reign over or govern global market forces.[3] Referred to variously as "transnational social movements," "global civil society" or "civil society networks," this type of political activism has become a beacon of hope for those who see in it a mode of political participation linking individuals at the local level to issues of global concern.[4] Not surprisingly, thousands of activist groups from around the world have established a presence on the Internet. No non-governmental organization of consequence is without its own World Wide Web page. Almost every imaginable political or social campaign has its electronic listserv component. As a consequence, the Internet has become as vital to global civil society as telecommunications are to transnational corporations. So closely linked now are civil society networks to the Internet that among more optimistic observers the Internet itself has often been portrayed as a nearly mystical generator of democratic social change.

The enthusiastic linking of the Internet with recharged democratic participation has not gone uncontested, however. Tempering the optimism have been studies that question the extent to which real communities can actually thrive on the Internet.[5] One recent study published in *American*

Psychologist went so far as to suggest that extensive Internet use is associated with declines in the size of participants' social circle and increases in depression and loneliness.[6] As Craig Calhoun has remarked, "relationships forged with the aid of electronic technology may do more to foster "categorical identities" than they do dense, multiplex, and systematic networks of relationships."[7] If true, such implications would likely limit the long-term potential for the Internet to serve as a medium of global democratic participation and civil society activism.

In this chapter, I examine in detail the case of the networks that emerged to lobby against the proposed Multilateral Agreements on Investments (MAI), focusing in particular on the role played by the Internet, World Wide Web, and other information and communication technologies. The case is instructive for three reasons: First, the issue-area centres on an agreement at the heart of developments in the international political economy. While numerous detailed studies of civil society networks have emerged in issue-areas such as health, human rights, development, gender, and the environment, very few focus directly on global market forces.[8] The MAI case is one in which a network emerged to lobby against an agreement touching at the heart of economic globalization and the furthering of foreign direct investment – issues strongly endorsed by the most powerful economic actors in the world today. It is, then, a "hard case" for those who would argue that civil society networks offer a potential counter-hegemonic force against unbridled capitalism and the interests of large transnational corporations.[9]

Second, the case is instructive because the groups opposed to the agreement appeared to have won a temporary victory, pushing the MAI off the agenda at the Organisation for Economic Co-operation and Development (OECD), the international venue at which the MAI was being negotiated.[10] Notwithstanding the fact that the MAI will almost certainly reappear at a later time in a different guise and forum, the case offers potential lessons on how networks could be used in a campaign directed at a particular forum or treaty, rather than at broad public opinion. And the fact that the activists were successful in pushing the MAI off the agenda at the OECD certainly gives prima facie evidence that even in the "hard case" of economic investment rules, the lobbying practices of civil society networks can occasionally succeed.

Third – and most important for this study – the case is instructive because nearly all of the press accounts, some academic studies, and most state and civil society participants in the campaign drew a strong connection between the success of the campaign and the role of the Internet.[11] For example, following its withdrawal from the MAI negotiations, the French government noted in its official report that non-governmental organizations were better organized and informed because of the Internet, and that "the development of the Internet is shaking up the world of negotiations."[12] If the evidence supports such strong connections, then it is reasonable to assume that as the Internet continues to grow we will see more cases of successful campaigns such as the anti-MAI lobby. Those interested in resisting global market forces should direct most of their energies into the Internet accordingly. And we should expect a growing and vibrant Internet-based form of civil society activism as a significant presence on the world political stage. If the evidence suggests a more circumscribed role for the Internet, however, then civil society networks might have to take a more nuanced approach to the Internet relative to other, perhaps more familiar, strategies and tools. In other words, the question at issue here revolves around the nature of the activists themselves and their relationship to the Internet. Did the Internet itself spawn the anti-MAI civil society activism, or did it facilitate and amplify activism that was already in place?

Guiding the research of this chapter, then, are the following main questions: What role did the Internet play in the activism surrounding the MAI? How did civil society networks employ it? Did it generate an essentially new form of activism, or facilitate older ones? Would the campaign have been different and have produced different results without the Internet? And can we characterize the groups involved in the anti-MAI campaign as a "community"? Are they part of "global civil society"? Or are they simply a set of largely independent groups that came together briefly because of coincidental interests and which will now wither away?

As I will show below, the Internet did play a vital role in the anti-MAI activism, helping to coordinate information strategically among groups in the network, to pressure politicians, and to publicize anti-MAI views. Although it is almost certain that some type of anti-MAI activism would have emerged without the Internet, it seems reasonable to conclude that the activism would not have been as successful without it. Although the groups that came together to form the anti-MAI network are varied and diverse, the network itself shows signs of persisting indefinitely, turning its gaze to new fora and issue-areas and continuing to use the Internet in ways that evolved out of the anti-MAI campaign. While it would be misleading to characterize the anti-MAI network as a community, it is something more than a coincidental coordination of isolated groups. It has become a durable presence on the Internet and part of a significant new and vital force in world politics. Hence, while it would be misleading to suggest that the Internet generated the anti-MAI activism in a determinist sense, it did more than simply facilitate activism that was already in place. It has become the sinew of power for the coalescing nebulae of global civil society.

The chapter will proceed as follows. I will first describe the proposed

MAI and the process of the negotiations. As the process was very controversial, it is important to have some understanding of the contrary views surrounding the MAI. I will therefore briefly outline the opinions of MAI supporters and detractors. Finally, I will turn to a detailed examination of the role of the Internet in the anti-MAI campaign. I will conclude with some observations of how the case of the MAI will set a precedent for future relationships between civil society networks, states, the Internet, and world order.

The Multilateral Agreement on Investment (MAI)

The story of the MAI begins in the context of deepening economic integration among developed states through the latter half of the twentieth century. The acceleration of transnational production processes and the concomitant rise in foreign direct investment through this period pushed issues of domestic economic regulation into the international arena.[13] Today, capitalist states, under pressure from domestic firms operating increasingly in foreign jurisdictions, have found themselves more often having to address issues that go beyond cross-border barriers to trade, into the very regulation of the domestic sphere. Although the foreign direct investment issue has been most acute in the US-Japanese investment relationship, particularly because of perceived Japanese "informal" barriers to investment, it has confronted all industrialized and developing countries.

It is in this context of deepening economic integration that the pressures to develop multilateral rules on investment policies evolved.[14] At the 1995 Halifax summit of the G7, the final communiqué endorsed the idea of negotiating a multilateral framework for investment rules under the auspices of the OECD, and it was hoped that the agreement would be completed in two years.[15] The twenty-nine-member OECD had been producing policy reports on investment liberalization since 1961, and had been working closely on the issues of a multilateral agreement on investment since at least 1991.[16] Branded by its critics, with more than a little accuracy, as a "rich states' club," the OECD was also the forum in which the countries with the largest stake in global foreign direct investment were members. And the expectation among G7 ministers was clearly that the smaller, twenty-nine-member OECD would be able to avoid the collective action problems inherent in the much larger and ideologically diffuse World Trade Organization (WTO), and thus come to a much quicker agreement. Just as clearly, however, it was unforeseen at the time that a different type of collective action problem would emerge with the uninvited participation of hundreds of non-governmental organizations and activists.[17]

The goals of the proposed MAI can be found most succinctly in a 1995 report to OECD ministers by the Committee on International Investment and Multinational Enterprises and the Committee on Capital Movements and Invisible Transactions, two specialized OECD committees that set the initial negotiating frame of reference.[18] The report's central argument began by acknowledging the growth in foreign direct investment, particularly among "newly emerging markets." While applauding this trend, and the liberalization that had occurred to date, the report noted that further growth was still hampered by many government restrictions and regulations, a tendency to resort to unilateral measures to solve them, and the lack of a multilateral framework within which to pursue negotiations. The report suggested that a multilateral agreement on investment would help solve these problems by providing a broad multilateral framework for investment protection, the furthering of liberalization, and effective dispute settlement among members.[19] Finally, the report recommended that the MAI would be a freestanding international treaty open to all OECD members and the European Community, and to accession by non-OECD member countries after its implementation by the former. Following the release of the report, the formal negotiations began at the OECD.

Opinions on the relative merits of the MAI are as plentiful as they are sharply divided. Proponents have argued that the MAI would further international liberalization and foreign direct investment trends (which they see in a positive light) by making clear a set of multilateral rules and an effective dispute settlement mechanism that could be applied uniformly among signatories. Countering the view put forth by detractors that the MAI is a radical departure from existing international economic practices, proponents have pointed to the existing non-discrimination precedents found in the General Agreement on Trade and Tariffs (GATT) and the rules and agreements within the WTO, the investment provisions in NAFTA, as well as the liberalization measures already taken unilaterally or bilaterally by many industrialized states. The MAI would simply duplicate these principles in a wider, multilateral framework, one that would eventually be open to many more states.[20] Proponents have also argued that beyond non-discrimination, the MAI would not *force* states to behave in a specific way. Each participating country would retain the right to legislate in whatever way it saw fit, to achieve its own national objectives. The non-discrimination principle simply requires that such legislation not be biased against foreign, as opposed to domestic, investment. As many industrialized states' economies include large corporations that invest in foreign jurisdictions, the benefits to these states of having such non-discrimination principles widely entrenched are obvious.

MAI detractors include a wide array of different interest groups – as many as 600 non-governmental organizations (NGOs) from at least seventy countries by some estimates[21] – in areas such as environment, labour, and culture, each with its own set of sectoral criticisms.[22] Common objections, however, centre on several key themes, at the forefront of which is the issue of diminished state sovereignty and growing corporate power and rights. Detractors argue that the MAI is yet another building block in the extension of global economic neoliberalism – an agreement that pushes aside environment, labour, and cultural regulations in favour of big business and transnational capital. Most importantly, the MAI would give far too many political rights to corporations over states and citizens.[23] Under the proposed MAI, so the argument goes, corporations would have the right to sue states if they thought that local or national laws discriminated against them. Adding to this fear has been the *cause célèbre* suit of the Ethyl Corporation against the Canadian government – a case cited by nearly every MAI detractor.[24] Under the existing expropriation and compensation provisions of NAFTA, which were to be duplicated in the MAI, the Ethyl Corporation sued the Canadian government over environmental laws being debated in the Canadian Parliament, which would prohibit interprovincial trade of MMT – a gasoline additive that the Ethyl Corporation produces. Detractors have seen the US$250 million suit, and the ensuing US$13 million settlement and abandonment of the proposed legislation by the Canadian government, as an ominous portent of what would ensue under the MAI.[25] Thousands of wealthy, litigious corporations would threaten suits against states whenever environmental, labour, or cultural regulations were proposed. The likely outcome, critics believe, would be a "chilling" climate over such regulations, for fear that they would provoke costly suits.

The Ethyl suit and the provisions within the MAI that seem to tilt the balance in favour of corporate interests over state sovereignty have suggested to many critics above all else an increasing loss of democratic control over economic matters through traditional state structures of political participation. As one joint NGO statement noted, "The intention of the MAI is not to regulate investments but to regulate governments."[26] For most critics of the MAI, globalization and all that goes with it has become synonymous with an increasing marginalization of citizens' rights relative to big business and anonymous transnational market forces. Adding to this perception has been the sense among critics that the MAI was being negotiated in secret, without the participation of member states' deliberative assemblies and the knowledge of their citizens.[27] This stark dichotomy between seeming corporate control, inherent in the MAI, and democratic participation – however inaccurate or accurate the perception may be – has riveted many people's attention onto the MAI issue and brought together groups of widely varying interests in the name of a common cause. Clearly, elites who participated in the negotiation process were unprepared for the firestorm of criticism that was unleashed by the MAI.

The negotiating process at the OECD did not run according to the script envisioned by the G7 summit's final communiqué. Rather than finishing in 1997, as originally hoped, from mid-1997 onward – the time at which a draft text of the MAI was acquired by the Council of Canadians and posted to the Internet – the negotiations were dogged by civil society groups and activists, both at Paris and within the countries of the member states involved in the negotiations. By April 1998, it was clear that the MAI was in trouble, with OECD ministers announcing a five-month moratorium on negotiations so that member states could consult with their citizens. The official nail in the coffin of the MAI, however, was the withdrawal of the French government in October 1998, following the release of the Lalumière Report, a study commissioned by the Jospin government that was highly critical of both the negotiating process and the content of the MAI. While anti-MAI activists have been satisfied with the short-term victory signalled by the termination of the MAI process at the OECD, they fully expect the issue of multilateral rules on economic investment to continue in a different forum, most likely the WTO.[28]

The Role of the Internet

Initial news reports of the MAI process emphasized that the Internet was vital to the success of the civil society networks, a view that is corroborated by virtually everyone that was involved in the process directly. But how was it employed? What role did it play in facilitating the activism? The Internet played a part in the anti-MAI activism in three main ways. First, it was crucial for the swift communication of information among members of the anti-MAI lobby – a lobby that was dispersed across several state jurisdictions in both developed and developing countries. The fact that local activists from disparate regions around the world could communicate dense information across several time zones instantly may seem commonplace today, but it is remarkable in light of the fact that activists of even a decade ago did not enjoy the same benefits. Certainly phones, faxes, and regular mail were employed as a matter of practice among activists for decades and were employed alongside new media in the anti-MAI campaign. But the Internet formed the technological infrastructure of the campaign in ways that older, more traditional media simply could not accommodate.

At the centre of the infrastructure were and still are several electronic listservs – electronic mailing lists that distribute information among participants worldwide. These listservs are the material nerves linking the global anti-MAI campaign. Information from any one of the participants is immediately forwarded to everyone else on the list. In this way, members of the anti-MAI lobby are kept apprised of negotiations, meetings, protests, letter campaigns, editorials, news items, Web sites of interests, and general information.[29] The three most significant anti-MAI listservs are the STOP-MAI listserv, run out of Australia, the MAI-Not listserv, run by the Public Citizen group of the United States, and the MAI-NOT listserv, run out of Ottawa, Canada, although many other listservs contain discussions relating to the MAI as well. On a typical day, the traffic on each of the main MAI listservs runs at about thirty to forty postings a day, the volume increasing relative to current events on some days.[30] Appendix A (p. 160) shows a recent posting to the MAI-NOT listserv that provides an example not atypical of the type of posting that regularly threads its way through the listserv. The posting provides a notice of an important upcoming WTO meeting, the agenda of the meeting, the names of the ministers attending, and a sample letter that could be printed and faxed to the ministers to apply pressure. Only one posting among 13,000 in one listserv among many, the posting gives some sense of the strategic power conferred by one component of the Internet. By providing a form of distributed intelligence, the listservs helped to augment the knowledge, capacity, and responsiveness of the anti-MAI network in a way that telephones or faxes could not.[31]

Beyond enhancing the capacity of individual members of the anti-MAI network, however, the Internet also bound individual activists and groups from around the world together more closely into a cohesive force. The specific nature of the relationship that was forged by these disparate groups will be considered in more detail below. What is significant here is the way in which the Internet helped coordinate the day-to-day activities of anti-MAI groups, focusing their attention on common issues simultaneously, and helping to contribute to a sense of common purpose. While interaction among members of the anti-MAI network can be traced back to a time before the advent of the Internet, it was much more sporadic and formal then. For example, activists in the United States and Canada opposed to the 1988 Free Trade Agreement interacted with each other through faxes, telephone exchanges, letters, and formal conferences. Although these types of links were just as vital in the anti-MAI campaign, what the Internet did was to add a dense layer of daily interaction to these links, intensifying the bonds between disparate members and fomenting a sense of international commonality. As Maude Barlow, of the Council of Canadians, noted in the midst of the campaign, "We are in constant contact with our allies in other countries. If a negotiator says something to someone over a glass of wine, we'll have it on the Internet within an hour, all over the world ... If we know something that is sensitive to one government, we get it to our ally in that country instantly."[32]

Second, the Internet was important in publicizing information about the MAI – and the activists' interpretation of the MAI – to a wider community of Internet users and beyond. The most important component of the Internet in this respect was the various World Wide Web home pages of the anti-MAI groups, although the listservs served an important function here as well. Many anti-MAI sites – such as those of the Preamble Collective, Public Citizen, the Polaris Institute, and the Council of Canadians – were central nodes of information distribution that provided updates on the progress of negotiations, secondary interpretations and general essays on the MAI and globalization, tips on how to become an anti-MAI activist, and notification of speeches and demonstrations. Once again, the Internet proved to have an advantage here over older, more traditional forms of media. By enabling Web site creators with little technical expertise to post images, text, graphics, and even audio and video to a global audience, World Wide Web pages give individuals a sense of broadcasting power – a power that in the past was largely unavailable. Whereas in previous campaigns an activist might have set up an information booth on a university campus, in a downtown mall, or at local place of worships, today activists create "virtual" information booths that have the potential to reach thousands, perhaps millions, of people around the world, twenty-four hours a day. They also seem to confer legitimacy on the information contained in them (although it is difficult to be certain) simply because they are on the Internet.

An important collective dimension to the home pages that increased their overall exposure was the common practice of cross-referencing sites in the anti-MAI campaign. Nearly every home page in the network had a list of links to other sites in the campaign. In many cases, essays and articles from one site would be linked directly to dozens of other sites, giving their authors a public exposure that would have been unthinkable without the Internet. For example, a single essay by Tony Clarke, "MAI-Day: The Corporate Rule Treaty," was linked from over a dozen different sites around the world.[33] The Preamble Collective Web site was linked from at least fifty other Web sites.[34] The home pages also served as a repository of information useful for activists and central to the campaign, but too large to distribute over the listservs. Most pages included background overviews of the MAI negotiations and general essays about international political economy. One home page posted a lengthy survey of Canadian members of parliament (MPs) about their views and knowledge of the MAI. Another home page had a detailed list of addresses and phone and fax numbers of editorial pages of major North American newspapers.[35] Most of the sites provided information about the MAI in non-technical language, including background details on trade and investment issues, in sharp contrast to the arcane, specialized language used in the technical papers of the OECD and member states.[36] How much of this was consumed by the "already converted" is unclear, but certainly, for the members of the network, access to such a large stock of detailed information buttressed the strength and intellectual capacity of the campaign.

A third way in which the Internet was used was as a tool to put direct pressure on politicians and policy makers in member states. Many anti-MAI sites provided the e-mail addresses of MPs and state representatives.[37] Many included form letters to employ in order to voice concern about approval of the treaty – letters that could be sent with a click of a button.[38] This technological capacity may have been responsible for the creation of a new type of "armchair activism," through which people could get involved in campaigns like the anti-MAI network without even leaving their home or office, thus reducing the physical commitment made and/or risks taken by participating in traditional demonstrations. One site provided a series of sample city and county resolutions against the MAI, information about how to go about lobbying local councils to have them adopted, and stories from anti-MAI activists who were successful in doing so.[39] Significantly, many of the resolutions that were successfully passed – through the Berkeley City Council and the Corporation of the City of Mississauga, to give just two examples – contained identical texts supplied by a Web site based in Washington, DC. Other municipalities passed resolutions in which only minor modifications had been made to the text. On the listservs and Web sites, the times and locations where important MAI-related meetings were taking place were announced beforehand, so that protests could be coordinated strategically. Even the times and locations at which prominent politicians were meeting to discuss topics not directly related to the MAI would be announced, so that activists could have the chance to put pressure on politicians. Although it is unclear to what extent politicians and policy makers have become "desensitized" to e-mail bombardments and electronic petitions, certainly the concerted and dogged swarm of attention from around the world had to give some of them pause.[40]

What If the Internet Had Not Been Available to the Campaign?

The three ways that the Internet was employed in the campaign suggest that it was an integral component of the activism. But how important was it? Would the campaign have been different and have produced different results without the Internet? Virtually every activist involved says that the campaign would not have been as effective without the Internet.[41] Whether a campaign would have existed at all is a different question. Certainly a strong case could be made that the forces of liberalization were meeting growing resistance and criticism around the world, especially in light of market shocks in East Asia and elsewhere.[42] In the case of the MAI, many felt it simply went too far beyond what was acceptable in terms of trade-offs to state sovereignty and autonomy in the interests of facilitating global commerce. In other words, many people were becoming increasingly vocal about their opposition to transnational capitalist expansion regardless of where and by what means they voiced such concerns.

Perhaps the best evidence of the extent to which an anti-MAI network would have emerged in the absence of the Internet can be found in the very nature of the anti-MAI network itself. If the Internet itself had spontaneously generated the anti-MAI network,[43] one would have expected a more evenly distributed set of participants from across the Internet, corresponding roughly to Internet participant demographics on a country-by-country basis. Although there were groups in the United States – the Preamble Collective and Public Citizen, for example – that were prominent in the anti-MAI network, the relative importance to the network of these participants was nowhere near equivalent to the disproportionate number of Internet users that were drawn from the United States, compared to other countries. Also vital to the campaign were (and are) groups from Canada, France, New Zealand, Malaysia, and Australia. Groups from these countries that participated in the anti-MAI networks – groups such as the Council of Canadians, in Canada, or the Third World Network, in Malaysia – have had a long history of anti-corporate social activism, and their relationships to each other can be traced back to years before the MAI.[44] For these groups, opposing the MAI is simply one part of a struggle against neoliberalism and economic globalization that has been going on for well over a decade. Not surprisingly, groups such as these, along with their American counterparts, have been the most important nodes in the network. It is certain, then, that some form of citizen activism would have emerged, without the Internet, to lobby against the MAI. The way the Internet augmented the power and capacity of the network, however, suggests that it would have been a very different and less successful campaign.

Older forms of media, for example telephone-based networks, would have lacked the technological capacity to allow for the dense networks of information exchange crucial for the strategic coordination of information. Although form letters and notifications of demonstrations could have been and were distributed en masse via fax machines, the latter lack the interactivity, responsiveness, and flexibility of computer networks. On listservs, for example, information is posted and redistributed, often with comments by participants, such that the same core message may circulate dozens of times through the network, modifying and changing as it goes from listserv to listserv. Moreover, both telephones and faxes lack the publication capacities of World Wide Web pages. The only comparable means of publication prior to the Internet were hand-distributed flyers and pamphlets and makeshift information booths. The latter are certainly still staples of activism, and featured prominently on many university campuses during the anti-MAI campaign. But on the World Wide Web, such information is given at once a permanent presence and an international reach. If the anti-MAI network had emerged prior to the availability of the

Internet, it would likely have been at least a more disconnected and sluggish – and perhaps even an unsuccessful – campaign.

Some have suggested that the academic and popular press focus on citizen activism and the Internet is misplaced, and that the negotiations would have collapsed regardless of whether or not any activism (Internet-based or otherwise) took place. This argument rests on the view that the negotiations were mired in problems from the outset because of disagreements among member states over sectoral exemptions from the basic principles of the MAI.[45] Countries like Canada and France, for example, had strong reservations about applying the national treatment principles to cultural areas, while the United States was adamantly opposed to exemptions. These sceptical observers also point out that it was the French withdrawal from the negotiations that ultimately killed the MAI at the OECD. If true, such an argument would raise serious questions about the overall potential power of civil society networks and the extent to which the use of the Internet contributed to their success. However, short of re-running the MAI episode without the anti-MAI network to see if the negotiations would have collapsed on their own, it is impossible to determine with complete certainty whether or not this argument is correct.

Perhaps one way to get a handle on this question of the role of the Internet in civic activism, however, is to focus on the reactions of member states and international organizations *in the wake* of the MAI. If their impression were that the citizen activism was largely an inconsequential sideshow, then they would probably not make any substantive changes to the way they go about trade, investment policy, and negotiations. If their impression were otherwise, however, they would most likely take steps to adapt their activities to appease the new force of civil society activism. Fortunately, some time has passed since the collapse of the MAI and we can begin to ascertain what some governments and international organizations are doing vis-à-vis civil society groups. Although an exhaustive survey of all twenty-nine states is beyond the scope of this essay, it is instructive to consider some the policy responses of some high-profile states and one international organization, the World Trade Organization.

In the United States, the United States Trade Representative (USTR) has made some very modest steps toward disclosure of information and outreach with interested civil society groups, but has generally not altered its fundamental views on the benefits of economic neoliberalism. Civil society groups that had contact with the USTR during and after the MAI negotiations speak of a gradual shift from a nearly complete lack of transparency and a marginalization of NGOs, to more transparency and serious engagement once more publicity surrounding the MAI arose, to a situation today where the USTR is calling for more transparency in upcoming

WTO meetings and is meeting with civil society groups in cities throughout the country to solicit views.[46] While some of the civil society groups that have had contact with the USTR view the new disclosure and outreach as little more than window dressing, it is clear that the USTR believes that at least some change in operating procedures, if not ideology, is required, given the new environment of engaged civil society activism. In Australia, the initial MAI negotiations were handled by the Treasury Department, and were confined to a small number of bureaucrats until anti-MAI activists in the STOP-MAI coalition alerted other members of the government, and in particular the Australian Parliament.[47] Since the collapse of the MAI, the Australian Department of Foreign Affairs and Trade has asked for public input on what the Australian negotiating position should be, and is holding public hearings throughout Australia on trade policy. It has also posted a number of background discussion papers on its Web site as aids for those participating in the discussions.[48] In Canada, the Department of Foreign Affairs and International Trade has gone perhaps the furthest in adopting changes in standard operating procedures. The Department held a "multistakeholder" meeting with interested business and citizen groups on 20 May 1999, and constructed a detailed Web site, entitled "We Want to Hear from You" (now called "Consultations with Canadians"), that includes detailed background and discussion papers on trade and investment negotiations on which Canadians are asked to give their views.[49] In private conversations with me, officials from the Canadian Department of Foreign Affairs and International Trade said that many government changes in attitude, while having roots that reach back prior to the MAI, have been kicked into high gear as a direct result of the MAI experience.

The World Trade Organization has made some deliberate changes in standard operating procedures in the direction of increased transparency and engagement with civil society groups. In July 1998, the former World Trade Organization director, General Renato Ruggiero, announced a plan for increased engagement and consultation with civil society groups.[50] As part of the plan, NGOs are now being invited to WTO ministerial meetings and symposia. The WTO circulates to member states information provided by NGOs. And a special section of the WTO Web page, devoted entirely to NGO issues, was created. Civil society groups were invited to attend in a consultative role the 1999 ministerial meeting of the WTO – a meeting that featured enormous street protests.

While in none of the cases cited above can it be said that states are undertaking any fundamental re-thinking of the basic trade and investment agenda in the wake of the MAI, standard operating procedures for dealing with civil society groups are undergoing significant transformation. States are placing much greater emphasis on transparency. There is a more forthcoming attitude among government officials about the release of documents and background papers. Invitations for feedback from the public and civil society groups on official position papers have been prominent. Ministries have held consultations and meetings with interested civil society groups. To be sure, such a transformation in standard government operating procedures needs to be treated with a great deal of caution. Many civil society groups are worried that the agenda of states and international organizations is less genuine engagement than it is *co-optation* and most view the new openness as more window dressing or "show" than a serious shift in the way policy is formulated. These are reservations that need to be taken seriously. But at the same time one should not underestimate the extent to which such a transformation in standard operating procedures, however minimal, can raise expectations, create path-dependencies, and open doors that cannot be shut again. Ultimately, however, such a transformation suggests that at the very least, in the wake of the MAI, states and international organizations *perceived* an important change in the power of civil society activists that needed to be addressed.[51] Undertaking a "business-as-usual" position to civil society groups was clearly not seen as a viable option, and this shift suggests that the civil society activism did indeed matter.

Is the Anti-MAI Network a "Community"?

Clearly, the Internet has provided the basis for a more vibrant and dense international network of activists. But what is the nature of the relationships between the groups that make up the network? Can we characterize the groups as a "community"? Are they an example of "global civil society"? Getting a complete picture of the global anti-MAI network is difficult because the group is constituted of individuals as well as nongovernmental organizations, some of which have since dropped out of the network since the MAI negotiation process halted. One relatively clear picture of the overall network, however, was seen in a list of individuals and groups that signed petitions against moving the MAI from the OECD to the WTO that was posted on the Public Citizen Web site. Perhaps one of the most striking aspects of this particular list – apart from its sheer size – is the diversity of the members. The GAIA Foundation of the United Kingdom signed alongside the Council of Canadians. The Instituto Brasileiro de Analises Sociais e Economicas took part, as did the Sarawak Campaign Committee of Japan. Can such a large group of diverse individuals and activists be considered a "community" in any meaningful sense of the term?[52]

Furthermore, while there were some groups involved in the network that can be categorized as truly *multinational* – the World Wildlife Fund,

Greenpeace, and the Third World Network, for example – the vast majority of groups involved in the campaign are *nationally based* organizations.[53] Groups like the Council of Canadians, in Canada; the STOP-MAI coalition, in Australia; the Preamble Collective and Public Citizen, in the United States, all direct their primary energies to the politics of their country of origin. The links that have been established between the groups are enormously beneficial, to be sure, but the groups themselves have not abandoned their national identity and primary concerns in favour of a global or virtual identity. The anti-MAI network is fundamentally an international alliance of transnational and national non-governmental organizations and activists, rather than a social movement existing solely in cyberspace.

What the Internet has done, however, is to allow the existing nationally based organizations to link together with each other and with multinational organizations. The cross-referencing of the groups on the World Wide Web and the continued vibrancy of the listservs thus suggest something much more than mere coincidental interests of disparate national groups. In other words, having been created in response to the MAI, the network shows definite signs of being sustained into the future. Some of the prominent Web sites have now situated their campaign against the MAI within a wider campaign against "corporate rule" or "neoliberalism" in general. As protests of increasing numbers in Seattle, Quebec City, and Genoa indicate, civil society groups are growing in size and sophistication. What the Internet has generated is indeed a new "species" – a cross-national network of activists and individuals linked by electronic mailing lists and World Wide Web home pages that vibrate with activity, monitoring the global political economy like a virtual watchdog. This network shifts its focus comfortably among the local, the national, and the global, from issues in one national jurisdiction to those in another, and from issue-area to issue-area. So while it is true that the Internet did not generate the anti-MAI activism itself, it has done more than simply facilitate activism that was already in place. It has created a new formation on the world political landscape, one which states and international organizations are beginning to realize must be taken seriously.

Conclusion

The case of the MAI offers an instructive example of how the Internet has boosted the responsiveness and capacities of civil society networks. Through the Internet, local activists from around the world were able to consolidate their knowledge, expertise, and resources to build a supranational campaign. The network's flexibility, speed, and international reach allowed it to intrude on and disrupt the MAI negotiation process primarily by working back through the political processes of member states involved in the negotiations. Although the MAI is likely to reappear at a new venue under a different guise, the network that emerged to lobby against it has not disappeared either. In fact, it has begun to enlarge its ambit, as evidenced by mounting demonstrations in Seattle in 1999, Washington in 2000, and Quebec City in 2001, among others. It is likely that wherever such negotiations are held, the anti-MAI network will be in orbit, participating in an unofficial way in government deliberations.

What does the particular case of the MAI tell us about the potential power of global civil society networks generally? Clearly, these movements that together form "global civil society" do not have the same aggregate structural power as do global market forces. Most significantly, they lack the common commitment to a shared system of values that is so important in translating the micro-decisions of individual capitalists into a large-scale structural effect on states. Few occasions are likely to arise, for example, when networks of Muslims, gays, anti-corporate leftists, neo-Nazis, environmentalists, feminists, and anti-nuclear activists converge in their responses to a single public policy issue.[54] However, while they lack the structural power of global market forces, many of them do increasingly have what might be called (borrowing from Michael Mann) "interstitial" power – that is, legitimate influence on the borders and in the margins, over specific issue-areas.[55] In the "hard case" of the international political economy, the case of the MAI suggests that such networks might even be able to win short-term victories and concessions. The aggregate influence of these networks, then, lies not so much in their "structural" effect on individual state policies as in their "interstitial" influence over disparate public policy issues and mass attitudes.[56] Such influence reinforces the views expressed in this volume that globalization is a *process* within which a great deal of choice and agency is possible, albeit circumscribed by differential power resources wielded by global actors.

A more significant issue, however, centres on the legitimacy of civil society networks as participants in world politics – an issue that cuts to the core of who the main actors are in world politics. If it were not already clear before the MAI case, it certainly is clear now that no international negotiation process of significance will take place without dozens, perhaps hundreds, even thousands of non-governmental organizations and activists orbiting alongside. With the Internet as their information infrastructure, these activists have carved out an ethereal, non-territorial space, circulating in and around the traditional political spaces inhabited by states.[57] As illustrated above, states and international organizations are beginning to take steps to accommodate civil society groups in the policy-making process, but such moves are not simple. Beyond logistical nightmares, such a profound transformation in the world political landscape raises fundamental questions about the basic structures of political participation and representation. In the future, a great deal of controversy will centre on exactly *how* to incorporate NGOs and activists into international and national decision-making processes. The question of *whether* to include them is already moot.

Notes

1 See Ronald J. Deibert, *Parchment, Printing, and Hypermedia: Communication in World Order Transformation* (New York: Columbia University Press, 1997); and Manuel Castells, *The Information Age: Economy, Society, and Culture,* 3 vols. (Oxford: Basil Blackwell, 1996). For a more detailed analysis of the issues discussed here and for previously published sections of this chapter, see Ronald J. Deibert, "International Plug 'n' Play: Citizen Activism, The Internet, and Global Public Policy," *International Studies Perspectives* 1, 3 (2000): 255-72.

2 See David M. Andrews, "Capital Mobility and State Autonomy: Towards a Structural Theory of International Monetary Relations," *International Studies Quarterly* 38 (1994): 193-218; Stephen Gill, "Economic Globalization and the Internationalization of Authority: Limits and Contradictions," *Geoforum* 23, 3 (1992): 269-83; Stephen Gill and David Law, Global Hegemony and the Structural Power of Capital," *International Studies Quarterly* 33 (1989): 475-99; and Michael Webb, "International Economic Structures, Government Interests, and International Coordination of Macroeconomic Adjustment Policies," *International Organization* 45 (1991): 309-42.

3 See, for example, Daniele Archibugi, David Held, and Martin Kohler, eds., *Re-Imaging Political Community* (Stanford, CA: Stanford University Press, 1998); Robert Cox, "Civil Society at the Turn of the Millennium: Prospects for an Alternative World Order," *Review of International Studies* 25, 1 (1999): 3-28; Richard Falk, "Challenges of a Changing Global Order," *Peace Research: The Canadian Journal of Peace Studies* 24, 4 (1992): 17-24; Richard Falk, *On Humane Governance: Toward a New Global Politics* (Cambridge: Polity Press, 1995); and Jessica Matthews, "Power Shift," *Foreign Affairs* 76, 1 (1997): 50-66.

4 For a general discussion of the concept of "global civil society," see Ronnie Lipschutz, "Reconstructing World Politics: The Emergence of Global Civil Society," *Millennium: Journal of International Studies* 21, 3 (1992): 398-420; and Leslie Paul Thiele, "Making Democracy Safe for the World: Social Movements and Global Politics," *Alternatives: Social Transformation and Humane Governance* 18, 3 (1993): 273-306.

5 In an influential study of social movements, Sidney Tarrow suggests that the collective trust essential to social movements cannot develop without some shared experience through face-to-face contact, a factor that would obviously have constraining implications for Internet activism. See Sidney Tarrow, *Power in Movement: Social Movements and Contentious Politics* (Cambridge: Cambridge University Press, 1998), 193; and Vivek Krishnamurthy, "Global Civil Society and the Multilateral Agreement on Investment" (unpublished manuscript, University of Toronto, 1999).

6 Robert Kraut et al., "Internet Paradox: A Social Technology that Reduces Social Involvement and Psychological Well-Being," *American Psychologist* 53, 9 (1998): 1017-31.

7 Craig Calhoun, "Community without Propinquity Revisited: Communications Technology and the Transformation of the Urban Public Sphere," *Sociological Inquiry* 68 (1998): 373.

8 For examples, see Richard Price, "Reversing the Gun Sights: Transnational Civil Society Targets Land Mines," *International Organization* 52, 3 (1998): 613-44; Kathryn Sikkink, "Human Rights, Principled Issue-Networks, and Sovereignty in Latin America," *International Organization* 47 (1993): 411-44; and Paul Wapner, "Politics beyond the State: Environmental Activism and World Civic Politics," *World Politics* 47, 3 (1995): 311-40.

9 I say "potential" here because whether the most powerful economic actors in the world

actually endorsed the MAI through the entire negotiating process is debatable, as will be discussed in some detail below.

10 Again, whether the civil society networks actually "won" the campaign is debatable, inasmuch as there are alternative possible explanations, which I will discuss below, that attribute the death of the MAI to non-civil society factors.

11 See, in particular, Stephen Kobrin, "The MAI and the Clash of Globalizations," *Foreign Policy* 117 (Fall 1998); Peter Morton, "MAI Gets Tangled in the Web," *Financial Post,* 22 October 1998, 3; and Madeline Drohan, "How the Net Killed the MAI," *Globe & Mail,* 29 April 1998, A1, A13. Some MAI activists believe that academic and popular focus on the Internet overemphasizes the extent to which activism emerged spontaneously with the Internet. As I argue below, the Internet *facilitated* activism that would almost certainly have emerged without it. But it has also *generated* a new self-sustaining international sphere of activism that did not exist prior to it.

12 See "Rapport sur l'Accord multilateral sur l'investissement (AMI)," Rapport Interimaire – Septembre 1998, Government of France, <www.finances.gouv.fr> (25 September 1999).

13 For studies, see Suzanne Berger and Ronald Dore, eds., *National Diversity and Global Capitalism* (Ithaca, NY: Cornell University Press, 1996); Robert O. Keohane and Helen V. Milner, eds., *Internationalization and Domestic Politics* (Cambridge: Cambridge University Press, 1996); and Beth A. Simmons, *Who Adjusts?: Domestic Sources of Foreign Economy Policy during the Interwar Years* (Princeton, NJ: Princeton University Press, 1997).

14 See, for example, T.L. Brewer and S. Young, "The Multilateral Agenda for Foreign Direct Investment: Problems, Principles, and Priorities for Negotiation at the OECD and WTO," *World Competition* 18, 4 (1995): 67-83.

15 Alan M. Rugman, "The Political Economy of the Multilateral Agreement on Investment" (paper presented at the academic symposium, "Prospects for the Birmingham Summit 1998," hosted and sponsored by Clifford Chance, the University of Toronto G8 Research Group, and the Centre for Research on the USA, London School of Economics, London, 12 May 1998).

16 See the OECD Code of Liberalisation of Capital Movements (12 December 1961), <www.oecd.org> (25 September 1999). The principle of "national treatment," which would be at the heart of the MAI years later, was first spelled out in detail in the "investment area" in this document. See Part I, Article 1, section b., which states, "Members shall, in particular, endeavor to treat all non-resident-owned assets in the same way irrespective of the date of their formation, and to permit the liquidation of all non-resident-owned assets and the transfer of such assets or of their liquidation proceeds."

17 Some have criticized those involved in the early MAI negotiation process as being naive about the extent to which the agreement would be intruded upon by civil society networks. Others have argued that since much of what occurred at the OECD in the past was arcane and specialized, and hence of little interest to the public, it was reasonable not to anticipate such a furor.

18 OECD, Report by the Committee on International Investment and Multinational Enterprises and the Committee on Capital Movements and Invisible Transactions, 1995, <www.oecd.org> (25 September 1999).

19 Effective dispute settlement mechanisms are notoriously absent from most international organizations. For those who are wary of economic globalization, the implementation of dispute settlement mechanisms in international regimes reflects a further dispersal of authority away from sovereign states.

20 Kobrin, "The MAI and the Clash of Globalizations." Kobrin points out that around 1,500 bilateral international investment treaties existed prior to the MAI negotiations, a fact that would explain both the impetus for developing multilateral rules (to reduce transaction costs) and the argument that the MAI is not a radical departure from existing practice.

21 Ibid.

22 For an environmental perspective on the MAI, see Friends of the Earth, "Ten Reasons to Oppose the MAI," 25 November 1977, <www.foe.org> (25 September 1999). For a cultural perspective on the MAI, see Garry T. Neil, "MAI and Canada's Cultural Sector," October 1997, <www.culturenet.ca/cca/gnmai.htm> (25 September 1999).

23 See Steven Shrybman, "The Rule of Law and Other Impediments to the MAI," *West Coast Environmental Law* (April 1998), available at Vancouver CommunityNet <www.vcn.bc.ca> (25 September 1999).

24 For an analysis from the standpoint of an anti-MAI activist, see Janice Harvey, "*Ethyl Corporation* v. *Government of Canada,*" New Brunswick *Telegraph Journal,* 4 June, <www.flora.org/library/mai/harvey3.html> (25 January 2002).

25 See Timothy Pritchard, "Lawsuits Are Prompting Calls for Changes to Clause in NAFTA," *New York Times,* 19 June 1999, C2. Demonstrating that the relevant "chapter 11" clause of NAFTA works both ways, the Methanex Corporation of Vancouver, British Columbia, recently launched a $970 million lawsuit against the United States government, seeking damages suffered as a result of California's ban on imports of a different gasoline additive, methyl tertiary butyl ether, or MTBE.

26 "Joint NGO Statement on the Multilateral Agreement on Investment (MAI)," NGO/OECD Consultation on the MAI, Paris, 27 October 1997, <www.corpwatch.org> (25 September 1999).

27 The supposed secrecy of the MAI negotiations is a contentious issue. Critics charge that MAI negotiators were deliberately trying to pull off an agreement without widespread public knowledge, a charge that is buttressed by the fact that when many elected representatives in Canada, the United States, and elsewhere were made aware of the MAI by those opposed, they were furious that they hadn't been informed by their governments. MAI supporters and those involved in the negotiations counter that the MAI process was no different than other negotiations undertaken in international fora like the OECD in terms of disclosure of information – in other words, it was business as usual. For sample discussion, see Rosemary Spiers, "Marchi Tries to Demystify Treaty Issues," *Toronto Star,* 25 October 1997, E4. Roy Jones, the Senior Researcher with the OECD's Trade Union Advisory Council (TUAC), said that the negotiations were more secretive than usual because the OECD's Secretary General was not as closely involved as in previous negotiations, and because the United States representatives at the OECD made sure drafts did not circulate too widely. According to Jones, even with its close connections to and official standing with the OECD, TUAC had no more access to documents than did any of the NGOs in the anti-MAI coalition. Interview by author with Roy Jones, Senior Research with the OECD's Trade Union Advisory Council, 27 July 1999.

28 Interview by author with Richard Sanders, Australian STOP-MAI Coalition, 17 August 1999; and interview by author with Neil Watkins, the Preamble Center, Washington, DC, August 1999.

29 World Wide Web pages serve the same notification function as do listservs. For a good example from the Australian context, see "The International Week of Action against the MAI" and other notices at <www.avid.net.au/stopmai> (25 September 1999).

30 For example, on the MAI-NOT listserv from 5 May 1999 to 9 April 1999, 597 postings were logged by 57 people. The MAI-NOT listserv had a total of 13,823 postings in the last year, an average of 37 a day. Statistics available at Flora, <www.mai.flora.org>.

31 The Australian STOP-MAI coalition set up a listserv that attracted 400 subscribers. Richard Sanders, who headed up the coalition, said that the listserv worked as a "network of networks." In other words, the elite of the groups involved in the STOP-MAI coalition would pass on information from the listserv to their own individual grassroots memberships. Interview by author.

32 As cited in Drohan, "How the Net Killed the MAI."

33 The following sites are relevant here, though not all continue to function or to maintain the links: APEC Alert! (UBC), <www.cs.ubc.ca>; Links zum Thema MAI (Germany), <www.pdsnetz.de>; MAI Documents, Press Releases and Commentaries (independent Web site), <www2.murray.net.au>; PDS Niedersachsen (Germany), <www.nds.pdsnetz.de>; Progress Report on the MAI (Preamble Center), <www.progress.org/mai.htm>; Strategic Road (links to MAI-related sites from a variety of nations), <www.mayaconcept.com>; Canadian Centre for Policy Alternatives, <www.policyalternatives.ca>; Green Party of Canada <www.green.ca>; Danmarks Kommunistiske Parti/Marxister-Leninster, <www.dkp-ml.dk>; Flora, <www.mai.flora.org>.

34 Kobrin, "The MAI and the Clash of Globalizations."
35 See "Media Addresses in North America," <www.mai.flora.org/mai-info/media.htm> (25 January 2002).
36 For discussion see Drohan, "How the Net Killed the MAI."
37 For example, a detailed list, "Members of the House of Commons of the 36th Parliament," appeared at <www.mai.flora.org/mai-info/mps-list.htm> (25 September 1999); and "Members of the US House of Representatives: Mailing Addresses," at <www.mai.flora.org/mai-info/hor-mems.htm> (25 September 1999).
38 Though they are no longer available, one could find an example of a letter opposing the MAI, to be sent to a Representative or Senator, at <www.citizen.org/pctrade/mai/What%20you/congrs.html> (25 September 1999); an example of a letter opposing the MAI that could be sent by e-mail to the Australian Parliament directly from the Web site, <www.avid.net.au/stopmai/letter/> (25 September 1999); and a sample of Canadian letters to MPs at <mai.flora.org/mai-info/letters.htm#1> (25 September 1999).
39 See Public Citizen, "Multilateral Agreement on Investment (MAI)," <www.citizen.org/trade/issues/mai/> (25 January 2002).
40 During private discussions that I conducted with Canadian Department of Foreign Affairs and International Trade officials, my sense was that they were certainly now cognizant of the power of online activism and were not likely to dismiss electronic petitions or e-mail submissions – in fact, they have been encouraging such submissions on their own Web site in the wake of the MAI, as I will discuss in more detail below.
41 See the interviews listed throughout the study and cited in the notes.
42 Kobrin emphasizes this point in "The MAI and the Clash of Globalizations."
43 For an interpretation that suggests that the Internet spawned the MAI activism directly, see Guy de Jonquières, "Network Guerillas," *Financial Times,* 30 April 1998, 20.
44 See Krishnamurthy," Global Civil Society and the MAI."
45 For an overview of the disagreements, see Kobrin, "The MAI and the Clash of Globalizations."
46 Interview by author with Neil Watkins; and interview by author with Ruth Kaplan, Coordinator, Campaign against Economic Globalization, Alliance for Democracy, 16 August 1999.
47 Interview by author with Richard Sanders.
48 See Australia, Department of Foreign Affairs and Trade, "Public Hearings on Future Multilateral Trade Negotiations," 22 November 2000, <www.dfat.gov.au/trade/negotiations/hearings/index.html> (25 January 2002).
49 See Canada, Department of Foreign Affairs and International Trade, "Consultations with Canadians," <www.dfait-maeci.gc.ca/tna-nac/consult-e.asp> (25 January 2002).
50 See WTO, "Ruggiero Announces Enhanced WTO Plan for Cooperation with NGOs," WTO Press Release/107, 17 July 1998, <www.wto.org> (25 September 1999).
51 A minister involved in the negotiations told Stephen Kobrin that the protest raised the MAI issue from the civil-servant to the ministerial level. Kobrin, "The MAI and the Clash of Globalizations."
52 Public Citizen is at <www.citizen.org>. Other "strange bedfellows" include Pat Buchanan's American Cause Web site, with its links to sites condemning homosexuality and abortion alongside links to the left-wing anti-MAI site of Public Citizen. See <www.theameri cancause.org> (25 September 1999). I am grateful to Vivek Krishnamurthy for discovering this example.
53 This supports the argument of Craig Calhoun that the strength of civil society groups still lies largely in their local or national roots. Calhoun, "Community without Propinquity Revisited," 382.
54 Formal alliances and coalitions of NGOs are becoming more common, however.
55 Michael Mann, *Sources of Social Power,* vol. 1 (Cambridge and New York: Cambridge University Press, 1986), 15-19.
56 David J. Rothkopf, "Cyberpolitik: The Changing Nature of Power in the Information Age," *Journal of International Affairs* 51, 2 (1998): 325-59.
57 For discussion of "non-territorial" political spaces, see John Gerard Ruggie, "International

Structure and International Transformation: Space, Time and Method," in *Global Changes and Theoretical Challenges: Approaches to World Politics for the 1990s,* ed. Ernst-Otto Czempiel and James N. Rosenau (Lexington, MA: Lexington Books, 1989), 31. That many of these groups are "anti-globalization" activists reinforces the paradox (noted by other contributors to this volume) of how responses and resistances to globalization implicate actors more deeply in the globalization process itself.

5
Communication and Globalization: A Challenge for Public Policy

Marc Raboy

Amid the confusion and chaos surrounding the abortive World Trade Organization (WTO) negotiations in Seattle in late 1999, US Trade Representative Charlene Barshefsky was widely quoted as stating, "The single greatest threat to the multilateral trade system is the absence of public support."[1] In Canada, the absence of public support for the WTO project was palpable. The House of Commons Standing Committee on Foreign Affairs and International Trade, in a report released the previous June, had revealed that Canadians wanted the protection of cultural identity and cultural diversity to be priority issues in Seattle.[2]

This was consistent with Canada's historical attempt to use communications policy to negotiate the tension between commerce and culture. But that position was becoming increasingly difficult to maintain. For example, also in June 1999, the country's long-brewing dispute with the United States over access for US magazines to the Canadian advertising market came to a head as Canada agreed to change several pieces of legislation in exchange for which the United States abandoned procedures it had begun under the existing WTO accord.[3]

The magazine dispute was just one, albeit highly mediated, illustration of the new constraints imposed on national sovereignty by the emerging global economy. These constraints are beginning to reveal problems that various social actors have been trying to address. The Canadian government, for one, has consistently maintained the legitimacy of pursuing non-economic goals through public policy, notwithstanding its adherence to the international trade regime developing under the auspices of new governance structures, such as the North American Free Trade Agreement (NAFTA) and the WTO. But the nature of this new regime – in which Canada is an active participant and which Canadian negotiators have very much helped to shape – does not easily allow for the pursuit of social and cultural goals. This situation prompts the question: How can public policy be meaningfully developed in a context marked by a shift in decision making from the national to the transnational or global level?

As this chapter is being written, a de facto policy environment for global communications is taking shape.[4] Right now, this environment is evolving according to its own logic, requirements, protocols, and rules, while various players try to influence it as best they can. But the extension of the sphere of communications policy to the global level has both limitations and possibilities, as national debates on communications policy issues are not only constrained but also enhanced by global policy developments. Globalization, therefore, should be viewed as a policy *challenge* rather than simply a justification for the "end of policy" arguments presented as received wisdom in neoliberal, deregulatory discourse.

Why Communication?

The mass media, cultural industries, and communication and information technologies have become the major catalysts for cultural activity, mass consumption, and participation in public life. They are also increasingly the basis for direct communication, across vast distances and irrespective of time. Consequently, access to the resources that facilitate communication can be seen as one of the basic building blocks of citizenship – one that raises policy issues that are central to the development of civil society.

Communication and information technologies, while of little interest in themselves, are strategically critical in efforts to intervene in the economy on the one hand, and in the cultural sphere on the other. The stakes of communications policy revolve around struggles over who gets to use these technologies, under what conditions, to promote which projects, and in whose interests. Conceptually, "communications" is another way of describing the technological space at the interface of economic globalization and cultural globalization. This chapter looks at the policy implications of what is going on in that space.

Communication has always been linked to democratic struggles, and is increasingly relevant to thinking about broader issues, such as the role of the state and human rights.[5] Today, because of the particular situation of communication in the overall environment of globalization, communications policy issues have an important impact on a range of related questions.[6] The global policy framework for communications is therefore emerging as a key structural component of the emerging global governance framework in general.

In trying to grasp this, we need to delink explanations of the mechanics of globalization from the ideology of neoliberalism. Even if it is true that we are moving toward a global society, this does not mean that the need for law and regulation no longer exists. The neoliberal approach to global governance is a political choice, not a logical one, and the development of economic or market globalization does not in itself negate the need for rules. Indeed, the pragmatic neoliberal approach recognizes this and is constantly searching for new regulatory mechanisms appropriate to advancing its political project and the interests that project represents. In terms of democratic politics, on the other hand, we need to begin thinking about what one might mean by "global public policy," and of ways to capture and define a "global public interest."[7]

For example, what kind of transnational mechanisms need to be put in place in order to allow local (national) authorities to regulate public resources in the public interest; in order to meet historical policy objectives that have evolved until now largely at the national level; and in order to resolve cultural differences in a context of economic inequality and unequal development?[8] These questions now need to be addressed in a transnational framework, where global policy could be developed based on global norms, and national policy would be based on principles designed to allow for the local expression of particular social and cultural values.[9]

A key feature of globalization is the systematic integration of private transnational industry into decision-making processes, alongside the exclusion of civil society forces from the arenas where decisions are made. In this sense, the new global governance system is undoing the democratization features put in place in various spheres of activity in countries such as Canada, where there is at least transparency, nominal participation, and a possibility of making gains.[10] While more and more social actors are beginning to use the term "global civil society," very few have considered the policy requirements for ensuring that communications contribute to the development of the democratic system of global governance that they have in mind. In trying to imagine these requirements, we can take some inspiration from the experience of historical national efforts to orient communications toward public interest goals.

A point of departure for this argument is Robin Higham's claim that cultural and communications policy issues constitute an area of "horizontal policy overlays, an all-policies policy. These are objectives to be accommodated in the same manner that we now accommodate environmental issues, human rights and justice in decision making by governments and civil society."[11]

Higham goes on to state, "The trade policy/culture quarrel is probably where the contest between Canada's economic and human development priorities is most visible to the public."[12] This visibility takes on a certain importance for our project as well, insofar as any state intervention intending to reverse the trends of globalization will require widespread mobilization of political constituencies.[13] On the world scale, the contradiction between culture and commerce is emerging as one of the fundamental cleavages of the twenty-first century, as a leitmotif of globalization. In Canada, we are particularly well situated to deal with this contradiction.

On the one hand, we have recognized its importance since very early in our history, so we are sensitive to its symptoms and have built up a considerable expertise in dealing with the problems that result from it.[14] On the other hand, Canada has, more than most countries, a stake in the outcome of the issues. In many respects, the issue is survival – not "as a nation" but as however each of us defines his or her distinctiveness. Communications policy issues are directly tied to the politics of identity, and are, in this sense, tied to concerns about social cohesion as well.

Communications policy must also address a whole set of issues related to cultural development. In a 1993 study, a research team including the author of this chapter defined cultural development as "the process by which human beings acquire the individual and collective resources necessary to participate in public life."[15] In thinking this through, we noted that "the key to dealing with the challenges of cultural development in the new global context lay in rethinking the role of the state and public policy."[16] At the time, only a few years ago, it was still a novel idea to suggest that it was necessary to examine how a country like Canada could continue to use national policy to influence the sphere of culture and communications in the context of globalization. But the terrain was already shifting, and rather dramatically.

In 1993, we observed that traditional cultural practices, mass-mediated communication, and other spheres of activity such as education had become intertwined "through networks of communication and information resources, which are also fundamental to the conduct of global commerce."[17] This trend has continued and grown in importance in the intervening years. It is therefore important to understand the development of this trend, from its historical roots in the emergence of an international governance regime in information and communication technology in the nineteenth century, through the establishment of multilateral institutions for regulating international relations in communication, to the launching of a range of global projects that are defining the parameters of the new global environment in communications.

But since national governments are still key players in this new environment, it is also crucial to understand the rise and decline of national policy intervention in communication – an area in which Canada provides one of the most interesting historical examples. The Canadian experience enables us to consider the current possibilities for "blending" policy approaches across the national and transnational spheres, as we map the current and immediately foreseeable terrain in global communications policy.

This chapter will therefore briefly sketch the historical background to the emergence of a global communications policy framework, in Canada and internationally. But first, some preliminary observations are necessary.

A Communication Perspective on Globalization

As a semantic notion, "globalization" is not new.[18] From the perspective of the European elites of the early sixteenth century, the term could well have described the outward push of the frontiers they had grown up with and the new consciousness of the contours of their world. The Native populations of the Western Hemisphere may have chosen a different term to describe the process that began in 1492, but the leap in consciousness that they would have undergone invites a parallel. In theoretical terms, "globalization" can be seen as referring to a process whereby the introduction of external elements changes the context in which a given collectivity has hitherto evolved.

Beyond this notion of an extended horizon, "globalization" also refers to processes of integration. The period of colonialism and the growth of mercantile capitalism it spawned added new links to the embryonic global economy born of the trade in commodities such as silk and spices. This economy was made possible by early technologies of communication, and developed successively with every major new technological advance. From the slogan, "The sun never sets on the British Empire," to the notion of world war, to the concept of the "global village," the idea of a shrinking and increasingly interconnected world has a long history in Western culture.

So what is new about "globalization" as we now use the term? A great deal of anecdotal evidence exists to illustrate the sense that the term *is* being used to describe something new.[19] As I see it, the term "globalization" is being used to describe the following salient characteristics of the world in which we are living. Each of these characteristics raises a set of particular issues with respect to communication and, more specifically relevant here, communications policy.

The Diminishing Sovereignty of Nation-States

The emergence of the international system of nation-states and the system of international relations based on relations between states was a main characteristic of an earlier phase of globalization, marked by the signing of the Treaty of Westphalia in 1648. For roughly 300 years from that date, national sovereignty was on the rise, and world politics was characterized by the conflicts and disputes between sovereign states, between allied groups of sovereign states, or between imperial states and their colonies. For the past fifty years, however, the Westphalian system has been undermined by a number of factors, including the emergence of the United Nations' system of multilateral institutions based, in theory, on the equal participation of sovereign states and the parallel emergence of more than 100 new postcolonial states. The nation-state remains the principal mode of political organization and representation for both domestic and international purposes, but it is increasingly required to share its sovereignty with other actors. One of the main challenges of late-twentieth-century "globalization" is therefore the need to rethink and actualize our conception of sovereignty, as well as the role of the state.

Where they once made policy autonomously in the full range of areas of public concern, nation-states now negotiate on behalf of their constituencies in various fora where transnational policy issues are discussed and decided. With respect to communications, this raises questions about regulation, public funding, the appropriate balance between public and commercial service, access, freedom of expression, the pertinence of harnessing harmful content, and so on. Similar lists could be made for any sector of activity. But what distinguishes the issue of communications policy with respect to others is the fact that communications policy is a major determinant of the context in which other sectors (such as health care, education, and job training) will develop in the current phase of globalization. Communications infrastructures are the foundation for other activities, and these are increasingly elusive for national policy makers. The extent to which the Internet remains openly accessible and relatively non-commercial, for example, is an issue that can be decided only by transnational agreement. The marketplace will seek its own solutions independent of the public interest, and national governments cannot act individually to address this problem. On the other hand, communications policy has become one of the main battlegrounds where nation-states attempt to claw back lost bits of sovereignty on cultural grounds.

The Increasing Integration of the World Economy

Global economic integration, too, dates from ancient times. The present situation is unprecedented in terms of both speed and extent, however, and a source of both exceptional stability and instability. On the one hand, one can now purchase apparently unique copies of a seventeenth-century Murano glass vase in places like Paris, Tokyo, or Montreal for roughly the same price. On the other hand, dozens of venerable domestic industries such as shoe production are no longer viable in most parts of the world. Entire regions are excluded from participation in the increasingly global economy (in the same way that, in an earlier era, new social classes were created as a result of the emergence of industrial production). Consistent with the diminishing role of the nation-state, the global economy is characterized by the enhanced role of transnational corporations and the transnational concentration of corporate economic power. This situation leads to its own paradoxes. For example, contrary to popular myth, only three of the seven leading global cultural industry corporations are actually owned by Americans; more significantly, all seven have their main operational headquarters in a twenty-block area of central

Manhattan.[20] In political terms, economic integration represents an important shift because, unlike the state, democratic politics has no grapplehold on the corporate sector.

Global economic integration comes packed with a particularly seductive ideology that emerges powerfully in the sphere of culture and communication. The global cultural industries market not only a set of products but also a vision of a certain way of life. Thrust on to the global stage, all industrialized cultural production is reduced to entertainment, and its only value is commercial. National cultural policies, public service media, and alternative and community forms of communication have no place in this framework – except as exceptions to the rules of commerce. Under NAFTA, for example, Canada is allowed to protect its cultural industries, but only at the expense of US retaliation in other trade sectors. Some important embryonic alternatives are worth mentioning, however. In 1997, the European Union adopted a measure recognizing the rights of member states to continue funding public service broadcast media, notwithstanding the impact that such funding could have on the competitive advantage of private sector media. The European Union's justification for this measure was that the importance of public broadcasting as an instrument of democracy outweighed the economic rights of the private broadcasting corporations. Contrary to the NAFTA exemption, this was the first case in communications policy when the logic of a nation-state was successfully transferred to a transnational governing body charged with developing a new regime of transnational economic integration, without provision for retaliation.[21]

The Technologically Based Shrinking of Time and Space

New technologies of communication have strongly marked every successive phase of globalization. In the present phase, however, new technologies such as the Internet give the impression of actually making time and space disappear. Major financial transactions take place instantaneously at the touch of a computer key, and independent of distance. Stockbrokers in Hong Kong and hairdressers in Miami play bridge together in real time. In terms of the characteristics we have previously mentioned, communications technologies have contributed to undermining the unbridled power of nation-states and to the integration of the global economy. But they have also empowered new social actors, to the extent that these actors are able to claim and enjoy access to the technologies. On the periphery of the new ideology of the information society, a new conception of civil society is emerging. Issues surrounding the development and use of communication technologies are therefore – as they have always been – at the centre of contemporary social and political struggles. Where earlier struggles focused on issues such as freedom of expression vis-à-vis the authoritarian state, and later, public versus private enterprise, today's struggles add new issues characteristic of the contemporary phase of globalization. The Internet, for example, raises issues concerning national sovereignty and economic power as well as freedom of expression and access to the means of communication. On the one hand, a certain conventional wisdom states that the new communications technologies, such as the Internet, are ungovernable; on the other hand, high-powered global players, ranging from the Microsoft Corporation to the European Union, are seeking to put in place a global regulatory regime for governing the use and future development of the Internet.

As is well known, the new communication and information technologies bring with them an unprecedented explosion of channels of communication. They do not, however, provide content to fill those channels. Who gets to use the channels, how, and with what content, are therefore major areas of conflict. The marketplace is structuring the new communications environment on a pay-as-you-go basis, and the high end is essentially inaccessible to most people. This inaccessibility is creating a new democratic deficit and is a flaw in the otherwise powerful ideology of the information society: the communication explosion does one no good if one can not afford to take advantage of it. At the same time, the market in information empowers the already powerful and excludes the rest, creating an ever-widening chasm between the information rich and poor. New technologies notwithstanding, cultural flow continues to be skewed from centre to periphery, north to south. Information and cultural products still travel mainly one-way between Atlanta and Ouagadougou. At the same time, it is increasingly difficult for anyone, or any country, to withdraw from the global culture. This situation has both positive and negative implications. On the one hand, authoritarian states no longer enjoy monopolies of knowledge by simply controlling national communications media or what enters their national territory. On the other hand, it raises the stakes of the debate on cultural universalism, best captured in Benjamin Barber's celebrated dichotomy "Jihad vs McWorld."[22]

The Passing of Received Ideas about Identity

The contradictions of globalization with respect to the politics of cultural and identity questions are most striking in the area of communications. On the one hand, globalization creates a single world cultural environment in which everyone has access to the same messages, produced and disseminated through a tightly controlled, centralized network of networks. On the other hand – indeed, in response or resistance – globalization encourages a quest for individuality, distinctiveness, and assertion of difference. The weakening of the "national" as the primary reference category for identity is mirrored by the strengthening of categories that cut across national boundaries, such as religion, ethnicity, language, gender, social class, and sexual orientation. This shift has led to increasing debate around new conceptions of citizenship, particularly as the current phase of globalization is marked by the emergence of new cultural "hybridizations," diasporic communities, and a delinking of cultural issues from geographical territories. Some, like US State Department intellectual Samuel Huntington, see in this development the seeds of a geopolitical "clash of civilizations."[23]

The political phenomena of "nations without states" and non-national forms of identification pose a special problem with respect to new forms of governance. Not surprisingly, this problem emerges first in the cultural sphere. Recognizing very clearly the fine line between nationhood and sovereignty, entities such as Quebec and Catalonia demand representation in UNESCO (the United Nations Education, Scientific and Cultural Organization) rather than the United Nations, because UNESCO addresses cultural diversity issues while the UN deals with issues that can be binding only on nation-states (at least in theory!). However, distinguishing between cultural and political issues is going to become increasingly difficult as politics and culture become intertwined. This blurring of boundaries will create new pressure on nation-states as well as multilateral bodies. The former congruency between national media and nation-states also becomes problematic in this context. New transnational media are emerging to fit the contours of the new constituencies that they seek to address, and traditional national media are among the first institutions to suffer from the blurring of national frontiers.

The Emergence of New, Locally Based Global Networks

Perhaps the most striking contradiction of globalization as we know it is that all of the above phenomena have given rise to an unprecedented capacity for networking among ordinary individuals and groups in civil society who have not traditionally travelled or communicated internationally. In just about every area of social life, people are now connected. Some of these connections have given rise to influential transnational self-help, action research, and lobby groups. The international mobilization against the Multilateral Agreement on Investment (MAI), made possible by the Internet, was one dramatic case that serves to highlight thousands of lesser examples. The issue now is sustainability: Can social networks survive strictly on the basis of technological links and in the absence of economic or political ties? And will the facilitating technologies remain accessible to them? Meanwhile, the new transnational non-governmental organizations constitute one of the three poles of the new global governance framework that is emerging at the political level (along with nation-states and transnational corporations).

In this context, "the right to communicate" has become a metaphor for both what is possible and what is problematic with respect to globalization. Some are even arguing that international problems in communication will be the successor to the environment as the focal point of both global concern and grassroots activism. Again, the paradox we noted previously comes into play here: communication becomes both the object and the means of political struggle. The new global networks in communication are thus constituted around groups of practitioners in community radio, video, and computer communication; but they are focusing increasingly on global policy issues as they come to recognize the link between the politics that determine the nature of the global public sphere and the activities they try to undertake in order to participate in it. Globally networked community media activists thus constitute an important link in the practices and policy debates that are redefining communication.[24]

The Establishment of a New Framework for Global Governance

Regional groupings of states, the multilateral system, international agreements – the number and scope of sites of global deliberation and rule making are multiplying at a ferocious pace. With the decline in national sovereignty, the shift from the national to the transnational as the principal location of governance is the final and possibly most encompassing aspect of the present phase of globalization. This development obliges us to think historically about the ways in which governance regimes were used in different phases of human history and particularly in moments of fundamental change. It is sophistry to claim globalization means that political intervention in favour of a collective social project is no longer possible. Rather, the nature of the collectivity needs to be rethought, and new mechanisms invented. Globalization facilitates this process, by foregrounding the alternatives to the traditional state and the market, and making available the technological means for new modes of social organization. The new culture of communication fostered by globalization is also a positive factor here.

Political and economic arrangements involving various groups of states, such as NAFTA, the European Union, and the G8, create new transnational regulatory regimes for governing a range of activities, including communication. These groupings each operate differently, each according to its own raison d'être. Under NAFTA, the emphasis is on trade relations. Europe seeks to develop a regionally integrated economy operating under a common set of rules. Thus the European Union's "Television without Frontiers" directive seeks to protect the European audiovisual space for European cultural enterprise; it does not protect the individual member states from one another. The G8, meanwhile, operates more as a clearing house for projects in the common interest of the world's economically most powerful nations. It is therefore not surprising that the G8 is sponsoring the US-initiated "Global Information Infrastructure" project to create a single, seamless worldwide communication system (see below).

At the global level, the multilateral system is becoming the site of discussion and debate on communications policy issues. The United Nations Declaration of Human Rights provides a focus for issues regarding the right to communicate; the UN must also deal regularly with media-related problems in the context of its conflict resolution and human development efforts. More concrete work takes places in a range of specialized agencies such as the International Telecommunications Union (ITU) and UNESCO. Here, again, nation-states constitute the deliberative and decisional basis but, increasingly, corporate and NGO participants are becoming involved. The much-awaited reform of these multilateral agencies heralds the new system of global governance. Meanwhile, international treaties discussed under the aegis of these organizations are becoming the legislative building blocks of the new system. This is the case especially of the World Trade Organization, whose 1997 agreement on telecommunications opened the telecom markets of some ninety countries to foreign investment. In this respect, the interesting thing about the Multilateral Agreement on Investment is that it was being negotiated within the Organisation for Economic Co-operation and Development (OECD), a far more exclusive organization, grouping the world's thirty or so richest countries.

In short, the emergence of a global governance system raises some tantalizing questions about the possibilities for future policy intervention at the global level. We shall consider some of these later, in the final section of this chapter.

Communications Policy in the Canadian Context

Every country in the world today faces a similar set of issues with respect to information and communication.[25] The responses of these nations vary from one context to another, according to an array of political, economic, sociological, cultural, and historical circumstances. But the issues are the same. So if we want to look at the policy challenges of globalization for Canada from a communications perspective, we have to look at the context in which communications policy is made – in this country, elsewhere, and globally.

Public debate over communications policy has been one of the dominant themes of Canadian social discourse since the early days of radio broadcasting. Communication, in Canada, has been seen as a binding force for national unity, as a vehicle for social development, and as an instrument of cultural affirmation. In contradiction to these overriding themes, policy has also sought to promote the economic development of Canadian communication industries. In this respect, more so than in

Europe or the United States, where one or the other pole has conventionally dominated, communication in Canada has evolved according to the push and pull of the tension between economics and culture.

To illustrate, consider the following important moment in Canadian communications history. The year was 1932, and the government had just introduced legislation after a three-year hiatus that followed the report of Sir John Aird's Royal Commission on Radio Broadcasting. One of the key players at the Parliamentary Committee hearing on the Radio Broadcasting Act was the Canadian Radio League, one of the most extraordinary public interest pressure groups in the country's history, a vast coalition crossing linguistic, class, and regional lines. The League had campaigned vigorously for Parliament to enact legislation along the lines of the Aird Report, and at the hearings, its chief spokesman, Graham Spry, reiterated the view that radio had to be viewed as a public issue: "The position of the Canadian Radio League is that so powerful and useful an agency of communication should be used for the broadest national purposes, that it should be owned and operated by the people, that it should not primarily be adapted to narrow advertising and propagandist purposes by irresponsible companies subject to no proper regulation or control."[26]

Canada needed a policy, a program, for broadcast development, Spry argued. The Aird Report had provided a framework for such a program, proposing the creation of a full-scale publicly owned broadcasting system. Spry and the CRL supported that proposal, but with a sense of urgency.

The urgency was brought about by an upcoming international convention on radio, scheduled for Madrid in September 1932, where radio frequencies were to be allocated to the participating nations, to be redistributed by their national governments according to whatever national policies each one would put in place. Canada's national interest was at stake, the Radio League argued. The big US commercial groups, such as RCA, considered Canada part of their domestic territory. In Europe, governments were establishing national monopolies to occupy the air waves. What would happen to Canada, Spry asked, "wedged as she is between a fiercely competitive group of European nations and a dominant American group? Without a program, without a policy, how can Canada claim her share of the air?"[27] Canada had a choice, and the choice was clear, he told the Parliamentary Committee: "It is a choice between commercial interests and the people's interests. It is a choice between the State and the United States."[28]

This argument has driven communications policy in Canada since the turn of the century. Canada's policy has always been tied to defining, protecting, and promoting a national interest vis-à-vis both internal and external pressures of fragmentation, and always, as the above example illustrates, in a context of globalization.[29] For Canada, seeking to distinguish itself from the United States has always been not so much a reflex of withdrawal but part of an attempt toward openness to the rest of the world on its own terms.

Public Service versus the Market

A quick historical overview of Canadian efforts to make policy in communications and culture helps to highlight the contradictions of globalization as they have appeared from the very beginning of Canadian state intervention in this sphere. Canada adopted a Wireless Telegraph Act in 1905, only two years after the first international conference on the regulation of wireless radio-telegraphy took place in Berlin. This was followed by the Radiotelegraph Act of 1913. The Canadian state's entry into the sphere of radio broadcasting was slowed down by a jurisdictional dispute with several provinces, notably Quebec, which claimed the legal competence to intervene in this area.

The early development of Canadian broadcasting was strongly influenced by the two dominant models of the day: the US commercial model and the British public service model. Typically, broadcasting in Canada developed as a compromise between the two. But Canada was aggressive and innovative with respect to the protection and promotion of Canadian content. Canadian content quotas in radio and television, efforts to gain control of feature film screen distribution, foreign ownership regulations, and various subsidy programs, combined with a strong emphasis on public cultural institutions such as the Canadian Broadcasting Corporation and the National Film Board, kept Canada on the global cultural map.

A new Canadian strategy for the deployment of public funds and policy toward industrial development rather than the public sector emerged in the 1980s. Typical was the 1983 creation of Telefilm Canada, which essentially diverted funds previously allocated to the CBC to a new independent production sector aimed not only at the domestic market but increasingly at international markets. The cable industry was anointed as the favoured vehicle for Canadianization in broadcasting, and a plethora of Canadian pay TV and specialty services were licensed with that in mind. Since the 1980s, nationalist rhetoric notwithstanding, Canada's cultural policy has aimed at giving Canadian cultural industries a competitive advantage in the global marketplace. This has made Canada a willing partner in the global trend toward market liberalization, deregulation, and corporate concentration – to the perplexed irritation of US trade negotiators who see the cultural industries' "exemption" in the Canada-US Free Trade Agreement (carried over into NAFTA) as a not-so-subtle protectionism that has nothing to do with culture.

This historical overview also highlights the fact that policy is the result of the interplay of particular interests represented in the organizations of the political structure (the state, political parties, bureaucracies, etc.), the economy (private and public sectors and their related institutions), and civil society (organized and unorganized groups and individuals who intervene in the policy process).

Contemporary Canadian communications policy debates have settled firmly into this mould. We have seen this interplay of interests in a stream of recent documents, procedures, formal and ad hoc policy development initiatives,[30] and lobbying and public relations campaigns, as well as in high-state pronouncements, ministerial declarations, representations at the G8 and the WTO, negotiations under NAFTA, and in other fora. We have seen the various interests at work played out within Canada, in bilateral relations between Canada and others on the world stage, and at the geopolitical level where Canada (mainly its elites but also its citizens) participates in concert with the world's most powerful, dominant forces to design – and profit from – the new global communications environment.

But this context should not obscure the fact that in the course of establishing a tradition of policy intervention for sociocultural objectives in culture and communication, Canada has built a set of important institutional practices for policy making in this area. Among these are the principles that communications infrastructures constitute a cornerstone of national cultural heritage, that the main instrument for realizing cultural and communications policy is a mixed system of publicly owned industries and publicly regulated private industries, and that the participation of social groups is a central part of the policy-making process. In this respect, Canada provides a model for process in communications policy making that is emulated in many parts of the world.

A "New" Debate?

As in other countries, recent developments in communication, particularly the development of the new information infrastructure and the convergence of broadcasting and telecommunications technologies, are a cause for concern on the part of a range of Canadian interests. But is there anything really new in the way the debate on these issues is being framed? In a fundamental sense, it goes back to the 1960s and the creation of the federal Department of Communications (DOC), the launching of a domestic satellite program, and the decision to develop policy in the field of communications with an eye toward both cultural and economic concerns. National development and industrial development were to be the two poles of Canadian communications policy after 1969. The cornerstone of Canadian cultural policy was to be the broadcasting system, organized as a mixed public-private sector model and closely regulated by an independent agency, the CRTC, to ensure both a strong Canadian presence on radio and television and the development of strong domestic production and distribution industries. At the same time, communications policy aimed to develop communications infrastructure, mainly through the use of satellites – in some respects exporting the problem of national development north of the 49th parallel to the more comfortable reaches of outer space.

In February 1969, speaking in the House of Commons debate about the legislation creating the Department of Communications, the minister-designate, Eric Kierans, said, in the popular jargon of the day, that the new department would be concerned "with the medium, not with the message."[31] This approach has, to a great extent, held true to this day, but as every regulator knows, the two functions – media and messages, hardware and software, carriage and content, technology and culture – are interrelated and interdependent.

All these activities would be linked in a national communications policy, Kierans said. Just as Confederation had been built on the "mile upon mile of steel rails laid across this country," Confederation would be renewed "by a communications system that meets the needs of all Canadians."[32] Kierans's vision had a distinctly determinist thrust, and we now have a better appreciation of complexities of technology but are still waiting for the policy.[33]

Fast-forward to 1993 and the shutting down of the DOC. The dismantling of the Department of Communications and the bundling of its activities into the new Department of Canadian Heritage and the revamped and expanded Department of Industry signalled the end of a twenty-five-year process of attempts at national consolidation through communications policy making. Older narratives of Canada as an information society would now be rewritten. After decades of organizational difficulties, ministerial skirmishes, and low political priority, the Canadian "information highway" project was initiated only in the face of an American and global kick-start, demonstrating that the motor force behind the 1990s version of the information society was, as in the United States, "business and business demand." When the kick-start finally came, it was in a new political context where communications policy, telecommunications, and infrastructure decisions would now be developed from inside the Industry portfolio, while the "soft" areas of cultural development, such as broadcasting, would be assigned to the domain of Heritage, whose main responsibility was the promotion of national unity and social cohesion.[34]

This was the context in which the current Liberal government took office in 1993. Following the lead of US vice president Al Gore, who called for progressive nations everywhere to help build a Global Information Infrastructure, the Liberals' 1994 Speech from the Throne announced the government's commitment to pursuing and developing a Canadian information highway.[35] In the ensuing debate, a new notion of the public interest in communications would emerge.

Access to Communication

In Canada, as elsewhere, the idea of the public interest operates as a legitimization of both state intervention and corporate affairs. A vague and polysemic term, "public interest" is defined quite differently in different frameworks, the definition always depending on who is in control. In Canada's conventional broadcasting and telecommunications policies, the public interest has been conceptualized around two distinct models of communication and, more specifically, around two separate conceptions of public "access." In the broadcasting model, emphasis is placed on the active receiver and free choice, and "access" refers to the entire range of products on offer. In the telecommunications model, emphasis is on the sender and the capacity to get one's messages out, and "access" refers to the means of communication. The information highway proposes to converge these models and to work toward an eventual single framework for communicative action, combining the broadcasting and telecommunications models by incorporating each one's conception of the public interest. The policies that are currently being put in place will determine the shape and texture of a new hybrid model of communication, which will have to combine the social and cultural, as well as economic, objectives of both broadcasting and telecommunications.

This should remind us that, beyond the existing operational models for both broadcasting and telecommunications lies an even more fundamental issue regarding access in Canadian communications policy: the issue of access to the policy-making process itself. If the role of policy is to intervene in the way that society is organized, then access to policy intervention is one way in which citizens become able to act upon the institutional and organizational arrangements that structure their everyday lives. Such access is a fundamental building block of democracy. In Canada, this principle has been an important part of communications policy making since the time of the Aird Commission; and public hearings are still a legally required prerequisite for most CRTC procedures, providing an important channel of access to policy making for those who do not enjoy the privileged positions of power leveraged by corporate and industrial lobbies.[36] But in fact, the erosion of effective public consultation has been one of the most striking aspects of the current phase of globalization. This shift takes on dramatic proportions when one considers it in the context of the emerging global policy framework, where world citizens have no direct access whatsoever to the mechanics of policy making. Paradoxically, the new communications technologies could facilitate and enable democratic participation in policy making on an unprecedented scale, if the political will to organize it were there. From the perspective of thinking about democratic global governance mechanisms, communications policy thus becomes a major site of political struggle.

The Global Politics of Communications Policy

On the time-scale of human history, communication in global terms has existed for only a relatively short period; although globalization is commonly perceived as a very recent phenomenon, traces of an evolving global communications policy are visible throughout the past hundred years and more, and many of the early issues it raised are still with us today.[37]

A global arena for communications policy was launched in Paris, in 1863, at a conference convened to lay the foundation of an international postal system. For the next 130 years, international relations in communication were focused largely on managing the environment in which communications resources would be used at the national level, according to the goals and capacities of individual nation-states, and were minimally focused on relations across state borders. From the harmonization of technical standards to the development of a common rate-accounting system, to the allocation of radio frequencies and, later, geostationary satellite positions, the underlying assumption was that communication was a national affair requiring a minimum of international coordination.

The world's first permanent intergovernmental organization, the International Telegraph Union (ITU), was set up in 1865 to provide a framework for the development of international telegraph and telegram services.[38] This move was followed in 1875 by the Treaty of Berne, which created the General Postal Union, and an international convention on copyright (also in Berne) in 1886. The turn of the twentieth century saw the emergence of new communications technologies enabling direct point-to-point and point-to-mass sound communication. Radio presented a wide new range of issues that required international agreement. A first international conference on the regulation of wireless radio-telegraphy took place in Berlin in 1903, but it was not until 1927 that the Washington Radio Conference drafted a set of international regulations on radio communication. This event was followed by a second conference in Madrid in 1932, at which the convergence of telegraph and radio technologies was recognized in the broadening and renaming of the ITU, now (and to this day) known as the International Telecommunications Union.[39]

Dividing the World

The Washington and Madrid conferences divided the world into a series of regions and attributed a particular set of radio frequencies to each one. A series of regional conferences then distributed the frequencies among sovereign states within the region, and each state authority was responsible for overseeing the use of those frequencies. Consequently, various national broadcasting models emerged in different parts of the world during the 1930s, but a basic pattern was established and remains in effect to this day: initial distribution of communication resources and establishment of minimal mechanisms for coordination at the global level, and sovereignty over the conditions of use of those resources at the national level. Without exception, national authorities everywhere set up some type of system for regulating the use of the airwaves allocated to their jurisdiction.

A new era in international communication came into being in the immediate postwar period. Article 19 of the Universal Declaration of Human Rights underscored the right to freedom of information. UNESCO, created in 1946, began a series of activities that have been crucial to developing an understanding of the links between communication and culture and their importance for human development. New regional bodies like the Council of Europe have included communication in their sphere of concern, through periodic reference to specific themes and issues.[40]

At the same time, cultural and communications issues began to crop up in the wake of the new economic multilateralism that flowed from the Bretton Woods agreements and from the creation of institutions such as the World Bank and the International Monetary Fund (IMF). The first General Agreement on Tariffs and Trade (GATT), in 1947, generated a vigorous debate that culminated in the acceptance of foreign film import quotas, notwithstanding the GATT's general thrust toward liberalization of national markets. The extent to which cultural "products" constitute a specific type of commodity requiring its own set of international trade rules has been a constant feature of multilateral and regional trade negotiations since that time.

Toward a New World Order

The question of national sovereignty over communications took on a new colour in the political and technological context of the 1960s and 1970s. Dozens of new postcolonial states emerged and the development of satellite technologies made it possible to transmit sound and images irrespective of national borders. The unequal flow of information content from north to south and the increasing importance of technological resources led, conceptually, to the articulation of a "cultural imperialism" thesis and, politically, to efforts to create a "New World Information and Communication Order."[41] These issues were highlighted by the publication, in 1980, of the report of a UNESCO commission chaired by Irish jurist and human rights activist Sean MacBride, and by the subsequent withdrawal from UNESCO of the United States, United Kingdom, and Singapore.[42] Meanwhile, with far less fanfare, an ITU report of the same period documented the unequal distribution of technical resources for communication worldwide.[43]

UNESCO has since adopted a more low-key communications strategy, emphasizing the need for training of communications professionals and development of media institutions in the "transitional" states of central Europe, Africa, and Asia.[44] In 1995, however, the UN/UNESCO World Commission on Culture and Development published a major report that brought many of the lingering issues back on to the table, with an updated analysis.[45] One of the concrete results of this report was the Intergovernmental Conference on Cultural Policies for Development, held in Stockholm in 1998.[46]

Meanwhile, the collapse of the Berlin Wall provided the possibility for extending the development of a global communications system under the hegemony of the Western alliance. Cultural goods and services have been increasingly integrated into the international trade agreements of the 1990s, despite the resistance of a small number of countries – of which Canada is in the forefront. Under the auspices of the WTO, an open global market in telecommunications is emerging – paradoxically, one in which, because of a spate of mergers, there are fewer and fewer players.[47] Foreign ownership and content regulations are increasingly under attack and threatened with extinction in the blueprints for the future such as the MAI. New issues are emerging that can be dealt with only by a world community at the global level.

An Imperial Project

The world had its first real glimpse of the communications politics of the global village at a February 1995 meeting of information ministers of the G7 nations in Brussels. Largely written in Washington, the plan to establish a "Global Information Infrastructure," adopted by the G7 at that meeting, represented an imperial triumph of unprecedented scope. It enshrined a single vision, program, and policy framework for the role of communications technology as a means of achieving an idealized global society driven by the market forces of transnational capital. The irony of a so-called global project originating in a private meeting of the world's most powerful nations has been lost on most observers, as was the fact that, in Brussels, for the first time, non-government corporate representatives were granted official status at a G7 meeting.

First presented by US vice-president Al Gore at a meeting of the International Telecommunications Union in Buenos Aires, in 1994, the GII project emanated from the Clinton administration's 1993 "Agenda for Action," launching an initiative to build the National Information Infrastructure (NII), which it defined as "the aggregate of the nation's networks, computers, software, information resources, developers and producers."[48] The NII has been the object of vigorous debate in the United States, focused on the contradictions between the development of its public interest and commercial vocations.[49] But bumped up to the global level, it was presented as an apparently unproblematic plan for establishing an information- and communications-based utopia.

As outlined by the United States, the GII project traversed a continuum connecting public purpose and private enterprise by mobilizing such concepts as free trade, industrial development, modernization, and technological progress. After Buenos Aires, US strategy called for bringing aboard, under US leadership, its partners in the alliance of advanced capitalist countries. Having proposed and achieved the calling of a G7 ministers' meeting in Brussels, the United States concentrated on gaining support for the five basic principles announced in the GII plan – private investment, competition, flexible regulation, open access, and universal service – and identifying "policy actions" likely to advance these principles.

In Brussels, a more complex political dynamic set in, reflecting the range of important specific interests of different G7 members. The need to achieve favourable positioning for their own national representatives at the table of international capital, as well as to reflect key aspects of national policy (and thus speak to domestic public opinion), dictated that members negotiate a modified programme. The US version of the GII's original five points was thus expanded by the addition of references to equal access, content diversity, and international cooperation. The new eight-point GII exhibited a greater attentiveness to potentially explosive issues, such as social justice, the gap between richer and poorer nations, and perceived threats to cultural and linguistic diversity.[50]

The mediating role played by Canadian interventions here was noteworthy, as officials from the departments of Heritage and Industry presented the opposing views characteristic of Canadian communications policy. Thus, while Heritage Minister Michel Dupuy added Canada's voice to the European G7 members' insistence on including the principles of equal access, cultural diversity, and international cooperation to the agenda of the GII, Industry Minister John Manley was busy reminding the assembly of the aggressive pro-market stance that Canada would be bringing to its information highway policy. This split was emblematic of Canadian policy making's historically pervasive ambiguity in dealing with commerce and culture – its straddling of American and European policy approaches – as well as of the contradictions inherent in Canada's century-long effort to meld them.

In terms of global governance, the Brussels meeting represented a major shift: for the first time under the auspices of the G7, corporate enterprises met around their own separate table, with official status.[51] Groups representing civil society, meanwhile, were relegated to the margins of unofficial intervention – more reminiscent of the masses gathered outside the city gates in medieval Europe than of the social partners that could be imagined by a naive reading of the text of the GII project.[52]

The framework arrived at in Brussels, in other words, was inscribed directly within the trajectory of US communications policy over the past fifty years, the rhetoric of which has moved from emphasizing the free flow of information to the free trade of goods and services. Indeed, in every respect, the Global Information Infrastructure is a harbinger of both an emerging global system to regulate communications and a future system of world governance. It is an imperial project with enormous implications for the future of democracy and human rights, insofar as it is based on political decision making at a level where there is no accountability, on the recognized autonomy of private capital, and on the formal exclusion of the institutions of civil society. In terms of international relations, it entrenches the dependency of the so-called less-developed parts of the world. As a social project, it locates human development as a potential benefit of economic investment, rather than as the principal goal. As a challenge, it presents a tremendous opportunity to imagine a different role for communications in global society, and to organize politically to create and sustain a framework in which such an alternative can be achieved.

Policy Implications and Recommendations: Toward a Global Public Space

As we have seen throughout this chapter, Canada is playing an important yet ambivalent role in the evolution of a new global system of governance, as it tries to minimize the costs and maximize the benefits of globalization. Canada's role is important because it is trying at least minimally to articulate and defend some alternative values to those of the marketplace. It is an ambivalent role, however, because the interests Canada is promoting on the front lines appear to be primarily those of Canadian industries.[53] This basic contradiction points to a need to place the social and cultural dimensions of communications more clearly in the foreground of global policy development. Otherwise, attempts to promote cultural policy goals will be too easily revealed as no more than economic protectionism couched in nationalist rhetoric.

Multilateralism is clearly one of the central trends in global governance; but different players have different stakes and, consequently, need different strategies for intervening in a political system based on multilateral relations. According to Sylvia Ostry, Canada was an active player in the coalition of mid-range powers that pushed the proposal to create the WTO during the GATT Uruguay Round in 1993-4. Ostry points out that mid-size countries like Canada favour a rules-based system for international governance – one that combines international rules and domestic sovereignty – rather than a system based on economic or military power.[54] The rules can then provide a basis for preserving and enhancing internal sovereignty. Large powers have a different stake in a multilateral system.

Their first preference would be to rely on sheer power to assert their dominance over their partners directly.

But even large powers are recognizing the need for global coordination and regulation, to create the state of order necessary for the flourishing of their interests. Thus, for example, the European Union and the United States have each been floating proposals for some kind of formal regulatory framework to govern global communications.[55] The crunch occurs when it comes time to determine the nature of that framework – as is illustrated by the case of the Global Information Infrastructure project. From a democratic perspective, no agenda for action on the global regulation of communications will be worth implementing unless the process can be broadened to include the participation of civil society in the new regulatory framework and the structures it creates. Thus perhaps the most important challenge to the new regulatory environment is to open up spaces for such participation.

It will be crucial to keep this idea in mind as Canada continues to struggle against the situation created under the regime of the WTO, a situation that is incompatible with Canada's historical consensus-based position of protecting cultural development from the whims of the marketplace.[56] In this light, it is important to mention the role Canada has been playing in calling for "a new international instrument" to offset the impact of the WTO-based regime in the area of cultural policy. This proposal emanated from a committee set up under the auspices of Foreign Affairs and International Trade and has since been reiterated in various government policy documents.[57] The proposed new instrument would lay out the principles for cultural policies and trade and allow countries to maintain policies that promote cultural industries; would seek to develop an international consensus on the responsibility to encourage indigenous cultural expression and on the need for regulatory and other measures to promote cultural and linguistic diversity; would act as a blueprint for cultural diversity and the role of culture in a global world; and would stress the importance of cultural sovereignty.

This proposal dovetails with efforts spearheaded by the Department of Canadian Heritage since the 1998 Intergovernmental Conference on Cultural Policies for Development, organized by UNESCO in Stockholm. That conference adopted an "Action Plan for Cultural Policies for Development" and recommended a series of policy objectives to UNESCO's member states, in keeping with the general philosophical position that communications resources constitute part of "the global commons."[58] Recognizing that "in a democratic framework civil society will become increasingly important in the field of culture," the conference endorsed a dozen principles, including the fundamental right of access to and participation in cultural life, and the cultural policy objective of establishing structures and securing adequate resources necessary "to create an environment conducive to human fulfilment."[59]

Since the Stockholm conference, Canada has played a leadership role in creating an International Network on Cultural Policy whose purpose is "to build increased awareness and support for cultural diversity in an era of globalization and technological change ... promot[e] culture as a key component of sustainable development ... place culture front and centre on the international policy agenda ... [and] strengthen cultural policies so that governments, together with civil society, can create an environment which values diversity of identity, creativity and freedom."[60]

The stated role of the Network is "to ensure that culture is 'on the table' in international fora, either directly or indirectly, so that ministers can: raise awareness of the importance of cultural diversity; ensure cultural considerations are taken into account in international negotiations; [and] show the link between national cultural objectives and international development."[61]

This experience can be seen as an embryonic working model for developing a new basis for global policy making in communications. If an appropriate mechanism could be established, a global public policy approach to communication might then address a range of issues that currently have no forum, such as

- regulation of commercial activities in the public interest, to guarantee equitable access and basic services
- funding and institutional support for the creation and sustaining of public service and alternative media
- placement of limits on corporate controls resulting from transnational concentration of ownership in new and conventional media and telecommunications
- guarantees of access to available media channels on the basis of public interest criteria
- development of universal codes and standards for curtailing the spread of abusive contents
- facilitation of networking capacity through communications technologies of not-for-profit organizations
- provision of public communication spaces for conflict resolution and democratic dialogue on global issues.

The question of Internet regulation illustrates some of the most important issues at the cutting edge of global communications policy. The powerful technology of the Internet exacerbates many old problems related to communications policy at the national level and introduces new ones globally. Paradoxically, national regulators are tending toward the abandonment of attempts to regulate the Internet, just as the global issues it raises cry out for some kind of transnational regulatory intervention.[62] These issues have been developed at some length in a paper by New York University scholars John R. Mathiason and Charles C. Kuhlman. Their paper enumerates a list of problems resulting from the technological characteristics of the Internet which, they argue, indicate that "the Internet today has reached a level of political importance where some form of governance policy is needed." The challenge, as they point out, is "to determine which policies [would] govern which aspects of the Internet."[63]

Mathiason and Kuhlman indicate three possible approaches to Internet regulation: a self-regulating market, national regulation, or an international regime. In general terms, each of these models has serious limitations. It has been well established that market regulation, while possibly suitable for meeting certain economic objectives, does little to help achieve non-economic goals. As for national regulation, we have been staring its limitations in the face throughout this chapter. The tendency today in every area of communications regulation is toward an international regime; however, this process would logically need to be opened up to greater representation than is allowed by the present framework of multilateral institutions, a framework which, as we saw earlier, focuses on individual member states and their corporate clients.

Mathiason and Kuhlman suggest an "international framework convention" on the Internet, which would articulate basic norms for how the Internet is to be governed and establish a mechanism for monitoring compliance with those norms and determining future changes. A framework convention would be different from a treaty-based regime such as the one pertaining to trade under the auspices of the WTO. Its task would be to sort out the roles and responsibilities of the various national, international, and private actors involved in the development of this "global enabling technology." It would need to be negotiated, the authors suggest, on the basis that the Internet is part of the global commons.[64]

This type of proposal clearly depends on a broad consensus of opinion regarding what communications is about. It can only hope to work to the extent that communications technologies are recognized as a public good. In other words, the normative view one takes about something like the Internet is much more important in determining the limits and possibilities of policy than are the nature of the technology or the policy-making capacity of the state. Debates surrounding the normative definition of communications technologies are therefore a key prerequisite to any attempt at global policy making in this area. These debates should be as open and all-encompassing as reasonably possible, so that the positions taken by national governments in global policy arenas reflect some kind of social consensus.

Internationally, a general debate has begun about the need to address issues for ensuring the global public interest in communication.[65] The next step needs to be the creation of a permanent, democratic forum for developing appropriate policies.

The urgency of such a project is being driven home almost weekly by developments in the field. In mid-September 1999, CEOs of the world's most important communications companies met in Paris to discuss the global regulation of electronic commerce. According to the press release issued after their meeting, a consensus was reached. The Global Business Dialogue on Electronic Commerce (GBDe), as this group is known, "invited governments as well as international organizations" to join them in developing the tremendous potential of e-commerce: "A global medium like the Internet needs a global policy approach," said GBDe chair Thomas Middlehoff, also chair and CEO of the world's largest publishing company, Bertelsmann AG. "It is the consensus position of the GBDe that conflicting national patchwork regulation will deprive consumers of the economic benefits of an innovative marketplace and be a source of significant insecurity for them," he said. The GBDe therefore urged governments and international organizations to coordinate their regulatory efforts regarding e-commerce.[66]

It is fair to say that a week no longer goes by without a story such as this one making it into the business and mainstream press – not to mention those stories that remain untold. Such stories are but small examples pointing to the characteristics of the emerging global communications environment that I have been discussing in this chapter, of the increasingly seamless system of global communications that is evolving in a widely dispersed policy regime with no discernible centre. A policy framework is, however, unquestionably taking shape. The agenda is being driven by big business, and other actors are cordially "invited" to take part.

I have tried to show that this situation presents a significant challenge to conventional thinking about communications policy and public policy in general. We have to be concerned about communications policy because of the pivotal role of the new communications environment in structuring almost every other area of public policy that the state has traditionally sought to influence. Issues regarding communications policy are impacting not only on the area immediately concerned, but on every other area as well. Meanwhile, as the example of the GBDe, naïvely shows, it is simply untrue to pretend that the globalization of communications means the end of policy. Rather, the sites of policy making have shifted, vertically, from the national to the transnational, and horizontally, from the state to the boardroom. Influencing the global framework in which communications is evolving, therefore, should be treated as a crucial strategic goal for the policy community.

Credibility will need to be given to the idea that the global communications environment, from the conventional airwaves to outer space, is a public resource, to be organized, managed, and regulated in the global public interest. Broadening access will require appropriate transnational regulatory mechanisms, as well as mechanisms for a more equitable distribution of global commercial benefits. International appropriation of some air and space is needed, for distribution outside the country of origin of viable creative products that currently have no access to the new global agora that figures so prominently in utopian discourses on the new information technologies.

The convergence of communications technologies will require a parallel convergence in programs and policies, as well as the invention of new models, new concepts, and a general new way of thinking about communication. This is nothing less than a global political project. If globalization means that nation-states have to redefine their way of doing things, if it means that transnational capital must be brought into check as it becomes more and more of a determining force, it also means that democratic, civil society agents are going to need to organize and mobilize across national boundaries and along new axes of identity, common purpose, and solidarity. This process is beginning, especially among the emerging global networks of community and alternative media practitioners – as well as media users – in various parts of the world.[67]

Corporate-driven communications policy has been to all intents and purposes "globalized," but it is seeking a new basis for legitimacy that it can achieve only through the endorsement of nation-states, international organizations and, ultimately, civil society. This means that, at the present time, a political space exists in which global communications policy is disputed by various stakeholders. New rules are being written as you read this. The key question is: How can the participatory base of the new policy environment be broadened?

The centrality of communications for global human development further underscores the importance of the emerging communications governance regime. In this respect, what I have been discussing should be seen as an essentially political issue, as part of the struggle for the democratization of the new global governance system. Communications is central to the development of what political theorist David Held calls "cosmopolitan democracy."[68]

This centrality of communications indicates a need to develop democratic mechanisms for ensuring access to the communications policy-making process at the global level. Without such mechanisms, promoting a public interest through policy intervention in any area influenced by communications will soon be impossible.

At present, at least four models of access to communications policy can be identified:

1. *The libertarian model* This model is characterized by a complete lack of regulation. With regard to the new digital technologies like the Internet, this is the approach that is currently being taken by most national regulators (including Canada's CRTC – Australia is an important exception), mainly because they do not know what to do or how to do it. It is also largely favoured by grassroots activists who are benefitting from this open communications system. But the history of communications technologies shows that, left to its own devices, this open access is not likely to last. A libertarian model of Internet governance will probably lead eventually to closed doors, restricted access, and limited communication.
2. *Self-regulation* This is the approach most often favoured by industry players, with the encouragement of national regulators. It is currently being touted as the solution to problems such as abusive content and threats to basic rights, the argument being that consumers will respond if they are not satisfied. But as we saw in the example of the GBDe, even the promoters of self-regulation are recognizing the need for a global structural framework for communication activity, within which industry self-regulation would take place.
3. *The closed club, or top-down institutional model* In this approach, plans are negotiated in organizations such as the OECD, G8, or WTO, as well as in the new institutions emerging as the corporate sector fills the vacuum created by the retreat of national governments from regulatory issues. One such agency that we will be hearing more about in the future is the Internet Corporation for Assigned Names and Numbers (ICANN), an organization set up on the initiative of the US government in 1998 for the purpose of directing traffic on the Internet.
4. *The long march through the institutions* This process is tied to the broader project of democratization of global governance, reflected in some of the initiatives around UN reform and again in notions such as "cosmopolitan democracy." Access to global policy making is being fostered to some extent by some important initiatives in multilateral agencies such as UNESCO and the ITU, which have demonstrated some openness to the concerns of civil society and the inclusion of NGO representation in their activities.

The overall analysis put forward in this chapter appears to indicate that the last of these approaches is the most desirable. Indeed, the Canadian approach to communications policy is based on transparency and public participation, and some of Canada's most significant achievements in communications have grown out of the initiatives of civil society. These are values that are now worth promoting transnationally.

A clearer emphasis, in policy making, on the social and cultural role of communications would also provide a normative basis for proposals that Canada has been trying to develop in multilateral fora, such as the so-called "new international instrument," which would aim to offset the impact on culture of the WTO-based trade regime.

Finally, a global policy approach along these lines would help redefine the role of the state with respect to communications, both domestically and in its new transnational guise, while providing leverage for addressing a range of specific issues that are currently well off the agenda.

In the current context of globalization, communications can be either a vehicle for human development or just another technology of power and domination. Which it will be has not yet been determined, and that is why the stakes of the current policy debates are so great.

Notes

1 Quoted in "Free Trade under Fire," *Financial Times,* 11 October 1999, 1.

2 See Canada, House of Commons, *Canada and the Future of the World Trade Organization: Advancing a Millennium Agenda in the Public Interest,* Report of the Standing Committee on Foreign Affairs and International Trade (Ottawa: Public Works and Government Services Canada, 1999).

3 Canadian Heritage, "Canada and United States Sign Agreement on Periodicals," News release, Ottawa, 4 June 1999, <www.pch.gc.ca/culture> (17 December 2001).

4 A "shortlist" of issue areas and sites that characterize global communication policy is included as Appendix B, p. 163.

5 See Marc Raboy, "Communication Policy and Globalization as a Social Project," in *Communication, Citizenship, and Social Policy: Rethinking the Limits of the Welfare State,* ed. Andrew Calabrese and Jean-Claude Burgelman (Lanham, MD: Rowman and Littlefield, 1999); and Marc Raboy, "Global Communication Policy and the Realization of Human Rights," in *A Communications Cornucopia: Markle Foundation Essays on Information Policy,* ed. R.G. Noll and M.E. Price (Washington, DC: Brookings Institution Press, 1998).

6 In this respect, we can say that issues regarding the governance of communication are "metagovernance" issues – that is to say, issues whose outcome impacts not only the area concerned, but all other areas as well.

7 See Wolfgang H. Reinicke, *Global Public Policy: Governing without Government?* (Washington, DC: Brookings Institution Press, 1998).

8 For a portrayal of the problem as it affects Canadian cultural policy, see Ivan Bernier and Richard Collins, "Politiques culturelles, intégration régionale et mondialisation," *Cahier-Médias* (Centre d'Études sur les médias, Quebec City) 7 (July 1998).

9 See Reinicke, *Global Public Policy,* on strategies for implementing national "opting out" mechanisms in global policy development.

10 For a case study of the playing out of this process in Canadian broadcasting policy, see Marc Raboy, "Influencing Public Policy on Canadian Broadcasting," *Canadian Public Administration* 38, 3 (1995): 411-32; and Marc Raboy, "The Role of Public Consultation in Shaping the Canadian Broadcasting System," *Canadian Journal of Political Science* 28, 3 (1995): 455-77.

11 K.R. Higham, "The Politics of Culture in Canada: Creating an Environment for Maximising Human Development," (paper presented at the meeting of the Canadian Cultural Research Network, Ottawa, 4 June 1998), 8.
12 Ibid., 9
13 This area is covered by Ronald Deibert in Chapter 4 of this volume.
14 In the 1960s, communications guru Marshall McLuhan – a genuine Canadian contributor to thinking on globalization if there ever was one – parodied the use of communications technology for military defence purposes in the Canadian north, by declaring that Canada itself was a Distant Early Warning system of global social and cultural trends. See Marshall McLuhan and B.R. Powers, *The Global Village* (Oxford: Oxford University Press, 1989); and Marshall McLuhan, ed., *The McLuhan DEW Line* (New York: Human Development Corporation, 1968-70).
15 The study was conducted as part of a joint initiative of the Social Sciences and Humanities Research Council of Canada (SSHRCC) and the federal Department of Communication (now Canadian Heritage), entitled "Cultural Development and the Open Economy." See Marc Raboy, Ivan Bernier, Florian Sauvageau, and Dave Atkinson, *Développement culturel et mondialisation de l'économie: Un enjeu démocratique* (Quebec: Institut québécois de recherche sur la culture, 1994).
16 Marc Raboy, Ivan Bernier, Florian Sauvageau, and Dave Atkinson, "Cultural Development and the Open Economy: A Democratic Issue and a Challenge to Public Policy," *Canadian Journal of Communication* 19, 3/4 (1994): 291-315.
17 Ibid.
18 General sources for this section include: Arjun Appadurai, "Disjuncture and Difference in the Global Cultural Economy," in *Global Culture: Nationalism, Globalization, and Modernity,* ed. M. Featherstone (London: Sage Publications, 1993); Daniele Archibugi and David Held, *Cosmopolitan Democracy: An Agenda for a New World Order* (Cambridge: Polity Press, 1995); Manuel Castells, *The Information Age: Economy, Society, and Culture,* 3 vols. (Oxford: Blackwell, 1996); Noam Chomsky, *Year 501: The Conquest Continues* (Montreal: Black Rose Books, 1993); Richard Falk, *On Humane Governance: Toward a New Global Politics* (Cambridge: Polity Press, 1995); Mike Featherstone, ed., *Global Culture: Nationalism, Globalization, and Modernity* (London: Sage Publications, 1993); Howard H. Frederick, *Global Communication and International Relations* (Belmont: Wadsworth, 1993); Jan Nederveen Pieterse, "Globalisation as Hybridisation," *International Sociology* 9, 2 (1994): 161-84; Roland Robertson, *Globalization: Social Theory and Global Culture* (London: Sage Publications, 1992); and Immanuel Wallerstein, *Geopolitics and Geoculture: Essays on the Changing World-System* (Cambridge: Cambridge University Press, 1991).
19 A database search of books and specialized journals done by World Bank economist and author Wolfgang Reinicke produced no title from 1971 with the words "global" or "globalization" in it; for 1995, Reinicke's search produced 1,200 results. See Reinicke, *Global Public Policy.*
20 These statistics are drawn from an *Economist* article, from 1998, at which time the seven corporations were Time-Warner (US), Disney (US), Viacom (US), Sony (Japan), Bertelsmann (Germany), News Corp. (UK/Australia), and Seagram (Canada). Time-Warner has since become AOL-TimeWarner, and Seagram has since been absorbed by Vivendi (France), but the basic premise of the *Economist* article remains unchanged. Emma Duncan, "Wheel of Fortune: A Survey of Technology and Entertainment," *The Economist* 21 (November 1998): 11.
21 Council of the European Union, "Draft Treaty of Amsterdam," Protocol on the System of Public Broadcasting in the Member States, Brussels, August 1997, <www.europa.eu.int/eur-lex/en> (17 December 2001).
22 See Benjamin Barber, *Jihad vs. McWorld* (New York: Times Books, 1995).
23 See Samuel P. Huntington, *The Clash of Civilizations and the Remaking of World Order* (New York: Simon and Schuster, 1996). These observations have taken on a new sense of meaning and urgency in the aftermath of the events of 11 September 2001.
24 See, for example, the Virtual Conference on the Right to Communicate and the Communication of Rights, hosted by Videazimut, 11 May-26 June 1998, <http://commposite.uqam.ca/videaz> (17 December 2001).

25 Unless otherwise mentioned, details in this section are taken from Marc Raboy, *Missed Opportunities: The Story of Canada's Broadcasting Policy* (Montreal: McGill-Queen's University Press, 1990).
26 Ibid., 39
27 Ibid.
28 Raboy, *Missed Opportunities,* 40.
29 The case of "split-run" magazines referred to at the beginning of this chapter is thus only one recent example of this phenomenon.
30 See for example, the extensive literature on Canada's "Information Highway Policy" debate. Several years after the government's official launching of that debate, much has been said, much is to be read, but Canada is still operating in a policy vacuum with respect to overall goals and direction of communications infrastructure development.
31 Cited in Raboy, *Missed Opportunities,* 193.
32 Ibid.
33 The closest we have come at the moment is the government's response to the preliminary report of its Information Highway Advisory Council (IHAC). This document indicates a general orientation and several specific pathways that Canadian communications policy may take in the future, but cannot be said to constitute the type of encompassing policy that has been so long awaited. National policy in communications, as in many areas, continues to be made on an ad hoc basis, often in response to crisis or conjunctural needs. See Industry Canada, *Building the Information Society: Moving Canada into the 21st Century* (Ottawa: Minister of Supply and Services Canada, 1996); Information Highway Advisory Council, *Connection, Community, Content: The Challenge of the Information Highway,* Final Report (Ottawa: Minister of Supply and Services Canada, 1995); and Information Highway Advisory Council, *Preparing Canada for a Digital World,* Final Report (Ottawa: Industry Canada, 1997).
34 Marc Raboy, "Cultural Sovereignty, Public Participation and Democratization of the Public Sphere: The Canadian Debate on the New Information Infrastructure," *Communications et stratégies* 21 (1996): 51-76; and Bram Dov Abramson and Marc Raboy, "Policy Globalization and the 'Information Society': A View from Canada," *Telecommunications Policy* 23, 10/11 (1999): 775-91.
35 Al Gore, "The Global Information Infrastructure: Forging a New Athenian Age of Democracy," *InterMedia* 22, 2 (1994): 4-6.
36 Marc Raboy, "Influencing Public Policy on Canadian Broadcasting," *Canadian Public Administration* 38, 3 (1995): 411-32; and Marc Raboy, "The Role of Public Consultation in Shaping the Canadian Broadcasting System," *Canadian Journal of Political Science* 28, 3 (1995): 455-77.
37 Details in this section are drawn from Cees J. Hamelink, *The Politics of World Communication* (London: Sage Publications, 1994); and Armand Mattelart, *La mondialisation de la communication* (Paris: Presses universitaires de France, 1996).
38 Provision was made for private sector participation at the organization's second conference in Vienna in 1868, and non-government, corporate members were first admitted as early as 1871.
39 Today's ITU is composed of 184 government and 375 private members. According to its former director-general, Pekka Tarjanne, the role of the private sector in the ITU is perhaps the single most important strategic issue it has to face. See Pekka Tarjanne, "The Limits of National Sovereignty: Issues for the Governance of International Telecommunications," in *Telecom Reform: Principles, Policies and Regulatory Practices,* ed. W.H. Melody (Lyngby, Denmark: Technical University of Denmark, 1997), 41-50.
40 See, for example, Council of Europe, *The Media in a Democratic Society,* Draft Resolutions and Draft Political Declaration, 4th European Ministerial Conference on Mass Media Policy, Prague, 7-8 December 1994, MCM-CDMM (94) 3 prov. 1 (Strasbourg: Council of Europe, 1994).
41 See John Tomlinson, *Cultural Imperialism: A Critical Introduction* (Baltimore: Johns Hopkins University Press, 1991); and Johan Galtung and Richard C. Vincent, *Global Glasnost: Toward a New World Information and Communication Order?* (Cresskill, NJ: Hampton Press, 1993).

42 UNESCO, *Many Voices, One World,* report of the International Commission for the Study of Communication Problems, chaired by Sean MacBride (London: Kogan Page, 1980).

43 See also International Telecommunications Union/UNESCO, *The Right to Communicate: At What Price? Economic Constraints to the Effective Use of Telecommunications in Education, Science, Culture and in the Circulation of Information* (Paris: ITU/UNESCO, 1995). This was a joint study that wondered to what extent societal goals could be reconciled with commercial objectives in telecommunications. This interagency report represented a rare effort to bridge the gap between technical and sociocultural aspects of international communications policy.

44 UNESCO, "New Communication Strategy," Adopted by the general conference at its 25th session, Paris, 1989, <www.unesco.org> (17 December 2001).

45 United Nations/UNESCO, *Our Creative Diversity,* Report of the World Commission on Culture and Development, chaired by Javier Perez de Cuellar (Paris: World Commission on Culture and Development, 1995).

46 UNESCO, "Action Plan for Cultural Policies for Development," Adopted at the Intergovernmental Conference on Cultural Policies for Development, Stockholm, 30 March-2 April 1998, <www.unesco-sweden.org/Conference> (17 December 2001).

47 In 1999, telecom mergers and acquisitions in play included Deutsche Telekom / Telecom Italia (Europe), Bell Atlantic / GTE (USA), AT&T / TCI (USA), Ameritech / Bell Canada (US-Canada), AT&T Canada / Metronet (Canada), BC Tel / Telus (Canada), and the four Atlantic telecommunications companies (Canada).

48 See Brian Kahin, "The Internet and the National Information Infrastructure," in *Public Access to the Internet,* ed. B. Kahin and J. Keller (Cambridge, MA: MIT Press, 1995), 3-23; United States, "The Global Information Infrastructure: Agenda for Cooperation," Washington, 1994, <www.iitf.nist.gov/documents/docs/gii/giiagend.html> (17 December 2001); and United States Information Agency, *Toward a Global Information Infrastructure: The Promise of a New World Information Order* (Washington: USIA Pamphlet Series, 1995).

49 See Patricia Aufderheide, *Communications Policy and the Public Interest: The Telecommunications Act of 1996* (New York: Guilford Press, 1999); and William Drake, ed., *The New Information Infrastructure: Strategies for U.S. Policy* (New York: Twentieth Century Fund Press, 1995).

50 G7, "A Shared Vision of Human Enrichment," Chair's Conclusions to the G7 Ministerial Conference on the Information Society, Brussels, 27 February 1995, <www.unix-ag.uni-kl.de/~lippold/g7-conclusion.html> (17 December 2001).

51 The main transnational companies involved in information and communication technologies have since set up a Global Information Infrastructure Commission (GIIC) to continue pursuing their common interests in this area. Among the companies involved in the GIIC are Mitsubishi, Motorola, Viacom, Time-Warner, Olivetti, Sprint, AT&T, Nokia, Oracle, NEC, Alcatel Alsthom, Teleglobe Canada, and Nippon Telegraph and Telephone. See Michel Venne, "Le secteur privé s'interroge: Où mènent les inforoutes?" *Le Devoir* (Montreal), 12 February 1995.

52 Civil society organizations have, however, been playing a crucial monitoring role with respect to the GII, attending on the periphery such meetings as the one in Brussels, circulating information, and seeking representation through whatever channels happen to be available. See, for example, Alain His, ed., *Communication and Multimedia for People: Moving into Social Empowerment over the Information Highway* (Paris: Transversales Science Culture, 1996).

53 This impression is strengthened by the trend toward private sector development in domestic cultural policy. The most recent spate of CRTC decisions on television, published in May-June 1999, unequivocally confirmed this trend. See Canadian Radio-Television and Telecommunications Commission, Public Notice CRTC 1999-97, "Building on Success – A Policy Framework for Canadian Television," CRTC, Ottawa, 11 June 1999, <www.crtc.gc.ca> (17 December 2001).

54 This fits Reinicke's model of internal and external sovereignty. Reinicke, *Global Public Policy.*

55 In September 1997, European telecommunications commissioner Martin Bangemann, author of a high-profile blueprint for communication liberalization that bears his name,

called for an "international charter" to govern the new world order in global communication. Within days, his remarks were endorsed by White House policy adviser Ira Magaziner, who stated that the United States believed that there was a need for international understanding on information policy issues, "some of which may need to be formal agreements, some informal understandings and common approaches." See Suzanne Perry, "U.S. May Back Internet Charter, Not Formal Body," ZDNet News Channel (Reuters), 2 October 1997, <www.zdnet.com> (17 December 2001). This project – which may some day soon lead to a global agreement on communication governance – has been developing slowly and steadily, but entirely behind closed doors. It is yet another example of the need for transparency and democratic policy mechanisms.

56 Support for this position in Canadian public opinion was confirmed most recently in the June 1999 report of the House of Commons Standing Committee on Foreign Affairs and International Trade, referred to at the beginning of this chapter. Canada, House of Commons, *Canada and the Future of the World Trade Organization: Advancing a Millennium Agenda in the Public Interest,* Report of the Standing Committee on Foreign Affairs and International Trade (Ottawa: Public Works and Government Services Canada, 1999).

57 SAGIT (The Cultural Industries Sectoral Advisory Group on International Trade), *Canadian Culture in a Global World: New Strategies for Culture and Trade,* report, Ottawa, February 1999, <www.infoexport.gc.ca/trade-culture> (17 December 2001).

58 The proposals presented to the Stockholm conference were based largely on the 1995 report of the World Commission on Culture and Development. United Nations/UNESCO, *Our Creative Diversity*; and UNESCO, "Action Plan."

59 UNESCO, "Action Plan."

60 The Network was the direct result of a meeting of ministers responsible for culture from some twenty countries, convened by Heritage Minister Sheila Copps in Ottawa in June 1998, to explore strategies for negotiating a general cultural exception from international trade agreements. See International Network on Cultural Policy, "Welcome to the INCP," <http://64.26.177.19> (29 January 2002).

61 Ibid.

62 Including Canada's. See Canadian Radio-Television and Telecommunications Commission, "Broadcasting Public Notice CRTC 1999-84 / Telecom Public Notice CRTC 99-14," New Media, CRTC, Ottawa, 17 May 1999. In this public notice, Canada's communications regulator proudly proclaimed that it would not regulate new media activities on the Internet.

63 Including, among others, the problem of preserving national, regional, and local culture. Mathiason and Kuhlman cite the issue of domain name assignment as one that stands "at the interface between the technological issues of Internet management and the economic and social issues that have emerged." John R. Mathiason and Charles C. Kuhlman, "An International Communication Policy: The Internet, International Regulation and New Policy Structures" (unpublished manuscript, New York University, 1999), 12.

64 Ibid.

65 *Javnost/The Public,* theme issue "Global Media Policy: A Symposium on Issues and Strategies," edited by Marc Raboy, 5, 4 (1998).

66 PR Newswire, "GBDe Paris Meeting World Business Leaders for the First Time Agreed on the Fundamental Principles of Global Electronic Commerce," 13 September 1999, <www.prnewswire.com> (15 September 1999).

67 Some examples of such networks are the Association for Progressive Communication, which brings together Internet activists; Videazimut, an international NGO of video practitioners; and AMARC, the World Association of Community-Oriented Radio Broadcasters. The People's Communication Charter, to take another type of example, has accumulated thousands of adherents since its launch in 1993, <www.pccharter.net>. In 1999, a new global initiative called Voices 21 was launched, with a view toward building what its statement called "A Global Movement for People's Voices in Media and Communication in the 21st Century," <www.comunica.org/v21> (17 December 2001).

68 See Daniele Archibugi and David Held, *Cosmopolitan Democracy.*

6
The State As Place amid Shifting Spaces

David R. Cameron and Janice Gross Stein

The Global Challenge

For at least the last 200 years, the nation-state has been the dominant form of political organization, and, since the Second World War, the dominant economic force on the globe. Citizens in the industrialized world forged social contracts with their governments and held these governments accountable not only for their security, but also for their well-being. However, the continuing economic and political pre-eminence of the state is no longer accepted conventional wisdom. Indeed, some argue that the state may be involuntarily retreating from its position of unchallenged control of the economic and political space within its territorial boundaries. This retreat may have profound implications for the social contract with its citizens, for accountable governance, and more broadly, for configurations of political identity. The state, it is argued, may lose its pre-eminence as the principal focus of political identity and become one among many actors bidding for the loyalty of its members in a competitive political marketplace.[1]

As processes of globalization accelerate, the state, some argue, is increasingly "hollow," because its borders no longer correspond broadly to the relevant economic, cultural, and social spaces.[2] As globalization proceeds, borders become more permeable and fluid, and identities multiply and reorder as structures of governance change. For a good part of this last century, the authoritative reach of the state overlapped almost entirely with the economic, cultural, and social spaces of its citizenry; cultural, social, and economic borders largely converged with the political. At the beginning of the twenty-first century, however, the reach of the state has retreated from a portion of the economic and cultural spaces that are important to citizens, and is shrinking from some of the social and even the security spaces.[3] The disjunction is clear: political boundaries continue to remain largely fixed, while cultural and economic spaces are reconfiguring.[4] Mathematicians would represent this changing configuration as sets that overlap less and less. Some see a continuing retreat of the state in the face of these changing configurations as both inevitable and irreversible, with disturbing consequences for national identities, legitimate and accountable governance, and the redress of social inequalities.

While we agree that globalization is having a profound impact on politics and society, we do not accept the proposition that the processes of globalization are inevitable. Nor do we accept the corollary argument that the state is largely hollowed out and increasingly irrelevant. The authors contributing to this volume have illuminated just how complex and multifaceted the phenomenon of globalization is, and how diverse its effects can be.

In this chapter, we advance four central arguments. First, the uncertainties in the pace and trajectory of globalization are very large. The future is contingent rather than determined, and even the parameters of future development are unknown. The processes of globalization are neither irreversible nor linear; rather there is a range of outcomes that are possible when we imagine the future.[5] Thinking about globalization needs to stretch to accommodate several possible futures.

Second, globalization is a "layered" process. Some of the threads of globalization may thicken more quickly than others, and, indeed, some may thin out. It is highly unlikely, for example, that the connections among societies that have been facilitated by the revolution in information and communication technologies will be reversed, but the density of economic integration among societies could well be.

Third, the nation-state remains an indispensable institution, under virtually all foreseeable contingencies. It is still the primary provider of social justice, and uniquely accountable to its citizens for their governance. The state will not continue to function, however, with its established roles and responsibilities unchanged from the last half-century; it faces new and powerful challenges to its core mandates.

Finally, the state has the capacity and the opportunity to make important strategic choices about what roles it will play and what kinds of economic, social, and cultural investments it will make. These choices will differ depending in part on the pace and intensity of globalization, in part on the specific impact of globalization on a particular state and particular sectors, in part on the institutional capacity of the state, and in part on the quality of political leadership and the resilience and vibrancy of society.[6]

We will develop these arguments, acknowledging the reality of an uncertain future, by fashioning alternative scenarios.

Contingent Scenarios: Globalization Triumphant and Globalization in Retreat

Is Globalization Inevitable?

The powerful effects of the revolution in information and communication technologies suggest that the current phase of "globalization," while not new, is qualitatively different from previous phases in some respects: its scope is unprecedented – it reaches literally around the globe – and the nature of technological development appears to make it irreversible. This argument needs qualification, however.

This is not the first time in history that economies have been integrated and culture spread broadly across the globe. In earlier phases of globalization, however, cultural homogeneity occurred largely through force, as religious proselytization swept through large swaths of population and as imperial powers imposed cultural idioms and languages on the peoples they conquered. The imperial powers were typically rooted in place: Rome, Constantinople, Madrid, Paris, and London.[7] Currently, culture spreads globally as economic product, pushed by the market or pulled by consumer demand. The contemporary equivalent of imperial power, the market, is everywhere and nowhere. The pace of the spread and the depth of the penetration of global culture are certainly unprecedented, but dependent in large part on thriving global markets. In the past, global markets have slowed and even collapsed.

Could such a reversal occur again? Shocks are not difficult to imagine, and the capacity of the current global system to brake and insulate against shocks is clearly limited. Historically, unexpected exogenous shocks to the system have always occurred, and we have no reason to think that these kinds of unanticipated "wildcards" will not continue to occur in the future.

War among the major powers in 1914 was an unexpected and dramatic shock to the system. While war among the great powers is unthinkable today, a nuclear conflict between India and Pakistan is certainly conceivable. Nor is it difficult to construct a path to regional war in the Middle East. These conflicts would shock the global economic system. It is not only interstate wars that threaten the global economy. In 1973, the dramatic increase in the price of oil was anticipated by very few, yet it severely jolted the economic order. More recently, the bursting of the bubble in technology jolted stock markets around the world. Even more dramatically, the attacks on the World Trade Center in New York and the Pentagon in Washington created an unprecedented crisis of confidence for the global travel and tourist industries. More generally, the vivid example of global terrorism gave pause to optimistic forecasters of uninterrupted global economic integration.

The current phase of economic globalization is perhaps more vulnerable to shocks precisely because of the broad base of the investment pool. Unlike the system a century ago, where a relatively small group of knowledgeable investors accounted for the bulk of global capital, current investments are far more likely to be short term, widely held, leveraged, and speculative. They are able to move far more quickly in and out of vulnerable economies and, indeed, to exacerbate the very vulnerabilities that then provoke further capital flight.[8] The international institutions designed to manage the global economy are lagging far behind the electronic flows of capital and investment. Even if current reforms are implemented, the capacity of global institutions to brake real time capital flows and to regulate capital markets will remain questionable.

A slowing or reversal of globalization is one among several plausible futures. Scenarios of possible contingent futures are appropriate when the uncertainties are large and exogenous shocks are a credible possibility. We develop only two contingent scenarios of globalization, each at opposite ends of a spectrum of possible futures, and consider the plausible impact of each of these on Canada in 2010. We do so fully conscious that these are stylized narratives, designed to highlight different tendencies. In 2010, Canada will likely find itself somewhere along the spectrum between these extremes.

Globalization Triumphant

It is easy to imagine the quickening and deepening of processes that are currently in play. Global capital markets, direct foreign investment, and trade continue to expand more rapidly than national economic flows. International institutions lag behind global economic flows, but nevertheless extend their capacity to monitor and regulate.

Processes of globalization reward innovation, analytic thinking, independence, and the capacity to "lead" flexible networks rather than command hierarchically organized, bureaucratic organizations. Those without the analytic skills to participate become further marginalized as global economic activity generates an increasing share of gross domestic product measured nationally.

Population movements continue to grow as people migrate in search of economic opportunities. A global underclass of the unskilled and their families move from village to metropolitan centre seeking a better life. It is more difficult, and getting harder all the time, for the unskilled to cross national borders. For the skilled, barriers to mobility decrease and "transilient citizens" move back and forth among multiple centres. They live "somewhere" but work "everywhere." Legal jurisdictions blur as projects and people become increasingly global, endowed with global identities and sharing a global culture.

"Global cities" – in Canada: Vancouver, Toronto and Montreal – grow in dynamism, in their attractiveness to new immigrants, and in their capacity to create wealth. They become the "hubs" connecting diverse populations to hubs worldwide. These cities become powerful global players, generating resources that dwarf those of provincial and federal governments. They become primary producers of cultural products that play directly in global markets. Cities invest their tax revenues primarily in infrastructure, safety, and tourism to increase their attractiveness as hubs. That these cities do not have an adequate tax base to meet the needs of those marginalized by new forms of wealth creation becomes a growing problem. In the cities, social inequalities grow.

Control, but not always authority, continues to migrate up to a vibrant global economy and to international institutions, out to non-governmental organizations and global associations, and down to local communities. Local communities become more important as a haven from global pressures and as an arena of effective political action. The state, an authoritative voice increasingly disconnected from capacity and control, becomes the referee that seeks to enforce fair practices. It retreats as the commanding focus of political loyalty and identity for many, and extracts less revenue from its citizens through taxation as mobility and global market pressures grow. Nevertheless, the state remains central to the marginalized population who seek to mobilize political resources to press the state to honour the pre-existing social contract.

Globalization in Retreat

Processes of globalization could be slowed, stopped for a considerable period, or even reversed, as they have been in the past. It is unlikely that the growth of global production through intrafirm trade could be stopped for very long, and difficult to foresee how interlocking networks of information could be stopped at all, but the pace of expansion could be significantly slowed and processes of economic integration could be reversed. It is, unfortunately, not difficult to build a credible scenario.

A fresh wave of attacks by a global network of terror targets economic and civilian infrastructure in Los Angeles, Chicago, and London. Unconventional weapons are used to spread panic, destroy confidence, and limit global mobility. Stock markets around the world drop sharply, responding to the threat to global commerce and mobility. The market contraction is exacerbated by a significant and prolonged decline in commercial as well as tourist travel, and by a decline in foreign investment. Vulnerable economies sink quickly into recession and several default on payments of their debt. International financial institutions are unable to manage the cascading series of defaults, and political leaders of vulnerable economies, reacting to enraged populations, impose temporary currency controls in an effort to halt the devaluation of their currencies. In the wake of declining economic confidence and heightened fears about security, widespread restrictions on the mobility of people are put in place. Global economic activity – trade and direct foreign investment – declines significantly as a proportion of gross domestic product. The "global cities" experience real declines in housing prices, increasing unemployment, and intense pressure on a social infrastructure that is already inadequate to meet social and economic needs.

Under these conditions, the state moves prominently to the foreground of the political landscape. Only the state can address the requirement for heightened security, the primary demand of frightened publics everywhere. The public also presses governments to rescue industries and sectors at risk of bankruptcy, to shore up currencies where devaluation would threaten life savings, and to reignite engines of economic growth and fulfil social contracts. The state again becomes the focal point of both political loyalty and public demand.

The State in the Two Scenarios

Clearly, globalization sets different constraints for the state in each of these two scenarios. Equally important, however, is the fact that states have strategic choices under each set of constraints. Before we examine these pairs of constraints and choices, we will make four general points.

First, states can and do follow noticeably different paths in their response to globalization. Consider, for example, how differently Japan and the United States, Singapore and Hong Kong, have addressed the challenges of globalization. Consider as well the distinctive responses of the countries of Southeast Asia to the regional economic crisis which all experienced in the last few years. It is apparent that "one size" does not "fit all." The neoliberal policies allegedly necessary for participation in the global economy permit more degrees of freedom than is commonly thought.[9] Indeed, mounting evidence demonstrates significant differences in the way in which countries have been adjusting or protecting their welfare systems in response to the pressures of globalization.[10]

Second, countries do not start from similar terrain when they respond to globalization. Globalization does not level the past. States and societies bring with them their own territorial space, population, and resource base, as well as the traditions, culture, and political institutions of their community, built up over long periods of time. These shape their response to globalization as they have shaped earlier stages of their national development. A major reason for the "biodiversity" of global states lies precisely in these deeply rooted historical traditions and institutional resources.[11]

Income inequality in the United States, for example, has grown much more dramatically than in Canada in the last twenty-five years. Indeed, income inequality among families in Canada after taxes and transfers does not appear to have grown between 1980 and 1995, the years of intensifying exposure to American and global markets.[12] Canada has spent more than the United States on social programs and the gap has widened since 1980.[13] Canadian programs have also been more strongly redistributive than equivalent programs in the United States. It appears that the Canadian state, rooted in its political values, culture, and institutions, has in the past mediated the impact of global market forces more aggressively than has its counterpart in the United States, although less so than many of the states of Europe.

Third, large chunks of the social policy field have not migrated out into the global system as have, for example, the formerly national dimensions of the economy, culture, information, and communications. Most social needs and demands, and consequently most social policy, remain domestic, not global, in character. For better or for worse, the state remains the principal, at times exclusive, repository of demands for social benefits. If states are able to generate budgetary surpluses as deficits recede in a period of expanding growth, they may have additional resources to meet these demands. Assuming that they do and that they choose to allocate resources in response to these pressures, they may recapture some of their centrality as focal points of loyalty, especially among that part of the population that is marginalized by globalization.

Fourth, inequality, exclusion, and marginalization on a global level have become increasingly acute in the last two decades and show evidence of deepening.[14] In fact, if states do not respond by reducing inequalities, and globalization deepens, two societies may develop: one composed of "global citizens" – skilled, mobile, urban, autonomous of government, capable of exploiting the opportunities the global economy presents; and an unfortunate underclass – impoverished and poorly educated, whose status as economic refugees in their own country encourages them to look to their government as their only source of support.

With these four caveats, we develop four models of the state, two under the "Globalization Triumphant" scenario and two under the "Globalization in Retreat" scenario.[15] Drawing on our analyses of these pairs, we argue that the choices open to the state, should globalization retreat, are significantly affected by the choices it makes when globalization is moving forward. Path dependence limits the trajectory of the state should the parametric condition of globalization change. We examine the consequences of these restrictions in our conclusion.

Globalization Triumphant: The Position of the State

Should globalization triumph, we can imagine two models of the state. We label the first the "handmaiden state" and the second the "social investment state."

In both models, state capacity decreases relative to the growing power of other institutions. The state attempts to mediate between the forces of globalization and its citizenry. It supports the efforts of its citizens, corporations, and private organizations to participate and compete successfully in global markets. Within its borders, it becomes the referee that seeks to ensure fair practices and compliance with international norms and regulations. The state defines its role as mediator, referee, and facilitator.

The state retreats as the commanding force of political loyalty and identity for many of its citizens, particularly those capable of participating successfully in global markets. Nationalism declines as a source of identity for these globalizing elites. In Canada, both Canadian patriotism and Quebec nationalism recede. As globalization triumphs, the state faces a fundamental challenge: How can the state address the increasingly acute problems of social and economic inequality and secure the inclusion of the marginalized and excluded population into the global community? We present two different stylized responses to this challenge.

The Handmaiden State

State leaders define as their central mission securing the "competitiveness" of their population. They seek to create and maintain the conditions generally understood within a neoliberal framework as critical requisites for an adaptive and attractive response to globalization: a balanced budget, low taxes, a skilled and literate work force, an accommodating regulatory environment, and a climate conducive to research and innovation. Public policy concentrates on building the economic infrastructure and the trained human resources required for participation in the global economy.

The state's capacity and willingness to support the weakest and most vulnerable members of society are limited by two factors. First, social justice is not at the core of the neoliberal state's mandate in a global economy; at best, it is secondary and instrumental. Second, the discipline imposed by global markets reduces government revenues as a proportion of domestic earnings and, consequently, its capacity to meet social needs, either directly, by spending, or indirectly, through taxation and redistribution. Governments, for example, are pressed to lower taxes to satisfy mobile corporations and retain the talented professionals and innovators who participate effectively in the global economy, but doing so limits the capacity of the government to address the growing social inequality that accompanies deepening globalization when it is unmediated. Although economic growth continues as globalization deepens, redistribution in the service of social justice becomes more difficult.

Mark Neufeld calls this state, which seeks to adjust its society to the exigencies of the global economy rather than adjust the impact of the global economy on its society, the "national competitiveness/forced-adjustment state."[16] In this kind of state, the space for political and economic policy choices shrinks, and state capacity to make the choices in the space that remains declines.

The Social Investment State

States need not choose to be handmaidens of globalization, even when it triumphs. Globalization sets the parameters of policy, but the range of choices within these constraints is still large. Especially as publics begin to focus on the unacceptable social consequences of the handmaiden state, the space for leaders to choose different priorities grows.

The social investment state recognizes that effective participation in the global economy and engagement with the revolution in information and communications are necessary to generate wealth. It has a more expansive view, however, of the requisites of global competitiveness than the neoliberal handmaiden state. Crime, social disorder, disease, and poverty all reduce a country's competitiveness; other things being equal, people and firms will prefer to locate in areas where the quality of life is good. Cities that work – where pollution is low, where crime is not a threat to safety, where neighbourhoods thrive, where communities cohere, where schools teach – make good economic sense, and, they are good places in which to live. A strong economic case can be made for an attempt to reduce the social inequalities that breed poverty and social disorder, for seeking to include the excluded.

The case for including the socially excluded is more than economic. Leaders of the social investment state continue to feel a responsibility toward their citizens and their citizens' needs. In a social investment state, policy is justified in social as well as economic terms, and leaders seek to balance needs. Much of what the handmaiden state does the social investment state will do, too: balance the books, reduce taxation, and seek efficiencies in government and innovation in the delivery of public services. Both will probably want to provide high-quality economic infrastructure and equip talented citizens with the capacity to participate in the global economy. Their reasons for doing so, however, are different.

The generation of wealth is not the sole priority of the social investment state. The state is accountable to the whole community and the community encompasses not only those who are agile in the global marketplace, but also those who are excluded from it. Some of the resources generated by the expanding economy are dedicated to support those unable to participate directly in its functioning. We observed earlier that, unlike economies and cultures that have partly migrated out into the global world, societies have remained largely, though not exclusively, at home. The social investment state responds to the needs of its national community and invests broadly in the needs of its society.

The Standing Senate Committee on Social Affairs has observed that, in the era of the welfare state, security used to mean protection from change, but that it now means building the capacity to change.[17] The Committee argues that the new concept of security implies a shift from an emphasis on social expenditure to social investment, a shift away from the traditional welfare state, based on direct provision of social services, to a new social investment state. Yet it acknowledges and accepts the limits to that approach. It recognizes that "the need for insulating or providing social insurance for those in the country who suffer from the socially corrosive forces of globalization and technology has not diminished. If anything, the need has become greater as a consequence of globalization."[18] The Committee argues that Canada has not yet responded adequately to the challenge: "We have not yet found or agreed on a solution on how to achieve a more sustainable balance between economic globalization and social cohesion. Canada lacks a social consensus on this question. There has been no comprehensive blueprint of a social contract for the new global era."[19]

The Committee identifies the central challenge for those who wish to construct a social investment state rather than a handmaiden state in response to the challenges of globalization. In an earlier era, the welfare state achieved a rough balance between economic productivity and social justice. That balance, along with the welfare state, is gone.[20] The challenge is to develop policies of social investment to rebalance economic and social needs, not only because a vibrant and functioning society enhances competitiveness, but also because the state has a responsibility to all of its citizens.

Globalization in Retreat: The Repositioning of the State

Processes of globalization do not necessarily march forward in an uninterrupted, smooth, linear sequence. As we argued earlier, globalization has proceeded historically in uneven, bumpy sequences. The scenario we described is a narrative of a bumpy reversal of some of the processes of economic globalization. It is only one of several plausible scenarios of globalization reversed.

Citizens, seeking security and protection, reinvest national governments with enhanced responsibilities. As concerns about public safety and security deepen and economic uncertainties intensify, citizens come "back home" to the state, which has a real if diminished capacity to act and retains substantial democratic legitimacy. National governments are reinvested with authority as well as control.

In a climate of enhanced insecurity, borders begin to matter more. The state promises protection as it restricts the mobility of people, goods, and services, its role as referee becomes less relevant, and government becomes an active player in national security and the national economy, in some cases challenging the dominance of international regulations and institutions. The global entrepreneurs and professionals, who worked everywhere and lived nowhere, are now being shed by retrenching multinational corporations as global trade and foreign investment declines and states begin to erect barriers to protect their domestic markets. These global entrepreneurs return "home" and look to the state as an engine of protection and economic recovery.

Social inequality remains an acute problem, although for reasons dramatically different from those related to scenarios of globalization triumphant. The political authority to redistribute income expands, but so does unemployment and social dislocation. The fiscal capacity necessary to act is limited by the shrinking economy that accompanies globalization's retreat, as well as by the low-tax regime put in place to remain competitive when the global economy was expanding and creating significant new wealth.

As the nation-state regains some of its prominence, loyalty to it and its institutions grows. Both patriotism in Canada and nationalism in Quebec intensify. In Canada, as in many industrialized countries, hostility to immigration grows, flexible migration and multiple citizenship decline, and citizens demand tighter control of entry into the country. When globalization retreats, the central question facing the state becomes: How can the state re-ignite the engines of economic growth in a "postglobal" world of re-emergent national economies and national communities and, at the same time, address the social dislocation that is the consequence of a contracting global economy?

We develop two prototypes of the state under the condition of a retreat of globalization. Each responds differently to the central question we have identified. The first we call "the state of unrequited dreams," and the second, "the state as guardian."

The State of Unrequited Dreams

Weakened and diminished during the period of globalization, the state is shorn of some of the critical capacities it needs in order to respond proactively to retreating processes of globalization. Its logical precursor is the handmaiden state, which put its faith in the power and utility of now retrenching global markets. During the state's relative lack of concern for social cohesion as globalization moved forward, important institutions and policy capacities decayed, leaving the state of unrequited dreams ill equipped to address the painful social dislocations that are part of a retrenching global economy. What is more, its capacity to serve as a focal point not only for the rising demands of its citizens, but also for their loyalty, has been crippled. Captured by neoliberal ideology, the state has shrunk not only in size, but in its ambition. Conceptualizing a positive and proactive role for government is unfamiliar, uncomfortable, and difficult after years of restricted service as referee, mediator, and facilitator. The state finds itself now unable to meet the new demands of its citizenry because of choices it has made in the past.

Neoliberal analysts will have little that is critical to say of this passive and limited role of the state as the wave of globalization retreats. Firm in their belief that governments can do little or nothing directly to encourage economic recovery, they will consider the government's policy appropriate. Neoliberals will applaud the state for seeking to get the fundamentals right and then leaving the field to markets to do what they do best: generate economic activity, profits, and employment.

Those who argue that government has an obligation to intervene when markets fail will consider the inactivity of the state of unrequited dreams frustrating and shortsighted. The critics of the handmaiden state during the era of globalization triumphant will take cold comfort from the accuracy of their forecast of a state shorn of its capacity to meet social needs, even if it were to have the vision to try to do so.

The Guardian State

The guardian state metamorphoses naturally from the social investment state as economic conditions change. The public-sector capacity, which the social investment state maintained during the period of expanding globalization, serves it well in the period of retrenchment. Habituated to adapting global pressures to domestic needs, and to using society's resources to support its weakest members, the guardian state has both the capacity and the predisposition to assume the role of society's protector in a time of crisis. Its public sector is larger than that preserved by the handmaiden state, and its core capacities to make social policy are more or less in place. The guardian state has the capacity to accommodate itself to a more activist role in times of economic difficulty and threats to security, and an interest in doing so. Since its priorities have been not only an efficient adjustment to the global marketplace but also the social well-being of its citizenry, it is well able to respond to citizens' renewed support of national sovereignty and national responsibilities, which are likely outcomes of globalization in retreat. The guardian state has meaningful choices to make, whereas the state of unrequited dreams has few if any at all.

Conclusion

We have sketched four stylized models of the state, each pair embedded in two very different narratives of globalization – the first of triumph, the second of retreat and even reversal. The two narratives of globalization present different plausible futures, each difficult to dismiss with confidence. Globalization at either parametric value, we argue, offers more degrees of freedom than is conventionally thought.[21] We do not enter into the debate about whether one or the other future of globalization is the more likely. Nor do we maintain that these are the only plausible scenarios of the future. We do argue that both scenarios are plausible – and possible. We develop these two scenarios to help discipline the arguments, vary the conditions, and reflect upon state and society in a contingent future.

We develop at least two models under each condition of globalization to dramatize our argument that Canada and Canadians do have choices in their response to globalization. Globalization triumphant creates one set of constraints, principally through international institutions, international law, and global markets, all of which limit the fiscal and economic autonomy of the state. Even then, the Canadian state can respond in different ways. It can significantly reduce the size of government and choose to concentrate on mediating and assisting the adjustment of its citizens to global processes so that they are better positioned to compete. If the state makes this choice, it sheds much of its capacity to make social policy, but it continues to play an important, even essential, role in building all the relevant infrastructures and platforms for participation in the global economy. Or, the Canadian state can choose to invest socially, to enhance and broaden the basis of participation in global markets, but also to strengthen society by compensating and sustaining those excluded by the current phase of globalization. We argue that Canadian values, political culture, and institutions, as well as the history of most of the last hundred years, predispose the government as well as the citizens to favour a social investment state.[22]

Yet the challenge will be real. As national identity declines in salience, and as the state loses control of some of the important levers of growth, public trust and social solidarity will decline. In the face of a growing "democratic deficit," the social investment state must be able to persuade its most globally active citizens to invest at home in order to support and enhance the capacity of those who are marginalized by the latest phase of globalization. Skilled political leadership, reinforced by continuing reference to the values that Canadians share, will be needed to persuade Canadians to continue to invest, in order to bridge the gaps that exist.

Despite all the challenges, the social investment state is the prudent and conservative choice. How the Canadian state responds when globalization is in its triumphant phase will have a significant impact on its capacity to respond should globalization stumble. The capacity that is eroded in the handmaiden state cannot easily be rebuilt when the parametric value of globalization changes. The handmaiden state, we suggest, creates a path dependency that seems to preclude the subsequent emergence of the guardian state. Should globalization reverse or slow significantly, it is very likely that the handmaiden state will be followed by the state of unrequited dreams. Ours is a cautionary tale of states that act purely as handmaidens to the processes of globalization.

Our stylized portraits of two pairs of states are heavily weighted toward an assessment of the capacity and inclination of the state, under varying conditions, to respond to social – and cultural – needs. We, and our fellow authors in this book, chose to examine the social dimensions of globalization in part because less attention has been paid to its social consequences than to its other dimensions, and in part because inattention to social justice in a period of rapid economic, cultural, and political change will be terribly costly in human misery. It will also jeopardize the promise that globalization brings to many who have been excluded from traditional structures of authority.

Broadly, the chapters in this book explore two interrelated ways in which social justice, equality, and inclusion might be addressed in the new environment. The first is via the state, and is relevant to the extent that national governments and national populations have the necessary levers of reform and protection under their control. The difficulty here, which all of the authors in this volume recognize, is that major elements of culture, society, and identity have migrated beyond the state to the global sphere, and, as such, lie beyond the conventional ambit of national governments. The second way in which these challenges might be addressed is through the development of responsible, democratic systems of governance, nurtured by an active civil society, at the global level. The authors in this volume have explored that option as well, in the context of their specific topics. They recognize that the barriers to progress in this area are immense. National governments, when they are acting together internationally, are effectively beyond democratic control, and a global civil society and the attendant supranational institutions of a civil order are, at this stage, embryonic at best.

Contemporary globalization has come upon us so rapidly that collectively we hardly know what questions to ask, let alone how to answer them. Who, for example, should be included in – or excluded from – the international fora where crucial decisions affecting culture and society are made? States are understood to have a right of participation, based on the principle of sovereignty. But on what basis does a citizens' group acquire the legitimacy to participate? Does Greenpeace or the Business Council on National Issues get a seat at the bargaining table, but not the Grandmothers Against Free Trade or the Vancouver East Side Anarchist League? If so, why? On what basis? And who is to judge?

Currently, citizens and networks are not subjected to anything like the standards of accountability, transparency, and representativeness imposed on democratic governments, despite all the legitimate criticisms that can be made of these state-based processes. More formal involvement would require that this issue be addressed. How is this to be done?

Furthermore, how are non-state actors to be included in these global decision-making processes? The Internet and the World Wide Web seem to offer part of the answer, as they allow for substantial circulation of information between and among state and non-state actors, but it is hard to see how they could ever become the central media for political deliberation. Face-to-face meetings and direct negotiating fora will remain as central to international decision making as they are to domestic political life. How is a potentially vast array of organized interests and voices introduced into a governing process without crippling its effectiveness? Countries have not been very successful at sorting out this dilemma at the national level; the problem multiplies exponentially at the global level.

Finally, what are the appropriate political institutions of a global governance system, and how can one best frame the appropriate global policy issues that need to be addressed? Most of the institutions have grown up in a "pre-global" world; is there any particular reason to believe that they are the most appropriate organizations, simply because they are there? And as for the appropriate policy issues, defining or framing the problem to be addressed can often be the most crucial step; who frames problems and through what process?

It is precisely because of these kinds of challenges that we have paid careful attention to the continuing and important role of the state, under widely varying conditions of globalization. Each of the authors in this volume, in his or her own way, has borne witness to a significant, evolving role for the modern democratic state, buffeted though it may be by global winds of change. Hannigan considers alternative ways in which the state could respond to the domestic impacts of the global entertainment economy, noting that an activist, regulatory response is inhibited in the Canadian case by agency, departmental, and jurisdictional fragmentation, and by the absence of international policy and negotiating fora (unlike in the field of telecommunications). Given that the strategic entertainment market in any country is concentrated in the large metropolitan centres, Canada is particularly vulnerable to the relatively unregulated ambitions of transnational entertainment corporations, because of its constitutional incapacity to fashion a coherent national urban policy. Raboy's chapter on communications points to the need for governments to build a stronger international public policy-making capacity to extend the national logic of the public interest into the international sphere. From a democratic perspective, he insists as well that any agenda for action on the global regulation of communication will have to include the broadened participation of civil society in the new regulatory framework and structures it creates.

Wong depicts the ways in which conceptions of citizenship and identity are shifting as a result of modern communication technologies and contemporary forms of migration. His critique of the Canadian government's attempt to tighten immigration policy, despite the contrary logic of contemporary migration patterns, is an implicit acknowledgment of the power of the state in the immigration and settlement field. He argues for a "thin but strong" citizenship, which can be differentiated and multicultural and based on civic engagement rather than shared values and common identity, and notes several inconsistencies in the Government of Canada's position as it seeks to negotiate this contested terrain.[23] Similarly, Deibert's report on the successful blocking of the MAI focuses on resistance groups and their use of the Internet, but they were opposing state representatives and it was governments that were unsuccessfully negotiating the investment agreement. Whatever the chain of reasoning, the agencies that display the potential to shape the forces of globalization, to confront the massive concentrations of private interest, and to protect the interests of citizens, are governments, acting either individually or collectively.

Some would disagree: they see an increasingly enfeebled state competing for political loyalty with multiple centres of authority. The state came into being at a particular historical moment and, as globalization advances, it will be but one among many focal points of political identity.[24] A few do not regret the decline of the state: citizens will enjoy multiple opportunities and a rich diversity of experience in global civil society, freed of the strictures of and obligations to the state. We disagree.

Our analysis suggests that the state still matters. It matters not only because globalization still permits significant state choices, or even because the state is still best equipped to address social inequalities. It matters even more because in constitutional democracies the state remains the most important repository of legitimate and accountable governance.[25]

Our fellow authors have identified the thickening of international institutions and faint signs of the emergence of a global civil society. But they have also recognized the degree to which private economic power and unaccountable political power is shaping social, cultural, and economic reality, both at home and abroad. Although not logically connected, neoliberal ideology and globalization walk hand in hand in the contemporary era, and many politicians, not just businesspeople, have accepted the interlocking logic that these linked forces represent.

Much of the analysis in this book has explored a set of dialectical tensions that constitute our modern world: between the state and the market; between national governments and emergent global institutions; between loyalties of place and loyalties of purpose; between citizens and elites; between the demands of justice and the allegedly beneficial operation of self interest; and between those inside the charmed circle of globally driven prosperity and those on the outside looking in.

Not surprisingly, identifying the tensions is easier than dissolving them. A recurrent theme in this book, for example, has been the limited writ of the modern democratic state; it can no longer do on its own most of the job that needs to be done. Yet while one can point to several international institutions and practices that may represent the first green shoots of an emergent global civil and political order, these are not subject to even rudimentary, much less systematic, democratic control. As Mark Zacher observes, an explosion of international agreements, treaties, and tribunals has occurred in recent years, yet most remain executive-led and heavily bureaucratic, thickly insulated from popular pressures.[26]

Canadians already have plenty of experience with the democratic deficiencies of executive federalism in the Canadian context.[27] "Executive federalism," disconnected from the publics it is allegedly serving, is as problematic at the global level as it is in the Canadian federation, or in the European Union. David Held has sought to develop a model of cosmopolitan governance that creates an overarching set of rights, obligations, and standards to govern the behaviour of all institutions, local, national, and international.[28] In this model, international institutions would become open, responsive, and accountable. Although groups of citizens are mobilizing to hold institutions accountable and to increase transparency, at present the accountability of international institutions is at best embryonic. International institutions remain a poor alternative to democratic, legitimate, and accountable states.

Democratic states, constitutionally governed by the rule of law, will continue for some time to be the venue where the exercise of power is best held accountable and where legitimate and representative governance is best assured. Indeed, it is likely that demands for representation and accountability will grow if globalization deepens, as citizens seek to assert control over important areas of public policy that directly affect their lives. The most promising arena for rule-governed popular contestation remains the democratic state. Certainly, international organizations, global private-sector corporations, military alliances, and even coalitions of non-governmental organizations do not provide the same opportunity. Nor, domestically, do cities, self-regulating industrial sectors, churches, or cooperative associations – at least, not yet. The modern, rule-governed democratic state is still unmatched in its capacity to provide accountability and representation. Whether connections among societies thicken as globalization advances, or borders re-emerge as globalization falters, our analysis suggests that it will be more important than ever to hold national governments accountable for their stewardship of society and to give voice to those who are excluded, as well as to those who are included, by current processes of globalization.

Notes

1 Yale Ferguson and Richard Mansbach, *Polities: Authority, Identities, and Change* (Columbia, SC: University of South Carolina Press, 1996).

2 As we saw in the opening chapter of this volume, Kenichi Ohmae, *The End of the Nation State* (New York: Free Press, 1995), argues that "traditional nation-states have become

unnatural, even impossible business units in a global economy." Susan Strange's similar argument is noteworthy: "The impersonal forces of world markets ... are now more powerful than the states to whom ultimate political authority over society and economy is supposed to belong ... the declining authority of states is reflected in a growing diffusion of authority to other institutions and associations, and to local and regional bodies." *The Retreat of the State: The Diffusion of Power in the World Economy* (Cambridge: Cambridge University Press, 1996), 4.

3 Janice Gross Stein, "The Privatization of Security," *International Security Review* (2002), forthcoming.

4 See Manuel Castells, *The Rise of the Network Society,* 2nd ed. (Malden, MA: Blackwell, 2000); and John Ruggie, *Winning the Peace: America and World Order in the New Era* (New York: Columbia University Press, 1996).

5 David Held, Anthony McGrew, David Goldblatt, and Jonathan Perraton, *Global Transformations: Politics, Economics, and Culture* (Stanford, CA: Stanford University Press, 1999), 437.

6 See Linda Weiss, *The Myth of the Powerless State* (Ithaca, NY: Cornell University Press, 1998).

7 Richard J. Barnet and John Cavanagh, *Global Dreams: Imperial Corporations and the New World Order* (New York: Simon and Schuster, 1994).

8 Thomas L. Friedman dubs this phenomenon "the electronic herd" in *The Lexus and the Olive Tree* (New York: Farrar Straus Giroux, 1999).

9 Weiss makes these arguments in *The Myth of the Powerless State.* Indeed she argues that current neoliberal orthodoxy that glorifies markets is an Anglo-American construction.

10 In *Degrees of Freedom: Canada and the United States in a Changing World* (Montreal: McGill-Queen's University Press, 1997), editors Keith Banting and Richard Simeon conclude that both countries retain a significant degree of autonomy in shaping domestic policy, despite being confronted with similar external and internal pressures. Guiliano Bonoli, Victor George, and Peter Taylor-Gobby explore the reasons for the failure to converge in Europe, in *European Welfare Futures: Towards a Theory of Retrenchment* (Cambridge: Cambridge University Press, 2000). Francis Castles and Christopher Pierson explore similar issues with respect to the United Kingdom, Australia, and New Zealand, in "A New Convergence: Recent Policy Developments in the United Kingdom, Australia and New Zealand," *Policy and Politics* 24 (July 1996): 233-45.

11 Paul Pierson explores the impact of politics and policy legacies in the resistance to welfare state retrenchment in *Dismantling the Welfare State: Reagan, Thatcher, and the Politics of Retrenchment* (Cambridge, Cambridge University Press, 1994). See also his article "The New Politics of the Welfare State," *World Politics* 48 (1996), 143-79.

12 A gini index measure of family income inequality after taxes and transfers shows a score of 0.294 in 1980 and 0.298 in 1995. See Statistics Canada, *Income after Tax, Distribution by Size in Canada: 1995* (Ottawa: Supply and Services Canada, 1997), Table VI. These data do not reflect the cuts to social programs that came on stream in 1997.

13 Organization for Economic Cooperation and Development (OECD), "Social Expenditures Statistics of OECD Member Countries: Provisional Version," *Labour Market and Social Policy Occasional Papers* 17 (Paris: OECD, 1996).

14 See the discussion of global and country inequalities in Chapter 1.

15 Our four models differ from the matrix developed by the Government of Canada in its "Governing in an Information Society" project. See Steven A. Rosell, ed., *Changing Maps: Governing in a World of Rapid Change,* 2nd report of the project on governing in an information society (Ottawa: Carleton University Press, 1995). Our models of the state – namely, the handmaiden state, the social investment state, the state of unrequited dreams, and the guardian state – are nested within two scenarios that vary the pace, scope, and intensity of globalization. The analytic purchase comes from identification of path dependence and obstacles of movement across the two scenarios.

16 Mark Neufeld, "Globalization: Five Theses" (paper presented at the Transatlantic Masters of Arts in Public Policy workshop, "Globalization and Public Policy," Toronto, 10-21 May 1999), <www.chass.utoronto.ca/tamapp> (29 January 2002).

17 The Standing Senate Committee on Social Affairs, Science and Technology, *Final Report on Social Cohesion,* June 1999, <www.parl.gc.ca> (24 December 2001), ch. 4, 4. Banting makes precisely this argument in "The Internationalization of the Social Contract."
18 Standing Senate Committee, *Final Report on Social Cohesion,* ch. 2, 10.
19 Ibid., ch. 4, 2.
20 Paul Pierson dissents and argues that despite austerity and retrenchment, the welfare state has demonstrated surprising endurance. See *Dismantling the Welfare State?,* 179ff.
21 Keith Banting, George Hoberg, and Richard Simeon, eds., *Degrees of Freedom: Canada and the United States in a Changing World* (Montreal: McGill-Queen's University Press, 1997). See also George Hoberg, Keith Banting, and Richard Simeon, "North American Integration and the Scope for Domestic Choice: Canada and Policy Sovereignty in a Globalized World" (paper presented at the Annual Meeting of the Canadian Political Science Association, Sherbrooke, Quebec, 6-8 June 1999).
22 Very loosely, one might suggest that the social democracies of Northern Europe represent empirical examples of the social investment state, and the United States and the United Kingdom empirical examples of the handmaiden state. Canada, typically, lies somewhere between these two poles.
23 First, there is the inconsistency of supporting freer trade, capital mobility, and the free flow of information while simultaneously seeking to erect constraints and barriers, both in the immigration and citizenship fields. Second, Canada encourages difference and cultural diversity through an official multicultural policy, yet citizenship policy really makes no movement toward recognition of differentiated citizenship or multicultural citizenship. Finally, if we consider Canada's current acceptance of dual and multiple citizenship as the institutionalization of the transnational ties people have, it seems inconsistent to support a continuation of this provision in the same piece of legislation that attempts to constrain forms of transnational expression.
24 Ferguson and Mansbach, *Polities: Authority, Identities, and Change.*
25 We are indebted to Ann Medina for insisting on consideration of this question.
26 Zacher, "The Global Economy and the International Political Order." See also Michael Th. Greven and Louis W. Pauly, eds. *Democracy beyond the State? The European Dilemma and the Emerging Global Order* (Lanham, MD: Rowman and Littlefield, 2000).
27 See David Cameron and Richard Simeon, "Intergovernmental Relations and Democratic Citizenship," in *Governance in the Twenty-First Century: Revitalizing Public Service,* ed. B. Guy Peters and Donald J. Savoie (Montreal: McGill-Queen's University Press, 2000), 58-118. Parts of the final paragraph of this chapter are drawn from this article, pp. 102-3.
28 David Held, *Democracy and the Global Order: From the Modern State to Cosmopolitan Governance* (Stanford, CA: Stanford University Press, 1995).

Appendix A
Posting to the MAI-NOT Listserv

STOP THE PROPOSED WTO "MILLENNIUM ROUND" – ASSESSMENT NOW!

Dear friends,
On May 9-10, the European Union's Trade Ministers will gather in Berlin to discuss the proposed WTO Millennium Round. The European Commission continues to push for a comprehensive new round of trade and investment liberalisation, including many of the elements we know from the MAI. The EU trade minister's meeting in Berlin will be an essential step in the building of the European Union position, so we need to get the message across: No new round – no to new issues – assessment now!

This message contains a list of ministers attending the EU trade ministers' meeting (Minister of Finance, Trade or Economics depending on your country) as well as a sample letter (prepared by Friends of the Earth Europe) which you can use for inspiration. You can also fax the "STATEMENT FROM MEMBERS OF INTERNATIONAL CIVIL SOCIETY OPPOSING A MILLENNIUM ROUND OR A NEW ROUND OF COMPREHENSIVE TRADE NEGOTIATIONS" (now signed by over 450 citizens' groups worldwide).

To

(YOUR TRADE OR FINANCE MINISTER)
XX
XY

EU trade ministers meeting on new millennium round, Berlin, May 9-10, 1999

Dear ——,
On May 9-10, 1999 the trade ministers of the European Union will meet to discuss the proposed WTO millennium round. We are writing to you to clarify the government's position on the proposed millennium round. Currently, the European Commission is pushing hard for a comprehensive new round of trade negotiations despite much opposition by many developing countries and large parts of civil society.

We call on our government not to support a new millennium round or a round of comprehensive trade negotiations which would include new issues such as investment, trade facilitation, competition policy and government procurement. We fear that a new round would increase the undermining of national and international environmental and health standards, lead to further dominance of transnational corporations, irreversibly destruct ecosystems, increase gaps in the distribution of resources and lead to more conflicts on a global scale.

Taking into consideration the global economic crisis, deficiencies of the WTO as an untransparent and undemocratic institution, and the dominance by strong developed countries and corporate interests in the WTO, we call for a moratorium on any further negotiation or any new issues that extend the competence and scope of the WTO. During the moratorium a comprehensive and in-depth review of existing WTO agreements should be conducted which looks at the WTO's impact on environment, development, health, marginalised communities, human rights, the rights of women and children and cultural diversity. The review should be conducted with civil society participation to formulate recommendations for a sustainable, equitable global trading system where the environment is protected and the world's wealth is equally shared.

We would like to make it very clear that rushing into new negotiations before assessing existing agreements would be irresponsible. We therefore ask you to make a strong statement in Berlin against a new round and ask for a comprehensive and in-depth review of the WTO and of existing agreements concerning its environmental, developmental and gender effects.

We also would like to know whether the Ministry for XX and XY (ADD YOUR MINISTRY DEALING WITH ENVIRONMENT AND DEVELOPMENT ISSUES) are consulted in the preparations of the 3rd Ministerial Conference of the WTO and how their position will be integrated in Berlin.

Last but not least, we also would like to express our disappointment with the European Commission, which publicly claims to be in consultation with "civil society." There is strong evidence that the EC shapes its negotiations strategy around the priorities of business interest groups which the EC identified as the Investment Correspondent Network (ICN). We find it unacceptable that the commission has not informed NGOs about these consultations with the ICN and that its public information policy is less transparent to non-profit citizens' organisations than to industry lobbies.

We hope that you will support us in this important matter and look forward to hearing from you,

Yours sincerely,

List of Ministers Attending the EU Trade Conference

Austria:
Dr. Hannes Farnleuter
Bundesminister fuer wirtschaftliche Angelegenheiten

Belgium:
Elio di Rupo, Vice Premier Ministre, Ministre de l'Economie et des Télécommunications
Charge du Commerce Extérieur

Denmark:
Gunnar Ortmann
State Secretary
Ministry for Foreign Affairs

Germany:
Dr. Werner Mueller
Bundesminister fuer Wirtschaft und Technologie

Finland:
Kimmo Sasi
Minister for Foreign Trade
Ministry for Foreign Affairs

France:
Jacques Dondoux
Secrétaire d'Etat au Commerce Exterieur
Ministère de l'Economie, des Finance et de l'Industrie

Greece:
Stefanos Avgouleas
Secretary General
Ministry of National Economy

Ireland:
Tom Kitt
Minister for Trade
Department for Enterprise, Trade and Employment

Italy:
Antonio Cabras
Sottosegretario di Stato
Ministerio del Commercio con l'Estero

Luxembourg:
Lydie Err
Staatssekretaerin fuer Auswaertige Angelegenheiten, Aussenhandel und Entwicklungshilfe
Foreign Ministry

Netherlands:
Gerrit Ybema
Minister for Foreign Trade
Ministry for Economic Affairs

Portugal:
Dr. Joaquim Pina Moura
Minister for Economic Affairs
Ministry for Economic Affairs

Spain:
Elena Pisonero Ruiz
Secretary of State for Trade, Tourism and SME
Ministry for Economic Affairs and Finance

Sweden:
Leif Pagrotsky
Minister for Trade
Ministry for Foreign Affairs

Appendix B
Global Communication Policy Environment

Issue areas	*Sites*
Global	
• Telecommunications	ITU
• Culture	UNESCO
• Development	World Bank
• Satellites	INTELSAT
• Intellectual property	WIPO
• Human rights	UN
• Internet regulation	To be determined
Multilateral	
• Global Information Infrastructure (GII)	G8
• Market liberalization	WTO
• Multilateral Agreement on Investments (MAI)	OECD
Regional	
• Cultural exception	NAFTA
• Television quotas	EU
• Principle of public broadcasting	EU
• Media concentration of ownership rules	EU
National (Canadian Examples)	
• Information highway policy	Industry Canada
• Broadcasting/telecom/Internet regulation	CRTC
• Cultural policy	Canadian Heritage
• Public cultural institutions	CBC, NFB, etc.
• Cultural industries subsidies	Federal and provincial governments
• International co-productions	FAIT

►

▶ *Appendix B*

Issue areas	*Sites*
Transnational Corporate Sector	
• Technical standards	ISO (ITU)
• Telecom pricing	ITUG (ITU)
• Infrastructure development	GIIC (G8)
• Investment	OECD input
• Ownership, mergers, acquisitions, market access	WTO input
• E-commerce	GBDe
• Direct lobbying of national governments and international organizations	—
Civil Society	
• Anti-globalization	ATTAC, Independent Media Centres
• Grassroots media	AMARC (radio), Videazimut (video), APC (Internet)
• Networking	Platform for Communication Rights, Voices 21
• Citizen mobilization	Cultural Environment Movement
• Right to communicate	People's Communication Charter
• Research	International Association for Media and Communication Research
"Homeless" Issues	

• Transnational media regulation
  • access requirements
  • tax on benefits
  • obligations
  • performance evaluation
  • offensive content	

• Transnational public service media
  • financing
  • access
  • accountability	

• A "WTO for culture"	
• Promotion of a universal right to communicate	

Bibliography

Web Sites

Many of the Web sites created in response to the MAI protests were transitory and have since been dismantled following the end of the negotiations and the termination of the MAI process at the OECD. Others still operate but MAI-related documents are no longer accessible.

American Cause. Pat Buchanan, founder. <www.theamericancause.org>.

APEC Alert! (UBC). <www.cs.ubc.ca>.

Canadian Centre for Policy Alternatives. <www.policyalternatives.ca>.

Danmarks Kommunistiske Parti/Marxister-Leninster. <www.dkp-ml.dk>.

Green Party of Canada. <www.green.ca>.

"The International Week of Action against the MAI" and other notices. <www.avid.net.au/stopmai>.

Links zum Thema MAI (Germany). <www.pdsnetz.de>.

MAI Documents, Press Releases and Commentaries (independent Web site). <www2.murray.net.au>.

MAI-NOT (Canada). Flora Community Web. <www.mai.flora.org>.

Media Addresses in North America. Flora Community Web. <www.mai.flora.org/mai-info/media.htm>.

Organisation for Economic Co-operation and Development. <www.oecd.org>.

PDS Niedersachsen (Germany). <www.nds.pdsnetz.de>.

People's Communication Charter. <www.pccharter.net>.

Progress Report on the MAI (Preamble Center). <www.progress.org/mai.htm>.

Public Citizen. Ralph Nader, founder. Multilateral Agreement on Investment (MAI). <www.citizen.org/trade/issues/mai/>.

Sample letters about the MAI (from Canadian citizens to their government). Flora Community Web. <www.mai.flora.org>.

Strategic Road (links to MAI-related sites from a variety of nations). <www.mayaconcept.com>.

Voices 21. <www.comunica.org/v21>.

World Trade Organization. <www.wto.org>.

Other Sources

Abrams, D., and M.A. Hogg, eds. *Social Identity Theory: Constructive and Critical Advances.* New York: Harvester Wheatsheaf, 1990.

Abramson, Bram Dov, and Marc Raboy. "Policy Globalization and the 'Information Society': A View from Canada." *Telecommunications Policy* 23, 10/11 (1999): 775-91.

Akin, David. "We're Becoming Less Like Americans: Poll." *National Post,* 21 June 2001, A1, A8.

Albrow, M. *The Global Age*. Cambridge: Polity Press, 1996.

Aleinikoff, T. "After Nationality, Then What?" *Research Perspectives on Migration* 2, 2 (1999): 14-15.

Alger, Dean. *Megamedia: How Giant Corporations Dominate Mass Media, Distort Competition, and Endanger Democracy*. Lanham, MD: Rowman and Littlefield, 1998.

Andranovich, Greg, Matthew J. Burbank, and Charles H. Heying. "Olympic Cities: Lessons Learned from Mega-Event Politics." *Journal of Urban Affairs* 23 (2001): 113-31.

Andrews, David M. "Capital Mobility and State Autonomy: Towards a Structural Theory of International Monetary Relations." *International Studies Quarterly* 38 (1994): 193-218.

Appadurai, Arjun. "Disjuncture and Difference in the Global Cultural Economy." In *Global Culture: Nationalism, Globalization, and Modernity,* edited by M. Featherstone, 295-31. London: Sage Publications, 1993.

–. *Modernity at Large*. Minneapolis: University of Minnesota Press, 1996.

–. "Sovereignty without Territoriality." In *The Geography of Identity,* edited by P. Yaeger, 40-58. Ann Arbor: University of Michigan Press, 1996.

Archibugi, Daniele, and David Held. *Cosmopolitan Democracy: An Agenda for a New World Order.* Cambridge: Polity Press, 1995.

Archibugi, Daniele, David Held, and Martin Kohler, eds. *Re-Imaging Political Community.* Stanford, CA: Stanford University Press, 1998.

Arthurs, Harry W. "Globalization of the Mind: Canadian Elites and the Restructuring of Legal Fields." *Canadian Journal of Law and Society* 12 (1997): 219-46.

Audley, Paul. *Canada's Cultural Industries: Broadcasting, Publishing, Records and Film.* Toronto: Lorimer, 1983.

Aufderheide, Patricia. *Communications Policy and the Public Interest: The Telecommunications Act of 1996*. New York: Guilford Press, 1999.

Australia, Department of Foreign Affairs and Trade, "Public Hearings on Future Multilateral Trade Negotiations." 22 November 2000. <www.dfat.gov.au/trade/negotiations/hearings/index.html> (25 January 2002).

Baade, Robert A. "Stadiums, Professional Sports and City Economies: An Analysis of the United States Experience." In *The Stadium and the City,* edited by J. Bole and O. Moen. Keele, 277-94. Staffordshire: Keele University Press, 1995.

Bader, V. "The Cultural Conditions of Transnational Citizenship." *Political Theory* 25, 6 (1997): 717-813.

Banting, Keith G. "The Internationalization of the Social Contract." In *The Nation State in a Global Information Era: Policy Challenges,* edited by Thomas J. Courchene, 255-85. Kingston, ON: John Deutsch Institute for Economic Research, 1999.

Banting, Keith, George Hoberg, and Richard Simeon, eds. *Degrees of Freedom: Canada and the United States in a Changing World.* Montreal: McGill-Queen's University Press, 1997.

Barber, Benjamin. *Jihad vs. McWorld.* New York: Times Books, 1995.

Barnes, Alan. "Unveiled: A New Downsview," *Toronto Star,* 25 April 1997, A1.

Barnet, Richard J., and John Cavanagh. *Global Dreams: Imperial Corporations and the New World Order.* New York: Simon and Schuster, 1994.

–. "Homogenization and Global Culture." In *The Case against the Global Economy: And for a Turn toward the Local,* edited by J.M. Mander and E. Goldsmith, 71-7. San Francisco: Sierra Club Books, 1996.

Bartelson, J. "Three Concepts of Globalization." *International Sociology,* 15, 2 (2000): 180-96.

Basch, L., N. Schiller, and C. Blanc. *Nations Unbound.* Langhorne, PA: Gordon and Breach, 1994.

Bauböck, R. *Transnational Citizenship*. Aldershot, UK: Edward Elgar, 1994.

Berger, Suzanne, and Ronald Dore, eds. *National Diversity and Global Capitalism.* Ithaca, NY: Cornell University Press, 1996.

Bernier, Ivan, and Richard Collins. "Politiques culturelles, intégration régionale et mondialisation." *Cahier-Médias* (Centre d'Études sur les médias, Quebec City) 7 (July 1998).

Beyard, Michael, Raymond E. Braun, Herbert McLaughlin, Patrick L. Phillips, Michael S. Rubin, et al. *Developing Urban Entertainment Centers.* Washington, DC: Urban Land Institute, 1998.

Blanc-Szanton, C., L. Basch, and N. Schiller. "Transnationalism, Nation-States, and Culture." *Cultural Anthropology* 36, 4 (1995): 683-6.

Bonoli, Guiliano, Victor George, and Peter Taylor-Gobby. *European Welfare Futures: Towards a Theory of Retrenchment.* Cambridge: Cambridge University Press, 2000.

Brent, Paul. "Bringing Americana to Europe." *The Financial Post,* 28 October 1998, C12.

Brewer, M.B. "The Role of Distinctiveness in Social Identity and Group Behavior." In *Group Motivation: Social Psychological Perspectives,* edited by M. Hogg and D. Abrams, 1-16. New York: Harvester Wheatsheaf, 1993.

Brewer, T.L., and S. Young. "The Multilateral Agenda for Foreign Direct Investment: Problems, Principles, and Priorities for Negotiation at the OECD and WTO." *World Competition* 18, 4 (1995): 67-83.

Brubaker, W. *Immigration and the Politics of Citizenship in Europe and North America.* New York: University Press of America, 1989.

Cairns, A. "The Fragmentation of Canadian Citizenship." In *Belonging: The Meaning and Future of Canadian Citizenship,* edited by W. Kaplan, 181-220. Montreal: McGill-Queen's University Press, 1993.

Calhoun, Craig. "Community without Propinquity Revisited: Communications Technology and the Transformation of the Urban Public Sphere." *Sociological Inquiry* 68 (1998): 373-97.

Cameron, James M., and Ronald Bordessa. *Wonderland through the Looking Glass: Politics, Culture, and Planning in International Recreation.* Maple, ON: Belston, 1981.

Canada. Department of Foreign Affairs and International Trade. "Consultations with Canadians." <www.dfait-maeci.gc.ca/tna-nac/consult-e.asp> (25 January 2002).

–. House of Commons. *Canada and the Future of the World Trade Organization: Advancing a Millennium Agenda in the Public Interest.* Report of the Standing Committee on Foreign Affairs and International Trade. Ottawa: Public Works and Government Services Canada, 1999.

–. Standing Senate Committee on Social Affairs, Science and Technology. *Final Report on Social Cohesion.* June 1999. <www.parl.gc.ca> (24 December 2001).

Canadian Heritage. "Canada and United States Sign Agreement on Periodicals." News release. Ottawa, 4 June 1999. <www.pch.gc.ca/culture> (17 December 2001).

Canadian Radio-Television and Telecommunications Commission. "Broadcasting Public Notice CRTC 1999-84 / Telecom Public Notice CRTC 99-14." New Media. CRTC, Ottawa, 17 May 1999.

–. Public Notice CRTC 1999-97. "Building on Success – A Policy Framework for Canadian Television." CRTC, Ottawa, 11 June 1999. <www.crtc.gc.ca> (17 December 2001).

Castells, Manuel. *End of Millennium.* Oxford: Blackwell, 1998.

–. *The Information Age: Economy, Society, and Culture.* 3 vols. Oxford: Blackwell, 1996.

–. *The Rise of the Network Society.* Cambridge, MA: Blackwell, 1996.

–. *The Rise of the Network Society.* 2nd ed. Malden, MA: Blackwell, 2000.

Castles, Francis, and Christopher Pierson. "A New Convergence: Recent Policy Developments in the United Kingdom, Australia and New Zealand." *Policy and Politics* 24 (July 1996): 233-45.

Cato, Jeremy. "Muscle in on this Action," *Globe & Mail,* 15 March 1999, D12.

Cerny, Philip. "Globalization and Other Stories: The Search for a New Paradigm in International Relations." *International Journal* 51 (1966): 617-37.

–. "Globalization and the Changing Logic of Collective Action." *International Organization* 49 (1995): 595-625.

Chan, K.B. "A Family Affair: Migration, Dispersal, and the Emergent Identity of the Chinese Cosmopolitan." *Diaspora* 6, 2 (1997): 195.

Chomsky, Noam. *Year 501: The Conquest Continues.* Montreal: Black Rose Books, 1993.

"Citizenship Act Would Toughen Rules." *Daily Courier* (Kelowna), 8 December 1998, A7.

Citizenship and Immigration Canada. "Citizenship of Canada Act. Strengthening the Value of Canadian Citizenship: The Government of Canada's Plan for Modernizing the *Citizenship Act.*" November 1999. <www.cic.ci.gc> (25 January 2002), under "Publications," "Policy and Legislation."

–. "Criteria for Obtaining Citizenship: Residency Requirements and Knowledge of One's New Country." News Release 3, Citizenship and Immigration Canada, Ottawa, 7 December 1998.

–. *Dual Citizenship,* Cat. no. Ci52-6/1998. Ottawa: Public Works and Government Services Canada, 1998. Available <www.cic.gc.ca> (25 January 2002), under "Citizenship," "Canadian Citizenship."

Cobb, Chris. "Pop Icons Bring Wealth into Canada." *National Post,* 21 June 2001, A8.

Cohen, Robin. "Diaspora and the Nation-State." *International Affairs* 72, 3 (1996): 507-20.

–. *Global Diasporas.* Seattle: University of Washington Press, 1997.

Cohen, Roger. "Building a Capital Where Triumph Is Taboo." *New York Times,* 11 April 1999, section 2, p. 33.

Cohen, R., and P. Kennedy. *Global Sociology.* London: MacMillan Press, 2000.

Commission on Global Governance. *Our Global Neighborhood.* Oxford: Oxford University Press, 1995.

Connor, W. "The Impact of Homelands upon Diasporas." In *Modern Diasporas in International Politics,* edited by G. Sheffer, 16-45. London: Croom Helm, 1986.

Council of Europe. *The Media in a Democratic Society.* Draft Resolutions and Draft Political Declaration, 4th European Ministerial Conference on Mass Media Policy, Prague, 7-8 December 1994, MCM-CDMM (94) 3 prov. 1. Strasbourg: Council of Europe, 1994.

Council of the European Union. "Draft Treaty of Amsterdam." Protocol on the System of Public Broadcasting in the Member States. Brussels, August 1997. <www.europa.eu.int/eur-lex/en> (17 December 2001).

Courchene, Thomas J., ed. *The Nation State in a Global Information Order: Policy Challenges.* Proceedings of a conference held at Queen's University, 14-15 November 1996. Kingston, ON: John Deutsch Institute for Economic Research, 1997.

–. *Room to Manoeuvre? Globalization and Policy Convergence.* Kingston, ON: John Deutsch Institute for Economic Research, 1999.

Courteaux, Olivier. "The Inner City for Fun and Profit." *National Post,* 19 March 1999, B5.

Cox, Robert. "Civil Society at the Turn of the Millennium: Prospects for an Alternative World Order." *Review of International Studies* 25, 1 (1999): 3-28.

Cummings, Scott. "Private Enterprise and Public Policy: Business Hegemony in the Metropolis." In *Business Elites and Urban Development: Case Studies and Critical Perspectives,* edited by Scott Cummings, 3-21. Albany, NY: State University of New York Press, 1988.

Davis, Mike. *City of Quartz: Excavating the Future in Los Angeles.* New York: Verso, 1990.

Deibert, Ronald J. "International Plug'n'Play: Citizen Activism, the Internet, and Global Public Policy." *International Perspectives* 1, 3 (2000): 255-72.

–. *Parchment, Printing, and Hypermedia: Communication in World Order Transformation.* New York: Columbia University Press, 1997.

De Jonquières, Guy. "Network Guerillas." *Financial Times,* 30 April 1998, 20.

Delanty, G. "Models of Citizenship: Defining European Identity and Citizenship." *Citizenship Studies* 1, 3 (1997): 285-303.

Dobrzynski, Judith H. "Heavyweight Foundations Throws Itself behind Idea of a Cultural Policy." *New York Times,* 2 August 1999, B1.

Doremus, Paul, William Keller, Louis Pauly, and Simon Reich. *The Myth of the Global Corporation.* Princeton, NJ: Princeton University Press, 1998.

Drainville, A. "The Fetishism of Global Civil Society: Global Governance, Transnational Urbanism and Sustainable Capitalism in the World Economy." In *Transnationalism from Below,* edited by M. Smith and L. Guarnizo, 35-63. New Brunswick, NJ: Transaction, 1998.

Drake, William, ed. *The New Information Infrastructure: Strategies for U.S. Policy.* New York: Twentieth Century Fund Press, 1995.

Dreidger, L. *Multi-Ethnic Canada.* Toronto: Oxford University Press, 1996.

Drohan, Madeline. "How the Net Killed the MAI." *Globe & Mail,* 29 April 1998, A1, A13.

Drucker, Peter F. "The Global Economy and the Nation-State." *Foreign Affairs* 76, 5 (1997): 159-71.

Duffy, A. "Citizenship Rulings a 'Sorry Mess,' Lawyer Says: Contradictory Judgments." 9 April 1999. <www.fact.on.ca> (27 November 2001).

Duncan, Emma. "Wheel of Fortune: A Survey of Technology and Entertainment." *The Economist* 21 (November 1998): 11.

Earl, Louise. "Entertainment Services: A Growing Consumer Market." *Service Indicators/ Indicateurs des Services – 3rd Quarter* (Statistics Canada) (1998): 17.

–. "Spending on Selected Recreation Items in Canada." *Focus on Culture* (Statistics Canada) 10, 2 (1998): 3.

Enchin, H. "Imax Scores Its Biggest Deal in 10-Theatre Sale to Regal," *Globe & Mail,* 25 June 1997, B8.

Fainstein, Susan S. *The City Builders: Property, Politics, and Planning in London and New York.* Oxford, UK, and Cambridge, MA: Blackwell, 1994.

Faist, T. "Cumulative Causation in Transnational Social Spaces: The German-Turkish Example." Paper presented at the International Sociological Association's meeting on "Inclusion and Exclusion: International Migrants and Refugees in Europe and North America," New School for Social Research, New York, NY, 5-7 June 1997.

–. "Transnationalization in International Migration: Implications for the Study of Citizenship and Culture." *Ethnic and Racial Studies* 23, 2 (2000): 189-222.

Falk, Richard. "Challenges of a Changing Global Order." *Peace Research: The Canadian Journal of Peace Studies* 24, 4 (November 1992): 17-24.

–. *On Humane Governance: Toward a New Global Politics.* Cambridge: Polity Press, 1995.

–. "The Making of Global Citizenship." In *Global Visions: Beyond the New World Order,* edited by J. Brecher, J. Childs, and J. Cutler, 39-50. Boston: South End Press, 1993.

Featherstone, Mike, ed. *Global Culture: Nationalism, Globalization, and Modernity.* London: Sage Publications, 1993.

Ferguson, Yale, and Richard Mansbach. *Polities: Authority, Identities, and Change.* Columbia, SC: University of South Carolina Press, 1996.

Firebaugh, Glen. "Empirics of World Income Inequality." *American Journal of Sociology* 104 (May 1999): 1597-631.

Fjellman, Stephen M. *Vinyl Leaves: Walt Disney World and America.* Boulder, CO: Westview Press, 1992.

Foot, David K., and Daniel Stoffman. *Boom, Bust and Echo: How to Profit from the Coming Demographic Shift.* Toronto: Stoddart, 1997.

France. "Rapport sur l'Accord multilateral sur l'investissement (AMI)." Rapport Interimaire – Septembre 1998, Government of France. <www.finances.gouv.fr> (25 September 1999).

Frank, Robert, and Philip Cook. *The Winner-Take-All Society.* New York: Simon and Schuster, 1995.

Frederick, Howard H. *Global Communication and International Relations.* Belmont: Wadsworth, 1993.

"Free Trade under Fire." *Financial Times,* 11 October 1999, 1.

Frideres, J. "Civic Participation, Awareness, Knowledge and Skills." In *Immigrants and Civic Participation: Contemporary Policy and Research Issues,* edited by Canadian Heritage, 33-48. Ottawa: Canadian Heritage Multiculturalism, 1997.

Friedman, Thomas L. *The Lexus and the Olive Tree.* New York: Farrar Straus Giroux, 1999.

Friends of the Earth. "Ten Reasons to Oppose the MAI." 25 November 1977. <www.foe.org> (25 September 1999).

G7. "A Shared Vision of Human Enrichment." Chair's Conclusions to the G7 Ministerial Conference on the Information Society. Brussels, 27 February 1995. <www.unix-ag.uni-kl.de/~lippold/g7-conclusion.html> (17 December 2001).

Gagnon, L. "Citizenship Rules for Homebodies." *Globe & Mail,* 19 December 1998, D3.

Galtung, Johan, and Richard C. Vincent. *Global Glasnost: Toward a New World Information and Communication Order?* Cresskill, NJ: Hampton Press, 1993.

Garrett, Geoffrey. "Global Markets and National Politics: Collision Course or Virtuous Circle?" *International Organization* 52 (1998): 787-824.

Garrett, Geoffrey, and Peter Lange. "Internationalization, Institutions, and Political Change." In *Internationalization and Domestic Politics,* edited by H. Milner and R. Keohane, 48-75. Cambridge: Cambridge University Press, 1996.

Giddens, A. *The Consequences of Modernity.* Cambridge: Polity Press, 1990.

Gill, Stephen. "Economic Globalization and the Internationalization of Authority: Limits and Contradictions." *Geoforum* 23, 3 (1992): 269-83.

Gill, Stephen, and David Law. "Global Hegemony and the Structural Power of Capital." *International Studies Quarterly* 33 (1989): 475-99.

Goldberger, Paul. "The Rise of the Private City." In *Breaking Away: The Future of Cities,* edited by J. Vitullo-Martin, 135-47. New York: The Twentieth Century Fund Press, 1996.

Gomery, Douglas. "Disney's Business History: A Reinterpretation." In *Disney Discourse: Producing the Magic Kingdom,* edited by E. Smoodin. New York and London: Routledge, 1994.

Gore, Al. "The Global Information Infrastructure: Forging a New Athenian Age of Democracy." *InterMedia* 22, 2 (1994): 4-6.

Graham, Stephen, and Simon Marvin, *Telecommunications and the City: Electronic Spaces, Urban Places.* London and New York: Routledge, 1996.

Grant, Don S. III, and Richard Hutchison. "Global Smokestack Chasing: A Comparison of the State-Level Determinants of Foreign and Domestic Manufacturing Investment." *Social Problems* 43 (1996): 21-38.

Greven, Michael Th., and Louis W. Pauly, eds. *Democracy beyond the State? The European Dilemma and the Emerging Global Order.* Lanham, MD: Rowman and Littlefield, 2000.

Griffiths, Franklin. "The Culture of Change." Paper presented at the "Analysing the Trends: National Policy Research" conference, Ottawa, 25-6 November 1999.

Guarnizo, L., and M. Smith. "The Locations of Transnationalism." In *Transnationalism from Below,* edited by M. Smith and L. Guarnizo, 3-34. New Brunswick, NJ: Transaction, 1998.

Habermas, J. *Between Facts and Norms: Contributions to a Discourse Theory of Law and Democracy.* Cambridge: Polity Press, 1996.

–. "Citizenship and National Identity: Some Reflections on the Future of Europe." In *Theorizing Citizenship,* edited by R. Beiner, 255-81. Albany: State University of New York Press, 1995.

Hamelink, Cees. J. *The Politics of World Communication.* London: Sage Publications, 1994.

Hanes, A. "Allegiance Oath Keeps Reference to Queen." *Ottawa Citizen,* 8 December 1998. <www.ottawacitizen.com> (20 December 1998).

Hannigan, John. *Fantasy City: Pleasure and Profit in the Postmodern Metropolis.* London and New York: Routledge, 1998.

Harvey, David. "Globalization in Question." *Rethinking Marxism* 8, 4 (1995): 1-17

–. "Urban Places in the 'Global Village': Reflections on the Urban Condition in Late Twentieth Century Capitalism." In *World Cities and the Future of the Metropoles,* edited by Luigi Mazza, 21-32. Milan: Electra, 1988.

Harvey, Janice. "*Ethyl Corporation* v. *Government of Canada.*" New Brunswick *Telegraph Journal,* 4 June. <www.flora.org/library/mai/harvey3.html> (25 January 2002).

Held, David. "Democracy: From City-States to a Cosmopolitan Order?" *Political Studies* 40, special issue (1992): 10-39.

–. *Democracy and the Global Order: From the Modern State to Cosmopolitan Governance.* Stanford, CA: Stanford University Press, 1995.

–. "Democracy and the New International Order." In *Cosmopolitan Democracy,* edited by D. Archibugi and D. Held, 96-120. Cambridge: Polity Press, 1995.

Held, David, Anthony McGrew, David Goldblatt, and Jonathan Perraton. *Global Transformations: Politics, Economics, and Culture.* Stanford, CA: Stanford University Press, 1999.

Helliwell, John F. *Globalization: Myths, Facts, and Consequences.* C.D. Howe Institute Benefactors Lecture 2000. Toronto: C.D. Howe, 2000.

Herman, Edward S., and Robert W. McChesney. *Global Media: The New Missionaries of Global Capitalism.* London and Washington, DC: Cassell, 1997.

Higham, K.R. "The Politics of Culture in Canada: Creating an Environment for Maximising Human Development." Paper presented at the meeting of the Canadian Cultural Research Network, Ottawa, 4 June 1998.

Hirst, Paul, and Grahame Thompson. *Globalization in Question: The International Economy and the Possibilities of Governance.* Cambridge: Polity Press, 1996.

His, Alain, ed. *Communication and Multimedia for People: Moving into Social Empowerment over the Information Highway.* Paris: Transversales Science Culture, 1996.
Hoberg, George, Keith Banting, and Richard Simeon. "North American Integration and the Scope for Domestic Choice: Canada and Policy Sovereignty in a Globalized World." Paper presented at the annual meeting of the Canadian Political Science Association, Sherbrooke, Quebec, 6-8 June 1999.
Hochschild, Arlie. *The Time Bind: When Work Becomes Home and Home Becomes Work.* New York: Metropolitan Books, 1997.
Holton, R. *Globalization and the Nation-State.* New York: St. Martin's Press, 1998.
Hulsman, Noel. "Fake Blood, Real Money," *Financial Post Magazine,* 1 July 1999, 18-24.
Huntington, Samuel P. *The Clash of Civilizations and the Remaking of World Order.* New York: Simon and Schuster, 1996.
Hurrell, A., and N. Woods. "Globalization and Inequality." *Millennium: Journal of International Studies* 24, 3 (1995): 447-70.
Hutton, T. "International Immigration as a Dynamic of Metropolitan Transformation: The Case of Vancouver." In *The Silent Debate: Asian Immigration and Racism in Canada,* edited by E. Laquian, A. Laquian, and T. McGee, 285-314. Vancouver: Institute of Asian Research, 1998.
Hyndman, J. "Border Crossings." *Antipode* 29, 2 (1997): 149-76.
Industry Canada. *Building the Information Society: Moving Canada into the 21st Century.* Ottawa: Minister of Supply and Services Canada, 1996.
Information Highway Advisory Council. *Connection, Community, Content. The Challenge of the Information Highway.* Final Report. Ottawa: Minister of Supply and Services Canada, 1995.
–. *Preparing Canada for a Digital World.* Final Report. Ottawa: Industry Canada, 1997.
International Network on Cultural Policy. "Welcome to the INCP." <http://64.26.177.19> (29 January 2002).
International Telecommunications Union. *The Missing Link.* Report of the Independent Commission for Worldwide Telecommunications Development, chaired by Sir Donald Maitland. Geneva: ITU, 1984.
International Telecommunications Union/UNESCO. *The Right to Communicate: At What Price? Economic Constraints to the Effective Use of Telecommunications in Education, Science, Culture and in the Circulation of Information.* Paris: International Telecommunications Union/UNESCO, 1995.
Ip, D., C. Inglis, and C. Wu. "Concepts of Citizenship and Identity among Recent Asian Immigrants in Australia." *Asian and Pacific Migration Journal* 6, 3-4 (1997): 363-84.
Ip, D., C. Wu, and C. Inglis. "Settlement Experiences of Taiwanese Immigrants in Australia." *Asian Studies Review* 22, 1 (1998): 93.
Jacobson, D. "New Frontiers: Territory, Social Spaces, and the State." *Sociological Forum,* 12, 1 (1997): 121-33.
–. *Rights across Borders: Immigration and the Decline of Citizenship.* Baltimore: Johns Hopkins University Press, 1996.
Javnost/The Public. Theme issue "Global Media Policy: A Symposium on Issues and Strategies," edited by Marc Raboy, 5, 4 (1998): 63-105.
Jenson, J. "Fated to Live in Interesting Times: Canada's Changing Citizenship Regimes." *Canadian Journal of Political Science* 30, 4 (1997): 627-44.
–. *Mapping Social Cohesion: The State of Canadian Research.* Canadian Policy Research Networks Study no. F-03. Ottawa: Renouf, 1998.
Jimenez, M. "It's Illegal for Canadians to Fight against Canada – RCMP Studying How Law Deals with Dual-Loyalty Issues," *National Post,* 28 April 1999, A10.
Joppke, C. "How Immigration Is Changing Citizenship." *Ethnic and Racial Studies,* 22, 4 (1999): 631-52.
Julier, Guy. *The Culture of Design.* London: Sage Publications, 2000.
Kacapyr, Elia. "Are We Having Fun Yet?" *American Demographics* 19, 10 (1997): 28-30.
Kahin, Brian. "The Internet and the National Information Infrastructure." In *Public Access to the Internet,* edited by B. Kahin and J. Keller, 3-23. Cambridge: MIT Press, 1995.

Kastoryano, R. "Transnational Participation and Citizenship." *Transnational Communities Working Papers Series,* WPTC 98-12. December 1998. <www.transcomm.ox.ac.uk/working_papers.htm> (28 November 2001).

Kearney, M. "The Local and the Global: The Anthropology of Globalization and Transnationalism." *Annual Review of Anthropology* 24 (1995): 547-65.

Keohane, Robert O., and Helen V. Milner, eds. *Internationalization and Domestic Politics.* Cambridge: Cambridge University Press, 1996.

Kobrin, Stephen. "The MAI and the Clash of Globalizations." *Foreign Policy* 112 (Fall 1998): 97-109.

Korzeniewicz, Roberto Patricio, Timothy P. Moran, and Angela Stach. "Trends in Inequality: Towards a World-System Analysis." Paper presented at the "Conference on Re-Inventing Society in a Changing Global Economy," University of Toronto, Toronto, 8-10 March 2001.

Krasner, Stephen. *Sovereignty: Organized Hypocrisy.* Princeton, NJ: Princeton University Press, 1999.

Kraut, Robert, Vicki Lundmark, Michael Patterson, Sarah Kiesler, Tridas Mukopadhyay, and William Scherlis. "Internet Paradox: A Social Technology That Reduces Social Involvement and Psychological Well-Being." *American Psychologist* 53, 9 (September 1998): 1017-31.

Krishnamurthy, Vivek. "Global Civil Society and the Multilateral Agreement on Investment." Unpublished manuscript. University of Toronto, 1999.

Krugman, Paul. *Development, Geography, and Economic Theory.* Cambridge, MA: MIT Press, 1995.

Krugman, Paul, and Robert Lawrence. "Trade, Jobs, and Wages." *Scientific American* (April 1994): 44-9.

Kymlicka, W. *Finding Our Way: Rethinking Ethnocultural Relations in Canada.* Toronto: Oxford University Press, 1998.

Kymlicka, W., and W. Norman. "Return of the Citizen: A Survey of Recent Work of Citizenship Theory. *Ethics* 104 (1994): 352-81.

Labelle, M., and F. Midy. "Re-reading Citizenship and the Transnational Practices of Immigrants." *Journal of Ethnic and Migration Studies* 25, 2 (1999): 213-32.

Laghi, B. "Ottawa to Tighten Citizenship Rules." *Globe & Mail,* 13 November 1998, A1, A8.

Lang, Amanda. "Starbucks Loses Its Mojo to the Internet," *National Post,* 2 July 1999, A3.

Lash, Scott, and John Urry. *Economies of Signs and Spaces.* London: Sage Publications, 1994.

Lasker, David. "A Virtual Disney World Close to Home." *Globe & Mail,* 27 March 1999, C20.

Leaf, Michael, and Ayse Pamuk. "Habitat II and the Globalization of Ideas." *Journal of Planning Education and Research* 17 (1997): 71-8.

Levine, Marc V. "Downtown Development as an Urban Growth Strategy: A Critical Appraisal of the Baltimore Renaissance." *Journal of Urban Affairs* 9 (1987): 103-23.

Lie, J. "From International Migration to Transnational Diaspora." *Contemporary Sociology* 24, 4 (1995): 303-6.

Lipschutz, Ronnie. "Reconstructing World Politics: The Emergence of Global Civil Society." *Millennium: Journal of International Studies* 21, 3 (1992), 398-420.

Lorimer, Roland W., and Jean McNulty. *Mass Communication in Canada.* 3rd ed. Toronto: Oxford University Press, 1996.

Losyk, Bob, "Generation X: What They Think and What They Plan To Do." *The Futurist* 31, 2 (1997): 4.

McLuhan, Marshall, ed. *The McLuhan DEW line.* New York: Human Development Corporation, 1968-70.

McLuhan, Marshall, and B.R. Powers, *The Global Village.* Oxford: Oxford University Press, 1989.

McQueen, Rod. "Declare Livent Canadian Content and Halt the Sale." *Financial Post,* 2 June 1999, C9.

Magder, Ted. "Franchising the Candy Store: Split-run Magazines and a New International Regime for Trade in Culture." *Canadian-American Public Policy* 3 (April 1998): 47.

Mahler, S. "Theoretical and Empirical Contributions toward a Research Agenda for Transnationalism." In *Transnationalism from Below,* edited by M. Smith and L. Guarnizo, 64-100. New Brunswick, NJ: Transaction, 1998.

Mander, Jerry. "Technologies of Globalization." In *The Case against the Global Economy: And for a Turn toward the Local,* edited by J.M. Mander and E. Goldsmith, 344-59. San Francisco: Sierra Club Books, 1996.

Mann, Michael. *Sources of Social Power,* vol. 1. Cambridge and New York: Cambridge University Press, 1986.

Martiniello, M. "Citizenship, Ethnicity, and Multiculturalism: Post-national Membership between Utopia and Reality." *Ethnic and Racial Studies* 20, 3 (1997): 635-41.

Mathiason, John R., and Charles C. Kuhlman. "An International Communication Policy: The Internet, International Regulation and New Policy Structures." Unpublished manuscript, New York University, 1999.

Mattelart, Armand. *La mondialisation de la communication.* Paris: Presses universitaires de France, 1996.

Matthews, Jessica. "Power Shift." *Foreign Affairs* 76, 1 (1997): 50-66.

Meehan, E. *Citizenship and the European Community.* London: Sage Publications, 1993.

Miles, Steven. "The Consuming Paradox: A New Research Agenda for Urban Consumption." *Urban Studies* 35 (1998): 1001-8.

Mitchell, K. "Transnational Discourse: Bringing Geography Back In." *Antipode* 29, 2 (1997): 101-14.

Morton, Peter. "MAI Gets Tangled in the Web." *Financial Post,* 22 October 1998, 3.

Neil, Garry T. "MAI and Canada's Cultural Sector." October 1997. <www.culturenet.ca/cca/gnmai.htm> (25 September 1999).

Neufeld, Mark. "Globalization: Five Theses." Paper presented at the Transatlantic Masters of Arts in Public Policy workshop, "Globalization and Public Policy," Toronto, 10-21 May 1999. <www.chass.utoronto.ca/tamapp> (29 January 2002).

Nevitte, N. "Canadian Values: Evolution or Revolution?" Paper presented at the "Policy Research: Creating Linkages" conference, Ottawa, 1-2 October 1998.

NGO/OECD Consultation on the MAI. "Joint NGO Statement on the Multilateral Agreement on Investment (MAI)." Paris. 27 October 1997. <www.corpwatch.org> (25 September 1999).

Obstfield, M., and A.M. Taylor. *The Great Depression As a Watershed: International Capital Mobility over the Long Run.* Working Paper no. 5960. Cambridge, MA: National Bureau of Economic Research, 1997.

O'Connor, P. *Mapping Social Cohesion.* Canadian Policy Research Networks Discussion Paper no. F/01. Ottawa: Canadian Policy Research Networks, 1998.

Ohmae, Kenechi. *The End of the Nation State.* New York: Free Press, 1995.

Ong, A. "On Edge of Empires: Flexible Citizenship among Chinese in Diaspora." *Positions* 1, 3 (1993): 745-78.

Oommen, T.K. *Citizenship, Nationality and Ethnicity.* Cambridge: Polity Press, 1997.

Organisation of Economic Co-operation and Development. "Code of Liberalisation of Capital Movements." 12 December 1961. <www.oecd.org> (25 September 1999).

–. Report by the Committee on International Investment and Multinational Enterprises and the Committee on Capital Movements and Invisible Transactions. 1995. <www.oecd.org> (25 September 1999).

–. "Social Expenditures Statistics of OECD Member Countries: Provisional Version." *Labour Market and Social Policy Occasional Papers* 17 (Paris: OECD, 1996).

Osiewicz, Estanislao, and Tu Thanh Ha. "Montreal's $1 Billion Coup Infuriates Lastman." *Globe & Mail,* 26 March 1999, A1.

Ostry, Sylvia. "Dissent.Com: How NGOs Are Re-Making the WTO." *Policy Options* (June 2001): 6-15.

–. "Globalization and Sovereignty." Paper presented at McGill Centre for the Study of Canada lecture series, 8 March 1999.

Papastergiadis, N. *The Turbulence of Migration.* Cambridge: Polity Press, 2000.

Pauly, Louis. *Who Elected the Bankers? Surveillance and Control in the World Economy.* Ithaca, NY: Cornell University Press, 1997.

Perry, Robert. *Galt, U.S.A.: The American Presence in a Canadian City.* Toronto: Maclean-Hunter Limited, 1971.

Perry, Suzanne. "U.S. May Back Internet Charter, Not Formal Body." ZDNet News Channel (Reuters). 2 October 1997. <www.zdnet.com> (17 December 2001).

Phillips, Patrick, and D. Wheatley. "Urban Chic." In *Developing Urban Entertainment Centers,* by Michael Beyard, Raymond E. Braun, Herbert McLaughlin, Patrick L. Phillips, Michael S. Rubin, et al. Washington, DC: Urban Land Institute, 1998.

Pierson, Paul. *Dismantling the Welfare State? Reagan, Thatcher, and the Politics of Retrenchment.* Cambridge: Cambridge University Press, 1994.

–. "The New Politics of the Welfare State." *World Politics,* 48 (1996), 143-79.

Pieterse, Jan Nederveen. "Globalisation as Hybridisation." *International Sociology* 9, 2 (1994): 161-84.

PR Newswire. "GBDe Paris Meeting World Business Leaders for the First Time Agreed on the Fundamental Principles of Global Electronic Commerce." 13 September 1999. <www.prnewswire.com> (15 September 1999).

Price, Richard. "Reversing the Gun Sights: Transnational Civil Society Targets Land Mines." *International Organization* 52, 3 (1998), 613-44.

Pritchard, Timothy. "Lawsuits Are Prompting Calls for Changes to Clause in NAFTA," *New York Times,* 19 June 1999, 2.

Putnam, Robert. *Bowling Alone: The Collapse and Revival of American Community.* New York: Simon and Schuster, 2000.

Raboy, Marc. "Communication Policy and Globalization as a Social Project." In *Communication, Citizenship, and Social Policy: Rethinking the Limits of the Welfare State,* edited by Andrew Calabrese and Jean-Claude Burgelman, 293-310. Lanham, MD: Rowman and Littlefield, 1999.

–. "Cultural Sovereignty, Public Participation and Democratization of the Public Sphere: The Canadian Debate on the New Information Infrastructure." *Communications et stratégies* 21 (1996): 51-76.

–. "Global Communication Policy and the Realization of Human Rights." In *A Communications Cornucopia: Markle Foundation Essays on Information Policy,* edited by R.G. Noll and M.E. Price, 218-42. Washington, DC: Brookings Institution Press, 1998.

–. "Influencing Public Policy on Canadian Broadcasting." *Canadian Public Administration* 38, 3 (1995): 411-32.

–. *Missed Opportunities: The Story of Canada's Broadcasting Policy.* Montreal: McGill-Queen's University Press, 1990.

–. "The Role of Public Consultation in Shaping the Canadian Broadcasting System." *Canadian Journal of Political Science* 28, 3 (1995): 455-77.

Raboy, Marc, Ivan Bernier, Florian Sauvageau, and Dave Atkinson. "Cultural Development and the Open Economy: A Democratic Issue and a Challenge to Public Policy." *Canadian Journal of Communication* 19, 3/4 (1994): 291-315.

–. *Développement culturel et mondialisation de l'économie: Un enjeu démocratique.* Québec: Institut québécois de recherche sur la culture, 1994.

Rae, Bob. *The Three Questions: Prosperity and the Public Good.* Toronto: Viking, 1998.

Rees, Emma. "Leisure Futures." *Design Week. The Big Picture: Leisure* (October 1998): 24-5.

Reguly, Eric. "Downsview Debacle Needs Leadership." *Globe & Mail,* 25 March 1999, B2.

–. "Reichmann: The Next Generation Takes a Shot." *Globe & Mail,* 6 April 1997, A10.

Reichl, Alexander. *Reconstructing Times Square: Politics and Culture in Urban Development.* Lawrence, KA: University Press of Kansas, 1999.

Reinicke, Wolfgang H. *Global Public Policy: Governing without Government?* Washington, DC: Brookings Institution Press, 1998.

Richmond, A.H. *Global Apartheid: Refugees, Racism, and the New World Order.* Toronto: Oxford University Press, 1994.

–. *Immigration and Ethnic Conflict.* London: MacMillan Press, 1988.

–. "Sociological Theories of International Migration: The Case of Refugees." *Current Sociology* 36, 2 (1988): 12.

–. "Sociology of Migration in Industrial and Post-Industrial Societies." In *Migration:*

Sociological Studies 2, edited by J. Jackson, 238-81. London: Cambridge University Press, 1969.

Rieff, David. "A Global Culture." *World Policy Journal* 10, 4 (1993/4): 73-81.

Robertson, Roland. *Globalization: Social Theory and Global Culture.* London, Sage Publications, 1992.

Robillard, L. "Speech to the House of Commons," 3 February 1999. *Hansard,* no. 173 [online]. <www.parl.gc.ca> (4 April 1999).

Robinson, John P., and Geoffrey Godbey. *Time for Life: The Surprising Ways Americans Use Their Time.* University Park: Pennsylvania State University Press, 1997.

Roche, Maurice. "Citizenship and Modernity." *British Journal of Sociology* 46, 4 (1995): 715-33.

–. *Mega-Events and Modernity: Olympics and Expos in the Growth of Global Culture.* London and New York: Routledge, 2000.

Rodrik, Dani. "Why Do More Open Economies Have Bigger Governments?" *Journal of Political Economy* 106, 5 (1998): 997-1032.

Rosell, Steven A., ed. *Changing Maps: Governing in a World of Rapid Change.* 2nd report of the project on governing in an information society. Ottawa: Carleton University Press, 1995.

Rosenau, J. "Citizenship without Moorings: American Responses to a Turbulent World." In *Citizenship and National Identity: From Colonialism to Globalization,* edited by T. Oommen, 227-60. New Delhi: Sage Publications, 1997.

Rosentraub, Mark. *Major League Losers: The Real Cost of Sports and Who's Paying For It.* New York: Basic Books, 1999.

Rothkopf, David J. "Cyberpolitik: The Changing Nature of Power in the Information Age." *Journal of International Affairs* 51, 2 (1998): 325-59.

Rubin, Michael S., and Robert Gorman. "Reinventing Leisure." *Urban Land* 52, 2 (1993): 26-32.

Ruggie, John Gerard. "International Structure and International Transformation: Space, Time and Method." In *Global Changes and Theoretical Challenges: Approaches to World Politics for the 1990s,* edited by Ernst-Otto Czempiel and James N. Rosenau, 31. Lexington, MA: Lexington Books, 1989.

–. *Winning the Peace: America and World Order in the New Era.* New York: Columbia University Press, 1996.

Rugman, Alan M. "The Political Economy of the Multilateral Agreement on Investment." Paper presented at the academic symposium "Prospects for the Birmingham Summit 1998," hosted and sponsored by Clifford Chance, the University of Toronto G8 Research Group, and the Centre for Research on the USA, London School of Economics, London, 12 May 1998.

Ruigrok, W., and R. van Tulder, *The Logic of International Restructuring.* London: Routledge, 1995.

Sachs, Jeffrey. "International Economics: Unlocking the Mysteries of Globalization." *Foreign Policy* 110 (Spring 1998): 97-111.

Safran, W. "Diasporas in Modern Societies: Myths of Homeland and Return." *Diaspora* 1, 1 (1991): 83-99.

SAGIT (The Cultural Industries Sectoral Advisory Group on International Trade). *Canadian Culture in a Global World: New Strategies for Culture and Trade.* Report. Ottawa, February 1999. <www.infoexport.gc.ca/trade-culture> (17 December 2001).

Sassen, S. "Territory and Territoriality in the Global Economy." *International Sociology* 15, 2 (2000): 372-93.

Schiller, Herbert. *Mass Communication and American Empire.* Boston: Beacon Press, 1971.

Schiller, N., L. Basch, and C. Blanc-Szanton. "From Immigrant to Transmigrant: Theorizing Transnational Migration." *Anthropological Quarterly,* 68, 1 (1995): 48-63.

–. *Towards a Transnational Perspective on Migration.* New York: New York Academy of Sciences, 1992.

Schiller, N., and G. Fouron. "Transnational Lives and National Identities: The Identity Politics of Haitian Immigrants." In *Transnationalism from Below,* edited by M. Smith and L. Guarnizo, 130-61. New Brunswick, NJ: Transaction, 1998.

Schor, Juliet. *The Overworked American: The Unexpected Decline of Leisure*. New York: Basic Books, 1991.

Schwinghamer, K., and P. Berkowitz. "New Ways of Seeing." *University Affairs* 40, 2 (1999): 6-9.

Searle, Glen, and Michael Bounds. "State Powers, State Land and Competition for Global Entertainment: The Case of Sydney." *International Journal of Urban and Regional Research* 23 (1999): 165-72.

Shrybman, Steven. "The Rule of Law and Other Impediments to the MAI." *West Coast Environmental Law* (April 1998). Available on Vancouver CommunityNet,<www.vcn.bc.ca> (25 September 1999).

Sikkink, Kathryn. "Human Rights, Principled Issue-Networks, and Sovereignty in Latin America." *International Organization,* 47 (Summer 1993): 411-42.

Simmons, Beth A. *Who Adjusts? Domestic Sources of Foreign Economy Policy during the Interwar Years*. Princeton, NJ: Princeton University Press, 1997.

Skeldon, R. "Emigration from Hong Kong, 1945-1994: The Demographic Lead-up to 1997." In *Emigration from Hong Kong: Tendencies and Impacts,* edited by R. Skeldon, 51-77. Hong Kong: The Chinese University Press, 1995.

Sorkin, Michael. "Introduction: Variations on a Theme Park." In *Variations on a Theme Park: The New American City and the End of Public Space,* edited by M. Sorkin. New York: The Noonday Press, 1992.

Soysal, Y. *Limits of Citizenship: Migrants and Postnational Membership in Europe*. Chicago: University of Chicago Press, 1994.

Spiers, Rosemary. "Marchi Tries to Demystify Treaty Issues." *Toronto Star,* 25 October 1997, E4.

Spiro, P. "Embracing Dual Nationality." Carnegie Endowment for International Peace – International Migration Policy. <www.ceip.org> (26 October 1999).

Spybey, Tony. *Globalization and World Society*. Cambridge: Polity Press, 1996.

Squire, Jason. "What's Your Major? Entertainment Studies?" *New York Times,* 19 April 1998, section 3, p. 13.

Stein, Janice Gross. *The Cult of Efficiency*. Toronto: Anansi, 2001.

–. "The Privatization of Security." *International Security Review* (2002), forthcoming.

Stein, Janice Gross, Richard Stren, Joy Fitzgibbon, and Melissa MacLean. *Networks of Knowledge: Collaborative Innovations in International Learning*. Toronto: University of Toronto Press, 2001.

Steinbock, Dan. *Triumph and Erosion in the American Media and Entertainment Industries*. Westport, CT: Quorum Books, 1995.

Strange, Susan. *The Retreat of the State: The Diffusion of Power in the World Economy*. Cambridge: Cambridge University Press, 1996.

Statistics Canada. *Income after Tax, Distribution by Size in Canada: 1995*. Ottawa: Supply and Services Canada, 1997.

Tambini, D. "Post-National Citizenship." *Ethnic and Racial Studies,* 24, 2 (2001): 195-217.

Taras, David. "Defending the Cultural Frontier: Canadian Television and Continental Integration." In *Seeing Ourselves: Media Power and Policy in Canada,* edited by H. Holmes and D. Taras, 174-87. Toronto: Harcourt Brace Jovanovich Canada, 1992.

Tarjanne, Pekka. "The Limits of National Sovereignty: Issues for the Governance of International Telecommunications." In *Telecom Reform: Principles, Policies and Regulatory Practices,* edited by W.H. Melody, 41-50. Lyngby, Denmark: Technical University of Denmark, 1997.

Tarrow, Sidney. *Power in Movement: Social Movements and Contentious Politics*. Cambridge: Cambridge University Press, 1998.

Telegdi, A. "Speech to the House of Commons," 5 February 1999. *Hansard,* no. 175 [online]. <www.parl.gc.ca> (4 April 1999).

Thiele, Leslie Paul. "Making Democracy Safe for the World: Social Movements and Global Politics." *Alternatives: Social Transformation and Humane Governance* 18, 3 (1993): 273-306.

Thompson, A. "Liberals Split on Birthright Proposal." *Toronto Star,* 14 May 1998, Migration Network E-mail listserv.

Tomlinson, John. *Cultural Imperialism: A Critical Introduction.* Baltimore: Johns Hopkins University Press, 1991.

Turner, B. "Contemporary Problems in the Theory of Citizenship." In *Citizenship and Social Theory,* edited by B. Turner, 1-18. London: Sage Publications, 1993.

–. "Outline of a Theory of Citizenship." *Sociology* 24, 2 (1990): 189-217.

Turow, Joseph. *Breaking up America: Advertising and the New Media World.* Chicago: University of Chicago Press, 1997.

UNESCO. "Action Plan for Cultural Policies for Development." Adopted at the Intergovernmental Conference on Cultural Policies for Development. Stockholm, 30 March-2 April 1998. <www.unesco-sweden.org/Conference> (17 December 2001).

–. *Many Voices, One World.* Report of the International Commission for the Study of Communication Problems, chaired by Sean MacBride. London: Kogan Page, 1980.

–. "New Communication Strategy." Adopted by the general conference at its 25th session. Paris, 1989. <www.unesco.org> (17 December 2001).

United Nations/UNESCO. *Our Creative Diversity.* Report of the World Commission on Culture and Development, chaired by Javier Perez de Cuellar. Paris: World Commission on Culture and Development, 1995.

United Nations Development Program. *Tenth Annual Report.* United Nations: New York, 1999.

United States. "The Global Information Infrastructure: Agenda for Cooperation." Washington, 1994. <www.iitf.nist.gov/documents/docs/gii/giiagend.html> (17 December 2001).

United States Information Agency. *Toward a Global Information Infrastructure: The Promise of a New World Information Order.* Washington: USIA Pamphlet Series, 1995.

Valpy, Michael. "Flocking to Lectures: Live and in Person." *Globe & Mail,* 30 March 1999, A11.

Van Hear, N. *New Diasporas.* Seattle: University of Washington Press, 1998.

Venne, Michel. "Le secteur privé s'interroge: Où mènent les inforoutes?" *Le Devoir* (Montreal), 12 February 1995.

Virtual Conference on the Right to Communicate and the Communication of Rights. Hosted by Videazimut, 11 May-26 June 1998. <http://commposite.uqam.ca/videaz> (17 December 2001).

Waddell, Ray. "SFX pays $93.6 Mil for Nederlander Interests." *Amusement Business,* 8 February 1999, 6.

Wade, Robert. "Globalization and Its Limits: Reports of the Death of the National Economy are Greatly Exaggerated." In *National Diversity and Global Capitalism,* edited by S. Berger and R. Dore, 60-88. Ithaca, NY: Cornell University Press, 1996.

Wallerstein, Immanuel. *Geopolitics and Geoculture: Essays on the Changing World-System.* Cambridge: Cambridge University Press, 1991.

"Wal-Mart Romps ahead in Canada." *Building* 47, 5 (1997): 34.

Wapner, Paul. "Politics beyond the State: Environmental Activism and World Civic Politics." *World Politics* 47, 3 (1995): 311-40

Warson, Albert. "Born again Shopping Centres." *Building* 47, 5 (1997): 30-4.

–. "Entertaining Canada." *Building* 48, 3 (1998): 32-4.

Watson, James. *Golden Arches East: McDonald's in East Asia.* Stanford, CA: Stanford University Press, 1997.

Watson, William. *Globalization and the Meaning of Canadian Life.* Toronto: University of Toronto Press, 1998.

Weale, A. "Citizenship beyond Borders." In *The Frontiers of Citizenship,* edited by U. Vogel and M. Moran, 155-65. New York: St. Martin's Press, 1991.

Webb, Michael. "International Economic Structures, Government Interests, and International Coordination of Macroeconomic Adjustment Policies." *International Organization* 45 (1991): 309-42.

Weiss, Linda. *The Myth of the Powerless State: Governing the Economy in a Global Era.* Cambridge: Polity Press, 1998.

Wellman, Barry. *Networks in the Global Village: Life in Contemporary Communities.* Boulder, CO: Westview Press, 1999.

Whitson, David. "Circuits of Promotion: Media, Marketing and the Globalization of Sport." In *MediaSport,* edited by Lawrence A. Wenner, 57-72. London and New York: Routledge, 1998.

Williamson, Jeffrey. *Globalization and the Labor Market: Using History to Inform Policy.* Milan: Lezioni Raffaele Mattioli, Banca Commerciale Italiana, Universita' Commerciale Luigi Bocconi, 1996.

Winland, D. "'Our Home and Native Land'? Canadian Ethnic Scholarship and the Challenge of Transnationalism." *Canadian Review of Sociology and Anthropology* 35, 4 (1998): 555-78.

Wolf, Michael J. *The Entertainment Economy: How Mega-Media Forces Are Transforming Our Lives*. New York: Times Books, 1999.

Wong, Lloyd. "Globalization and Transnational Migration." *International Sociology* 12, 3 (1997): 329-51.

Wong, L., and M. Ng. "Chinese Immigrant Entrepreneurs in Vancouver: A Case Study of Ethnic Business Development." *Canadian Ethnic Studies* 30, 1 (1998): 64-85.

World Trade Organization. "Ruggiero Announces Enhanced WTO Plan for Cooperation with NGOs." WTO Press Release/107, 17 July 1998. <www.wto.org> (25 September 1999).

Wu, David Y.H. "McDonald's in Taipei: Hamburgers, Betel Nuts, and National Identity." In *Golden Arches East: McDonald's in East Asia,* edited by J.L. Watson, 110-35. Stanford, CA: Stanford University Press, 1997.

Yum, Kenny. "Toronto's Blight Gets a Face Lift." *Globe & Mail,* 23 February 1999, B15.

Zacher, Mark. "The Global Economy and the International Political Order." In *The Nation State in a Global Information Order: Policy Challenges,* edited by T. Courchene, 67-95. Proceedings of a conference held at Queen's University, 14-15 November 1996. Kingston, ON: John Deutsch Institute for Economic Research, 1997.

Zuznek, Jiri, and Bryan J.A. Smale. "More Work-Less Leisure? Changing Allocations of Time in Canada, 1981 to 1992." *Loisir et société/Society and Leisure* 20 (1997): 73-106.

Contributors

David R. Cameron was formerly a senior official with the Government of Canada and the Government of Ontario. He has been a professor of political science at the University of Toronto since 1990. Born and raised in Vancouver, he studied at the University of British Columbia and did his graduate work at the London School of Economics. In Ottawa, he was Assistant Secretary for Strategic and Constitutional Planning in the Privy Council Office and Assistant Under Secretary of State in the Department of the Secretary of State. In 1985, he became a vice president at the University of Toronto. From 1987 to 1990, he was Deputy Minister of Intergovernmental Affairs at Queen's Park and has continued to provide constitutional, national-unity, and intergovernmental advice to the Government of Ontario. Author of several books on political theory, nationalism, federal and provincial politics, and Canadian studies, he has advised a number of foreign governments on constitutional and federal issues.

Ronald J. Deibert is an associate professor of political science at the University of Toronto, specializing in media, technology, and world politics. He is the author of *Parchment, Printing, and Hypermedia: Communications in World Order Transformation* (New York: Columbia University Press, 1997). He has published articles on topics relating to Internet politics, civil society and global politics, earth remote sensing and space policy, postmodernism, and social science epistemology in journals such as *International Organization, The Review of International Studies*, and *The European Journal of International Relations*. He currently serves on the editorial board of the journal *International Studies Perspectives*. At present, Dr Deibert is finishing a book on the politics of Internet security, entitled *Network Security and World Order*. He is also conducting research on the Internet and citizen networks, virtual reality, and the possibilities of cyberspace as a global public sphere.

John Hannigan is a professor of sociology at the University of Toronto. He attended the University of Western Ontario and Ohio State University, where he received his PhD in 1976. Dr Hannigan recently began a three-year term as Secretary of the Canadian Sociology and Anthropology Association (CSAA). He is the author of two books: *Environmental Sociology: A Social Constructionist*

Perspective (1995); and *Fantasy City: Pleasure and Profit in the Postmodern City* (1998), both published by Routledge. *Fantasy City* was nominated for the CSAA 1999-2000 John Porter Award. He is currently at work on a new book about the theming of the urban landscape.

Marc Raboy is a full professor in the Department of Communication, University of Montreal, where he has directed the Communication Policy Research Laboratory since 1993. He is the author or editor of a dozen books and over a hundred articles or book chapters on media and communication, including *Missed Opportunities: The Story of Canada's Broadcasting Policy* (Montreal: McGill-Queen's University Press, 1990) and a sixteen-country study for UNESCO, *Public Broadcasting for the Twenty-first Century* (Luton, UK: University of Luton Press, 1996). He is also a senior research associate in the Programme on Comparative Media Law and Policy at the University of Oxford. A past president of the Canadian Communication Association, he has been a consultant to the UN/UNESCO World Commission on Culture and Development, the European Institute for the Media, and the Japan Broadcasting Corporation, as well as public and private sector organizations in Canada. His most recent book is an international edited collection, *Global Media Policy for the New Millennium* (Luton, UK: University of Luton Press, forthcoming).

Janice Gross Stein is the director of the Munk Centre for International Studies and Harrowston Professor of Conflict Management and Negotiation in the Department of Political Science at the University of Toronto, a Fellow of the Royal Society of Canada, and holds the title of University Professor. Some of her publications include *Choosing to Cooperate: How State Avoid Loss* (Baltimore: Johns Hopkins University Press, 1993), edited with Louis W. Pauly; *We All Lost the Cold War* (Princeton, NJ: Princeton University Press, 1994), with Richard Ned Lebow; *Powder Keg in the Middle East: The Struggle for Gulf Security* (Lanham, MD: Rowman and Littlefield, 1995), edited with Geoffrey Kemp; and *Citizen Engagement in Conflict Resolution: Lessons for Canada in International Experience,* C.D. Howe Institute Commentary 94 (June 1997), with David Cameron and Richard Simeon. Her most recent books are *Networks of Knowledge: Collaborative Innovation in International Learning* (Toronto: University of Toronto Press, 2001) and *The Cult of Efficiency* (Toronto: Anansi, 2001). Janice Stein was the Massey Lecturer in 2001.

Lloyd L. Wong is an associate professor in the Department of Sociology at the University of Calgary. A graduate of York University, he conducted research and taught in the University of British Columbia Arts Program at Okanagan University College before joining Calgary. He currently conducts research in the areas of racism, migration, ethnic entrepreneurship, transnationalism, and citizenship. Among his recent publications are "Globalization and Transnational Migration," in *International Sociology* and "Chinese Immigrant Entrepreneurs in Vancouver," in *Canadian Ethnic Studies.*

Index